MODERN THEORIES OF PERFORMANCE

Modern Theories of Performance

From Stanislavski to Boal

Jane Milling and Graham Ley

palgrave

First published 2001 by
PALGRAVE
Houndmills, Basingstoke, Hampshire RG21 6XS and
175 Fifth Avenue, New York, N. Y. 10010
Companies and representatives throughout the world

PALGRAVE is the new global academic imprint of
St. Martin's Press LLC Scholarly and Reference Division and
Palgrave Publishers Ltd (formerly Macmillan Press Ltd).

ISBN 0–333–77541–4 hardback
ISBN 0–333–77542–2 paperback

This book is printed on paper suitable for recycling and made from fully managed and sustained forest sources.

A catalogue record for this book is available from the British Library.

Library of Congress Cataloging-in-Publication Data
Milling, Jane, 1967–
    Modern theories of performance : from Stanislavski to Boal / Jane Milling and Graham Ley.
        p. cm.
    Includes bibliographical references and index.
    ISBN 0–333–77541–4 — ISBN 0–333–77542–2 (pbk.)
    1. Theater—Philosophy. 2. Performing arts—Philosophy. 3. Acting––Philosophy. I. Ley, Graham. II. Title.

    PN2039 .M518 2000
    792'.01—dc21
                                                    00–062838

10   9   8   7   6   5   4   3   2   1
10   09   08   07   06   05   04   03   02   01

Printed and bound in Great Britain by
Creative Print & Design (Wales),
Ebbw Vale

Contents

Preface

The second half of the twentieth century in Europe and North America became distinctive, in terms of theatrical history, for its admiration for a range of outstanding theoretical practitioners. This was a phenomenon for which it would be difficult, if not impossible, to find a convincing parallel in the past, and admiration was often matched by influence, operating both on those who worked in the profession and on the increasing numbers of those who have studied theatre. Part of the attraction of these select figures was undoubtedly that they produced ideas as well as performances, and when juxtaposed they might be thought to present a methodology of theatre practice for modern times. Publication followed admiration, and by the close of the century few theatre intellectuals or students would have found it difficult to compile a canon of great names. Indeed, one leading institution, the Centre for Performance Research in Wales, established a series of study-conferences passing such figures under review, with the general title 'Past Masters'.

The phenomenon, like almost all others of a similar sort, is apparently a curious mixture of impulses, motives and needs. But one distinguishing characteristic in the selection or prominence of these figures is undoubtedly the presence of ideas, expressed in a form that can be read. Clearly, the rise of the director from the dominant figure of the actor-manager is as much a phenomenon of the twentieth century as the emergence of theoretical practitioners. Much the same might be said of the designer as a universal rather than exceptional figure, in moderate to large-scale performance and production. Yet even when the documentary history of directors or designers does exist, and has been brought to notice, there appears to be no similar spread of admiration for them. The later twentieth century was prone, on reflection, to a particular interest in theoretical practitioners, and at the root of that lay a fascination for theory.

The ideas associated with prominent names have gained much of their strength from the existence of writings. Yet in many cases those writings, while exercising fascination, have only rarely and sporadically received any critical attention. This book offers a critical introduction to leading texts by a number of those theoretical

vi

practitioners. It might be reasonably objected that no introductory book can claim to be truly introductory, when there is already so much published on various aspects of its subject. What this book aims to do exclusively is to provide a series of starting-points for those wishing to study modern theatrical theory, to do so by suggesting contexts, and to examine the texts which compose the theory. It is a critical introduction in that sense, directing students or other readers towards helpful contexts, and offering a concentrated critical analysis of a selection of the most relevant writings. It is not, of course, comprehensive, since any selection of theories or of texts is particular, and might arguably be replaced by another. But the selection here represents our experience of teaching theory to interested and committed people, and it includes those figures and subjects to which people have regularly turned their attention, and may well continue to do so for some time to come. We start with Stanislavski and end with Boal, and refer to publications or collections that are generally available. One prominent and notable exclusion is that of Brecht. Brecht wrote copiously; his plays, his poetry, short stories and writings about theatre form multi-volumed collections, of which seven volumes are his writings on theatre (*Schriften zum Theater*), although much less than this is translated into English. Our firm conclusion was that to offer an overview of his theoretical writing in a single chapter in this book would not be helpful, when the task has already been undertaken effectively and at length by many others. Indeed, Brecht is one of the very few theoretical practitioners admired in the twentieth century who has been subject to scrutiny primarily and avowedly for his writing of theatrical theory, which has gained quite as much attention as his dramaturgy.

The theoretical practitioner has been a characteristic of the twentieth-century theatre, a period which has often been embraced in the term 'the modern theatre'. Modernity, the modern and modernism are everyday but nonetheless critically fraught topics. We do not intend in our commentaries to advance a determined and decided contribution to debates on those subjects. But if there is such a thing as 'the modern theatre', then it will undoubtedly consist in some part of these theoretical practitioners, and of any conclusions that might be drawn about their theories, and about the contexts in which they were composed. Existing definitions of the 'modern' in theatre tend to be extremely vague, and some of the issues that arise in the course of the critical discussions here may help to suggest appropriate lines of enquiry into an enigma. Whether or not the 'modern' in any of its definitions can be shown to have changed decisively in the closing decades of the twentieth century into the postmodern, both the scope and inclination of theoretical writings on the theatre have changed in their nature. Our conclusion offers some brief indications of the genesis and divergent concerns of those writings; it is the subject for other major studies, but not immediately of this short book. The relationship between theory and practice, or between performance and theory, is obviously complex at any time or in any given case that might be isolated. To discuss the written texts, and then to discuss their implementation in or influence on performances, would be impossible. Our chosen emphasis results partly from the existence of many studies which take performance as their principal subject. What we offer here is complementary to those initiatives, and simply recognizes that theory is hard to read, even when there is a strong compulsion to approach it and sound it out for its inspiration and its value.

Theatrical theory tends to be difficult, and our commentary is bound to be both difficult and demanding at certain times. The alternative of an insistent simplification would hardly be of any value or likely to prove acceptable to most thoughtful readers. We have composed particular chapters individually, and then passed them for comment to each other, and we should not claim that the resultant approaches to the sources are uniform. There might be some value in submitting what is intensely diverse and varied to a uniform thesis, but there is possibly greater value in an appropriate diversity. Criticism is a vital act of reception. It is not, as is often assumed, immanently hostile; but equally it is under no obligation to be a cheer-leader. We are not seeking to promote or to demolish the theories that we discuss, merely to examine them sharply in the light of a history of considerable interest in them. Our hope is that, in some part or preferably as a whole, you will find this book helpful to your own questioning, and your interest.

We should like to register our thanks here to Margaret Bartley and Beverley Tarquini, our editors at the publishers, and to the anonymous readers who provided a constructive commentary on our ideas and our text.

University of Exeter   Jane Milling
                                                      Graham Ley

1
Stanislavski's Theoretical System

Stanislavski (1863–1938) is one of the most familiar names in the modern theatre, and yet he is known primarily as a theorist. This situation is to some extent puzzling. Theatrical reputations might be thought to be generally established by prominence or reputation in performance or in writing scripts: quite simply, those who are famous in the theatre have traditionally been actors or playwrights, and more recently directors. In fact, Stanislavski was a dedicated and admired actor, and a significant director, but his prominence is undoubtedly due to the fame and reputation of his 'system', which is a mode of preparation for actors. There was, in the history of the European theatre, no real precedent for this, nor, indeed, for a pedagogic system of acting which crossed cultural boundaries to such great effect. So perhaps the opening questions in relation to Stanislavski should be why he felt the need to prepare actors, and why that need was experienced (and still is) so universally, or at least in a wide range of cultures.

To the first of these questions there is no convenient answer, except to assume that the late nineteenth century saw a crisis of some sort in the capacity of actors to perform in those scripts judged by management and audiences to be most appropriate. What may well be the case is that we are witnessing, in the phenomenon centred on his name, a massive shift in taste or reception which created a break with the past, one in which we are still to some extent involved. There are two associated phenomena which make that likely: the first is the certainty which now surrounds the cultural changes summarized in the term 'modern', and the second is the apparent dominance of related concepts of realism in divergent western cultures, and indeed outside them. Stanislavski was as

1

important to psychological realism in the United States of America, in both the theatre and film, as he was to the uniform if problematic concept of socialist realism in the former Soviet Union, which was applied as readily to music as to the theatre.[1]

But the temptation to link Stanislavski conveniently to some definition of realism is likely to deny some crucial aspects of the historical and theatrical context. Even if we were to assume, loosely enough, that 'realism' is an acceptable term for plays written to reflect contemporary society, then it has to be admitted that the Moscow Art Theatre which Stanislavski founded with Nemiro-vich-Danchenko in 1898 did not exclusively concern itself with contemporary plays. To take one prominent example, in one of his earliest accounts of the preparation of an actor, Stanislavski chooses to discuss a leading role in the bizarre if classic verse drama by Griboyedov, *Woe from Wit*, which was neither contemporary (it was first performed in 1831) nor, by virtue of its verse rhythms, realist in any convincing sense we could bring to the term.[2] Nonetheless, it is plain that the portrayal that Stanislavski chooses to bring to a lead-ing role in the play, that of Chatski, and the exemplary place he grants it in his demonstration of what an actor should do, make it central to the continuing revolution which he inspired in acting.

Of course, *Woe From Wit* stood as a classic of the Russian literary theatre – in Stanislavski's time a complimentary term – and that readily explains its choice. But it is evident that the objective of inner or psychological conviction in the actor in his actions on stage represents a cultural value which is not restricted to a particular class of scripts. Nor is it tied to a particular kind of scenic conven-tion, which might choose to represent a material reality in some detail. The prevalent mode of production in the more radical com-panies was that of naturalism, but this was compiled of curiously disparate elements. So, in the early years of the Moscow Art Thea-tre, fidelity in the creation of scenic environments ranged from an archaeological tendency for plays with a historical setting such as *Julius Caesar*, which was heavily indebted to the influential Meinin-ger company, to the evocation of the underclass for a production such as Gorky's *The Lower Depths*.[3] But the plays of Shakespeare, Gorky and Chekhov, even if realized with an accent on detailed material illusion, do not inherently make a stylistic composite which might compel the actor to respond within a specific mode of performance. Even naturalism does not arise naturally out of the innate scenic or scenographic qualities of the plays themselves.

So I wish to point out that there is something enigmatic in the creation of the modern theatre, and that if we use Stanislavski as a marker in defining it we are doing no more than to return to a problem we do not fully understand. What is clear is that this is a context for Stanislavski, one with which he is struggling and to which he is constantly trying to bring some coherence. He is not, as some others are to do, formulating a manifesto for a particular and specific intervention, but creating an alternative performance text for acting in changing circumstances.

There are, in fact, many different contexts that might be applied to Stanislavski. The first is the work of the Moscow Art Theatre, which now has some reasonable documentary representation in English, through the publication of selections of correspondence with a commentary, and of a good analytical account of some leading productions over its many years of existence (Benedetti 1991 and Worrall 1996, respectively). A second is biographical, a trend in understanding that is not only conventional for leading practitioners of theatre, but which is prompted by Stanislavski's autobiography, *My Life In Art*.[4] This volume is, significantly, the first work that was published in English, although it is by no means the earliest writing of Stanislavski which is now available in English, even discounting the letters. It has an important role in providing a charter or a justification for the system of preparation for the actor, which Stanislavski was to record and promulgate both in English and his native Russian language, and I shall discuss it a little later in this chapter. It should be read alongside the related but distinctive autobiographical work by his partner in the Moscow Art Theatre, Nemirovich-Danchenko (1937), which helps to complete the link between the experience and values of the directors and the activity of the theatre company. Yet another context is provided by the history of theatre schools in Russia: at present the material available in translation on this topic is piecemeal, although it is vital to our understanding of theatrical education and training in Europe and America and beyond, and of the constitution of the modern theatre itself. I shall discuss it very briefly below.

There can be no doubt that Stanislavski as the phenomenon he is could not have come into existence without his propensity and talent for writing, which was in some respects motivated by the need for income. He not only worked in the theatre when he was ill, in later life, but he kept writing and preparing editions of his writing. There is a compulsion in this which has had lasting effects, and which could not have arisen from a mere inclination to record a few thoughts, or some good practice, to use the contemporary jargon. Nor is his approach to writing simply that of the enthusiast, who sees the written text as a transparent means to the communication of important perceptions or intuitions. His texts are carefully designed, and although we must allow for the intervention of editors who were originally quite close associates, the form his writings take is to a large extent the substance of his influence. What exactly the 'system' is, or was, or has become outside reference to and reliance on the writings is very hard to track. As the Stanislavski scholar Benedetti has observed, drawing on comments made by Grotowski, different disciples of Stanislavski have disseminated the theory at different times, and Stanislavski himself never came to finite conclusions about its tenor and exact content (Benedetti 1989, 72–3). One major aspect of this diaspora is the role and influence of Boleslavsky, whose emigration to the United States gave rise eventually to the formation of method acting by Strasberg at the Actors Studio, which has had an immense impact on postwar cinema.[5] In fact, interpretations of Stanislavski within practice or in institutions are immensely diverse, and it is quite beyond the scope of this book to track them.[6] But it is worth questioning whether there is such a thing as the 'system', or whether it has become one of the most influential myths of the modern theatre.

The publication history of Stanislavski's writings has been set out clearly by Benedetti, with additional commentary coming from other scholars (Benedetti 1989, Appendix: 76–9).[7] Stanislavski exists very firmly in both the English and Russian languages, but is different in each. This is a result of the timing of publication, which could not be coordinated, and of the effects of different editorial support and intervention, which have their own histories in the United States (with Norman and Elizabeth Hapgood) and in the Soviet Union and now Russia (with Gurevich, Kristi and others). One important characteristic is that publication came relatively late, and began (in English) after the decisive visit of the Moscow Art Theatre to the United States in 1922–23. The significant theoretical texts in English are these: *An Actor Prepares* (1936), *Building a Character* (1949), *Creating a Role* (1961), with *Stanislavsky on the Art of the Stage* (1950), a transcript from a student's notes of lectures given by Stanislavski to opera singers between 1918 and 1922. *An Actor Prepares* and *Building a Character* are essentially two parts of one work, *An Actor's Work on Himself*, of which the first alone was published

before Stanislavski's death in 1938. *Creating a Role*, although published last, combines studies written at different times on three
plays: the first (mentioned above, on Griboyedov's *Woe from Wit*)
between 1916 and 1920, the second (on *Othello*) between 1930 and
1933, and the last (on Gogol's *The Government Inspector*) in 1936–37.
Of other English translations, *Stanislavski's Legacy* is a collection of
minor pieces of little theoretical importance, and *An Actor's Handbook* is a dictionary of 'pithy statements' of Stanislavski's ideas.[8] The
whole sequence of texts has its prelude in the publication of the
autobiographical *My Life in Art* in its English version in 1924. New
English-language translations of the major works, taken from the
Russian editions, have been promised for some time, but it is
through those listed here that Stanislavski has been known in English during the twentieth century.

Tracing the genesis of the system is bound to be intriguing, and
much of Stanislavski's autobiography is dedicated to a sense of the
discovery of an artistic mission which must be accurately identified,
and of the promise and guarantee of artistic integrity that the
evolution of a method will embody. But *My Life in Art* is not
referring to an existing body of published texts, and so the charter
that it aims to offer is, paradoxically, in support of something that is
not as yet overtly expressed. As it seems, the context for the generation of a disciplined preparation for the actor is formed of many
constituents. The first of these is Stanislavski's work on himself as
an actor conceived ideally in a tradition of great actors of his
century, notably in succession to figures such as the Russian
Shchepkin (who died in the year of Stanislavski's birth) and the
Italian Salvini, who was seen by Stanislavski. Both are mentioned
regularly in the autobiography and in later writings. The demands
that Stanislavski placed on himself plainly form a core of experience, on which he draws to place demands through specific exercises and challenges on the performer in the company, or the actor
as student.

Secondly, there is the contribution made by the system of introducing a play to actors which was embraced by both Stanislavski
and Nemirovich-Danchenko for the Moscow Art Theatre (Nemirovich-Danchenko 1937, 94–5). The mechanical implementation of a
script without discussion or examination is recorded by Nemirovich-Danchenko as a standard feature of theatrical practice rejected
by both partners (*ibid.*, 96–8). Nemirovich-Danchenko complains
that in that prevalent scheme of rehearsal the actors quite quickly

'arrange the play by themselves', whereas a defining feature of the regime established by the pair was the continuing importance of the director, what Nemirovich-Danchenko calls 'the dictatorial will of the director-*régisseur*' (*ibid.*, 98 and 88 respectively). The model for this was undoubtedly the 'monarchical authority' of Kronek, the director of the Meininger company, which had visited Russia in 1885 and 1890 (*ibid.*, 104).[9] Both men acknowledged his influence upon them, and both had for some years exercised authority in their respective groups, Stanislavski in the Society of Art and Literature, and Nemirovich-Danchenko as head of the drama school at the Philharmonic Society, one of two in Moscow, which he ran from 1891.

This last fact introduces a third constituent, which is the pedagogic quality of their formation as directors. In his autobiography, Stanislavski makes no mention of the school he added to the Society of Art and Literature in 1888, but Nemirovich-Danchenko writes of both partners as pedagogues:

> To begin with, we were both of us in our groups absolute *régisseurs* and pedagogues. Both of us were accustomed to impose our sole will; more than that, we accustomed our pupils to submit to it. Furthermore, we were convinced it could not be otherwise. (*ibid.*, 106)

In this connection, Worrall has provided some useful information on the development of drama schools in Russia in the nineteenth century. He also gives a short account of the foundation of the Moscow Art Theatre school in 1901, and its early years, for which there is little documentation available in English (Worrall 1996, 65–7). The numbers admitted were small, and over three years of induction they regularly became smaller. Lastly, and in addition to the involvement of both directors in teaching the students, there is the intermediate status of the successive studios of the Moscow Art Theatre to take into account as a site for research into method. But the system itself became truly significant as a practical possibility when it was formally adopted as the company's rehearsal method in 1911, despite Nemirovich-Danchenko's doubts and reluctance.[10] To make matters more awkward, the principal accounts in English translation of Stanislavski's methods in rehearsal date from the later periods of his activity for the company, in the early 1920s and at the end of his life.[11]

This combination of factors makes the identity of the system hard to determine, in its different manifestations as an intensive process for production-preparation and rehearsal, or as an extended programme for student training. It is perfectly possible that the idea of a system, which will support and yet discipline the actor, is the primary ambition. This may then constitute what I referred to earlier as a myth, shifting in modes of re-telling from its inception in the aspirations of Stanislavski, through practical implementation and textual record, to the continuing promise of satisfactory induction and successful training.

The earliest component of the written theory that is available to us is the first part of *Creating a Role*, which is an exposition in three parts of Stanislavski's approach to the role of Chatski, the disillusioned lover, in Griboyedov's *Woe from Wit*. The background to this is interesting, because the play had been produced by the Moscow Art Theatre in 1906, after some delays, and revived in 1914, but in both these productions Stanislavski had taken and developed the role of Famusov, the father-figure of the satirical comedy, rather than Chatski.[12] Early in 1915 Nemirovich-Danchenko wrote to Stanislavski complaining that Stanislavski did not understand 'the actor's particular theatrical gift', and lamenting the inability of the partners to 'direct plays together' (Benedetti 1991, 299–300). In the letter he alluded to the history of that failure:

> In the past this was explained by the fact that you went from the outside, from the characteristics, from the 'picture', and I from the inner image, from the psychology, the 'sketch'. But then you moved over to the psychological.[13]

Nemirovich-Danchenko then claims that he offered Stanislavski a 'sketch' for the role of Famusov, 'acted it out' several times 'in order to make it clear' and was twice asked to repeat it by Stanislavski, but that the latter subsequently failed to credit him with any influence on the success of the role. Stanislavski apparently began writing his study of the role of Chatski in 1916, but as a compensation, it seems, for a sense of frustration in the actual productions, which had been directed substantially by his partner. So this is theory not documentation, presenting the preparation for a fantasy role in a fictional production.

The presentation is given as a direct address to the reader, and is clearly theoretical in its organization and its frame. The three parts of the process that are announced at the outset are an early version of the more familiar, later form of the developed theory of process, with inner preparation ('the period of emotional experience') in the second part, and physical realization supposedly the subject of the third. These correspond, in anticipation, to the first two parts of *An Actor's Work on Himself*, which we now find in *An Actor Prepares* and *Building a Character* respectively. In addition, there is included as the first part an opening period of study, which confirms the importance of the radical changes that Nemirovich-Danchenko and Stanislavski brought to the early period of preparation for rehearsal and production. The presiding imagery, which introduces and forms the continuing frame for the presentation, is that of sexual desire and union between a man and a woman. So the first reading of the play is like the 'first meeting between a man and a woman . . . who are destined to be sweethearts, lovers, or mates', and 'first impressions have a virginal freshness about them' which acts as a stimulus. They are also 'seeds', and they 'often leave ineradicable traces which will remain as a basis of a part, the embryo of an image to be formed' (*Creating a Role* = CR 3). In this sensitive moment, the reader who reads the play to the cast acts like a tactful go-between, and must not intrude his personal interpretation on the roles, since the actors must be free to feel the play emotionally, without obstacles (CR 5). Enticing as the imagery is, it also serves conversely as an dire warning against rushing carelessly into a script: 'You cannot erase a spoiled first impression any more than you can recover lost maidenhood.' The ideal reader sounds remarkably like Nemirovich-Danchenko, whose reputation as a writer and literary figure had confirmed for many years his predominance as the literary manager for the Moscow Art Theatre (CR 6–7).

The debt to Nemirovich-Danchenko may be more than that, or it may be that at this time Stanislavski the nascent writer and theorist is looking to his literary partner to provide assurance and validation. In the opening of part two, the imagery of the seed is ascribed to a comparison, or simile, made by Nemirovich-Danchenko, in which the seed of the author's script, planted in the actor, must decompose to emerge as a plant. In this vision, the metaphor of nature as creativity is simple and reassuring, but as presented it also suggests a dual authorship for performance and production, shared between actor and script-writer, which has an immense resonance in the twentieth century. The role of the director is noticeably marginal here. For Stanislavski, this second period is one of creation, equivalent to consummation and conception, and the organic quality which he asserts for acting offers a vital charter for the proper study of that discipline, and a high status for the activity itself:

> The creative process of living and experiencing a part is an organic one, founded on the physical and spiritual laws governing the nature of man, on the truthfulness of his emotions, and on natural beauty. How does this organic process originate and develop, of what does this creative work of the actor here consist? (*CR* 44)

Conceived in this way, the study of acting is a natural science like any other. The process of acting already exists as an organic entity, both physical and spiritual, and as such it has both truth and beauty: all that remains is for the natural scientist to discover its originating sources or inspiration, and to chart the stages of its progression and natural development. It is a model which will recur in the theatrical theory traced by this book. The completion of the imagery at the opening of part three, in which physical embodiment is compared to birth and early growth, is tame by comparison, since the work of the image has been done.

Much of the first part of the presentation is pragmatic, granted the premise that the play must be studied. But there are principles on which Stanislavski insists, and they reveal a particular profile for the kind of analysis that he envisages. For an actor, he states, knowing is feeling, and so an actor's analysis is an analysis of feeling. This must include a search for sensual memories which will be related or will relate the actor to the play, and these are stored in the actor's 'emotion memory' (*CR* 9). Stanislavski here concentrates on the principle to which he alludes at the opening of part two, one which characterizes his later theoretical position consistently: granted a creative process is organic, what matters above all is to find its sources. So creativity must find a root from its unconscious state into action, motion and effect, and that requires conscious preparation: 'Through the conscious to the unconscious – that is the motto of our art and technique.' (*ibid.*). Studying the course of the action in the play is working on one plane, and studying the social situation is working on another, but ultimately Stanislavski suggests reliance by the actor on imagination to put life into what he calls external circumstances. Through imagination the actor can exercise a mental version of what we might now call virtual reality, wandering about the house in which the play is set and confronting specific characters (*CR* 21–30). The actor may set up an imaginary dialogue with a character, and the imagination may also provoke the actor's own feelings into dialogue, by suggesting acceptable motives for characters whose behaviour is emotionally repellent (*CR* 32 and 36–8 respectively).

This approach continues for part two, in which the imagination prompts the actor to recreate a scene, offering the actor a path into the inner action that is so strongly desired (*CR* 45–8). It is this inner action which forms another essential principle, and Stanislavski spells out the paradox: the most decisive kind of action is internal. As such it must be lived by the actor, and it can only be lived if it is composed from the actor's own feelings and desires (*CR* 50). So desire is more than a suggestive image; it is an indication of a vital motive which must be coaxed rather than commanded from the actor. In order to coax it successfully, there must be an objective, which 'is the lure for our emotions' (*CR* 51). In relation to the role of Chatski, this objective, like the desire, is overtly sexual, that of preventing 'an unnatural and unaesthetic union' taking place. Stanislavski is, on this topic, not altogether clear whether this constitutes a conscious or unconscious objective, which is perhaps just as well in a performer who draws on his ability to 'be touched by his own efforts to save an inexperienced girl intent on destroying herself.' (*CR* 53–4). Furthermore, psychological objectives must be bound up with physical objectives, and in such a manner that the inner life of the character is not only manifest when the actor is speaking the character's lines. This means that the actor must create an alternative and complementary script to that of the play itself, something that Stanislavski designates 'the score of a role' (*CR* 56–62). Later, Stanislavski is to distinguish between two 'scores' for Chatski, that of a friend and that of a lover (*CR* 76).

The analysis of objectives, and alternative scores, is complex, and from it issue two more crucial components of Stanislavski's theoretical vision: contradiction, and the notion of the superobjective. Contradiction is a quality of genius in Stanislavski the writer, and one which is seldom noticed in dogmatic or mechanical accounts of the system. In some respects, the analysis here of process based on the role of Chatski degenerates into simplicity, as Stanislavski, caught by his own theoretical framework of desire, settles on passion as a central definition of the character. Yet, at the same time, this relatively uninspired simplicity – it is a perception adduced to add 'depth' to the portrayal – is combined with and qualified by the admonition that passions are formed from individual, varied, and even contradictory feelings: the example given is that of the passion and feelings of a loving mother when she strikes a child in anger after it was nearly run over. Similarly, he advises that the evil in a good character should be sought out, the stupidity lurking in intelligence, the gravity in an ebullient character (*CR* 67–8 and 69 respectively). Most impressively, the line of action for any character will encounter frustrations and obstacles, and be confronted and confused by those of other characters: life is a struggle, and those collisions and conflicts 'constitute the dramatic situation' (*CR* 80).

In some senses, this is far more subtle than the presentation of the superobjective, 'the objective of all objectives', the transcending principle of interpretation which is the ultimate and satisfying unity of all endeavour, and 'the quintessence of the play' (*CR* 78 and 79 respectively). This concept, incorporating as it does such theoretical absolutes as unity and transcendence, can inevitably only be realized by 'artists of genius', and so like many theoretical objectives remains withheld from most readers. It is paired with the far more comprehensible, analytical 'through line of action' which permits the actor to attain the superobjective, as it has allowed the writer to express it (*CR* 78–9). Yet this combination of the writer and the actor, although it looks attractive, makes the concept of the superobjective problematic at this stage. On the one hand it is banal, equivalent as it seems to the familiar idea of the dominant passion in any individual: this is the illustration that Chatski offers, of passion in its erotic form, and Stanislavski suggests further unremarkable examples in the miser's aspiration for riches, the ambitious person's 'thirst for honors', the aesthete's 'artistic ideals' (*CR* 79). But, in the writer, Stanislavski identifies spiritual and metaphysical superobjectives (Dostoyevski's 'search for God and Devil in the soul of man' in *The Brothers Karamazov*, 'the comprehending of the secrets of being' in Shakespeare's *Hamlet*) with thoroughly personal quests, such as Tolstoy's 'unending search for "self-perfection"' (*CR* 78). Whether and how these are contained or expressed in the work itself, or to be sensed of the author through the work, is unclear. But the final theoretical formula is already certain of its terms:

Thus the process of living your part consists of composing a score for your role, of a superobjective, and of its active attainment by means of the through line of action. (*CR* 80)

The third part, on physical embodiment, significantly fails to rise to these heights, with little even in the way of valuable instruction for the actor, apart from the pedestrian advice to rely on observation, or to make sketches.

Notes taken by a student rather than a text prepared by Stanislavski form the substance of *Stanislavsky on the Art of the Stage*, translated by Magarshack and published in the same year as his biography of Stanislavski (Stanislavski 1950). The notes date from 1918–22, when Stanislavski responded to a request to open a studio for singers of the Bolshoi Opera. In his autobiography Stanislavski states that in the first year of operation a small number of established singers came along, but that for subsequent years he insisted on having younger singers, for whom he constructed a syllabus (Stanislavski 1924, 558–62). Not much of that syllabus is apparent from the 30 talks that constitute the shorthand record, which carry the title 'The System and Methods of Creative Art'. Magarshack comments that Stanislavski 'did not believe in "lecturing"', and that these 'discourses were never prepared', and certainly they are inordinately repetitive and for the most part unrevealing about the nature of the teaching involved (Stanislavski 1950, 79). Stanislavski concentrates on the ethics of belonging to a studio, offering in the centre of the series observations on such topics as alertness, concentration, and even gladness. Momentarily, the discursive flow of exhortation is broken by allusions to specific examples or exercises, which are tantalizing. In talk XII Stanislavski fixes on a knife which is to be used, in a dramatic plot, to kill a rival, and starts with concentration on the implement itself. He then insists on the performer widening the circle of concentration to include the memory of the time when this enemy was a friend, in childhood, or the occasion on which he saved 'your' life, complicating the feelings by what I have called his technique of contradiction (*ibid.*, 145–8). This principle is repeated in talk XVII, in which the performer is urged to discover at least one moment when a villain has shown courage or been good. Stanislavski covers this advice with the ethical principle of 'courage' as a performer, but it is plain that contradiction is understood to be an intense quality of successful portrayal (*ibid.*, 185–6; he follows this with another reference to the relationship of mother and child, 186–7).

Apart from these moments, there are glimpses of theoretical ideas, notably the insistence, which is surely part of the 'system' to which Stanislavski constantly alludes, on the thought of '''I want to'' ' which must motivate every action and so every part of the script or libretto (*ibid.*, 157–9, 173 and elsewhere). Similarly, 'if' recurs throughout the talks, to mark significantly the difference between the mere fact of impersonation and the artistic challenge that should result from it: not 'I am this character', but 'if I am this character, then what follows from that'. The two principles should then combine, as Stanislavski explains: ' ''*If* I am Tatyana, I want to give my love, I want to disclose to you the inmost secrets of my heart…'' ' (*ibid.*, 180). Towards the end of the sequence, there is even a momentary reference to 'the little magic word "if"' (*ibid.*, 245). In fact, in these concluding talks, exercises and the style of teaching do begin to emerge: in talk XXVIII a Miss X is faced with the task of entering the studio and picking a quarrel with each of its members, starting with Stanislavski himself (we find here that there are five in the room). There is no representation of dialogue, but the talk contains a response in character from Stanislavski accused of infidelity in the opening gambit by Miss X, a self-critique by him, and then a critique of Miss X and her approach (*ibid.*, 239–44). In talk XXX, Mr Y is told to sit down and imagine himself to be an old, sick man. Instruction proceeds by way of an immediate criticism of Mr Y's representation, by re-setting the problem, by a second immediate condemnation of the results, and by the suggestion of a detailed score of physical actions that Mr Y then follows (*ibid.*, 251–3). The rehearsals of Massenet's *Werther* that conclude the series of talks are less revealing, and date from just before the Moscow Art Theatre left (in 1922) for its tour in Europe and the United States.

On the first foreign tour of European cities in 1906, Stanislavski had been accompanied by Nemirovich-Danchenko (Nemirovich-Danchenko 1937, 277–326). The second European tour was conducted by Stanislavski alone, and it concluded with a voyage to New York, and performances in New York, Chicago, Philadelphia and Boston (in 1923). After a period of rest in Europe, Stanislavski returned later in the year for a second season in New York, and toured other American cities in 1924. The American tour was marketed by the theatrical manager Morris Gest, and founded Stanislavski's individual reputation as a celebrity in the United States. As a companion to the promotion of the tour came an offer to publish a theatrical life, a stage autobiography by Stanislavski, and to this project he committed himself earnestly.

My Life in Art, is a complex, intriguing and charismatic account of its subject, and an immensely successful exercise in public relations. It was first published in English in 1924, and revised for a Russian edition published in 1926 (Benedetti 1989, 76–7). Like many autobiographies, it is vocational, which means that the narrative takes the reader through a series of false starts leading towards the goal. The book successfully communicates this sense of frustration, and by doing so supports the feeling that a great conclusion is eventually found. The spiritual history is confessional, with self-criticism and self-transcendence constant motifs, written in a manner which testifies to effort, dedication, honesty and survival, and which also leads the reader emotively towards the belief in a solution. There are other, signal characteristics of the narrative, of which the most telling is the emphasis on the inadequacy of the actor.[14] Stanislavski is a harsh judge at times of his own portrayals, and this critical self-consciousness is translated into what becomes at times almost an ideology of the actor's weakness, fallibility and sheer idleness. *My Life in Art* is ultimately a history of the revolution undertaken by Stanislavski against that debilitating *ancien régime*, and the announcement of his system promises the disclosure of the secrets of the art of acting held by 'the great masters of the stage', but rarely if ever passed on to another by them.

> The absence of this tradition sentenced our art to become dilettantism. From the inability to find a conscious path to unconscious creativeness, actors reached destructive prejudices which denied spiritual technique; they grew cold in the surface layers of scenic craft and accepted empty theatrical self-consciousness for true inspiration. I know only one method of combating this so dangerous circumstance for the actor. This is to describe in a well-balanced system all that I have reached after long researches...
> (Stanislavski 1924, 571)

Autobiographies should contain profound rejections, and may also issue in a sense of enlightenment. *My Life in Art* is an immense success in confirming celebrity and establishing the pattern of personal achievement, and it is a charter for a practice which has discovered, after a lifetime's effort, 'a few grains of gold.' What is promised is 'a guide, a series of exercises' that will lead to inspiration for the actor, and seldom has the hope of theatrical redemption found such devoted adherents (*ibid.*, 572 and 571 respectively).

An Actor Prepares is probably the most familiar of all Stanislavski's writings in English translation. It has, of the systematic works, the longest history since it was published in 1936, and *Building a Character*, the second of this English-language trilogy, appeared only in 1949, to be followed after another extended interval by *Creating a Role* in 1961. We may also detect, in this relative popularity, a bias in reception towards that part of the system or method which relates to work on the inner, emotional psychology of the role, which may take its lead from a preference expressed in the work itself. In *An Actor Prepares*, Tortsov says 'I do admit that I incline towards the emotional side of creativeness ...' (*An Actor Prepares* = *AP* 248). Alternatively, it may be that Stanislavski's supervision of this volume has resulted in something more convincing in printed form; a final possibility might be that it is simply more successful, more consistent and more thorough as a written presentation than its sequels.

An Actor Prepares is conceived most overtly in the form of a dialogue, and Stanislavski may have had any number of models for this. The origins of the literary dialogue lie with Plato who used it to expound, through the person of Socrates, the philosophical victory of right thinking over mistaken beliefs and arguments. Dialogue is ideally suited to contradicting error, and had precedents in theatrical theory of which Stanislavski was almost certainly aware, namely Diderot in the influential *Paradox on the Actor* and some of the writings of Edward Gordon Craig, with whom Stanislavski had collaborated.[15] Dialogue almost emerges from the final talks in the series from the Bolshoi Opera studio, and it is relatively plain that Stanislavski engaged his students in this kind of interrogation of realization and achievement. But a dialogue in literary form is not just a record of a conversation, pedagogic or not, and the framework of the narrative is carefully established. It transpires that we are reading an account recorded by a student Kostya of the instruction given by the Director, Tortsov, in a drama school or studio; we learn, in the course of the account, that Kostya has shorthand skills (*AP* 240). As has been pointed out by (for example) Benedetti, Kostya is the familiar version of Konstantin, and so Stanislavski can be present both as the narrator, the 'I' of the

account, and as the teacher Tortsov, whose name carries the con-
notation 'creator'.[16] In this way Stanislavski is able to chart learning
as well as instruction, and to incorporate a version of the autobiographical conviction he had constructed in *My Life in Art*.

An Actor Prepares covers the first year of training in this school,
and the narrative supposedly offers a record of between eighty to
one hundred lessons, almost exclusively with the Director, who is
himself called off infrequently to perform or to tour. There is occasional mention of other lessons – dancing, gymnastics, fencing,
voice-placing and diction is the largest list, without further detail
– and repeated reference is made to 'drill', which appears late in the
book to refer to exercises in muscular relaxation and concentration,
repeated from earlier in the course (*AP* 170 and 266 respectively).[17]
The students are introduced indirectly to aspects of lighting and
scene-design or scenic arrangement, which appear to be supervised
by the Assistant Director, Rakhmanov, who is also responsible for
discipline in the school, and for putting up the placards used to
announce a specific concept (*AP* 2–3 for discipline, and *AP* 223 for
the placard announcing 'adaptation'). The number of students is
small – six are characterized to some effect, but others are named –
and classes take place on the stage of the school for the most part,
with the stage curtain drawn for much of the time to obscure the
auditorium. The personal circumstances of any student are only
exceptionally revealed in any depth when they emerge unavoidably
into the lessons: one female student has had an illegitimate child
which died. The Director, Tortsov, relies on a small number of
improvised scenes, to which he makes the students return to some
purpose; some scenes from a shortlist of plays (*Hamlet, Othello,
Brand*) which partly stem from student choices; illustrative anecdotes; various, arranged stage environments; and a series of challenges, often given to individuals or to the class in turn. The
teaching is founded on a principle that Tortsov describes as 'learning by vivid practical example', and he declares that he is fearful of
'falling into philosophy and straying from the path of practical
demonstration' (*AP* 242–3). It is distinctly noticeable, from the narrative itself, that the students become more confused and recalcit-
rant towards the end of the year and of the book.

In some respects, the narrative is presented as seamless, as a
constant progression through exercises which concentrate on a particular perception or activity, and then move on, often abruptly, to
another. In fact, there are two major breaks in the flow. The first

occurs at ch. VI, when Kostya hurts himself and has to rest, and Tortsov interrupts what he calls 'the strictly systematic development of our programme', interposing exercises on the relaxation of muscles which properly belong to 'the external side of our training' (*AP* 95). This is, in fact, a distinction which has not been made as yet to the students, or the reader. The second break occurs at the end of ch. XI, when Tortsov states to the students that he has brought them 'temporarily to the end of our study of the internal elements necessary to the creative process in an actor' (*AP* 243). The remaining elements are displayed on placards, and they will be deferred to the second part of the training which we find in *Building a Character*, although that is not plainly stated at this point. So a potential second year and second part, on external training, haunt the narrative of the first and interrupt it, suggesting a design for the method or system which is not made explicit.

It may be helpful to see these three sections of *An Actor Prepares* as successively concerned with basic principles, theory and realization, all three in connection with what Stanislavski allows Tortsov finally to fix as the 'inner creative state' of the actor. The opening process is like an audition rather than a lesson, one in which the Director expressly does not teach, but allows the student's own sense of failure to illuminate a need. The primary statement of principle is framed by quotations from the actors Salvini and Shchepkin, and it insists on the need for feeling in acting to be moved by the subconscious, and for the actor to reach the subconscious by oblique or indirect means, so ensuring that acting is both natural and true (*AP* 12–14). This, for Tortsov, confirms that 'realism and even naturalism in the inner preparation of a part is essential, because it causes your subconscious to work....' That principle issues in an imperative, which in its two parts implicitly describes the organization of the system: 'An actor is under the obligation to live his part inwardly, and then to give to his experience an external embodiment' (*AP* 15). The method to be followed, which is identified with 'true art', is contrasted with other, unsatisfactory means of acting such as representation (a 'mirror' form), the mechanical (drawn from conventions), and over-acting (reliant on clichés); the final category of error is that of vanity, which forms part of Stanislavski's persistent caricature of the female student Sonya.

Other basic principles follow this induction. If it is necessary to act inwardly, then the 'fundamental principle' of 'unconscious creativeness through conscious technique' is best activated by introducing the 'if' as a stimulus to the imagination (*AP* 50). The 'given circumstances' of the play, 'its facts, events, epoch, time and place of action, conditions of life', the interpretations of actors and director, its *mise-en-scène* and production values will provide the 'if', and by this means the actor will 'bring to life what is hidden under the words' (*AP* 50–1). The imagination is vital, either in its visual and pictorial capacity of visualizing (students are asked to be a tree, and see what the tree sees) or in its capacity of displaying a virtual reality such as entering a house, which was explored in the study of Griboyedov's *Woe from Wit* (*AP* ch. IV, 54–71). This opening sequence of the statement and discovery of principles, and their exploration and validation through exercises, is concluded with work on the concentration of attention.

The brief hiatus granted by Kostya's accident and an excursus on the relaxation of muscles allows the narrative to move into its central, and heavily theoretical section. The actor must analyse a play and a role within the play, breaking both down into units, each of which should have an objective at its heart, and the succession of both units and objectives should form a 'channel', or 'a logical and coherent stream' (*AP* 115 and 117 respectively). The objectives may be physical and external (the approach to a formal handshake), or psychologically simple (a sincere, heartfelt handshake) or complex (apologizing for an insult) (*AP* 119–20). The objective is drawn from the unit by finding a verb – an active motive – rather than a noun to describe it. The simple technique is to apply 'I wish to do – so and so' to a unit to find the objective, and the students confirm by their own explorations that 'the *verbs* provoked thoughts and feelings which were, in turn, inner challenges to action' (*AP* 121–6).

By the middle of *An Actor Prepares*, Stanislavski is sufficiently confident to introduce the term 'psycho-technique', notably in a chapter which emphasizes that 'every physical act...has an inner source of feeling' (*AP* ch. VIII, 151 and 144 respectively). The introduction of this term announces the central theoretical position to be occupied by 'emotion memory', which must be distinguished from the more superficial 'sensation memory', associated principally, for Tortsov, with the senses of smell, taste and touch. Stanislavski's approach to this central concept, derived or adapted from the French psychologist Ribot, is to have Kostya witness and record an accident in the street, which a week later is displaced or adjusted in his memory by other incidents that happened earlier in his life.[18] Memories, in Tortsov's explanation of this phenomenon, are filtered by time, which produces a result like an archive, a source of inspiration in the actor's work for which a stimulus is required. This stimulus may be provided by the stage setting, or it may be activated by sympathy in the actor for the character. Since this is a theory that links the art of composing scripts – Shakespeare applied his own 'crystallized emotion memories' to stories received from others (*AP* 173) – to the art of acting we expect more here, but the theory falters on these two rather disparate and generalized stimuli. Indeed, it is not clear that sympathy is essentially a stimulus, because Stanislavski has Tortsov conclude that it is a parallel source to emotion memory as creative material (*AP* 190). The vocabulary of means is limited, and tentative in describing the process: so we read of a 'psycho-technical store of riches', but of a 'lure' or of the need to 'coax' out emotions, which are 'as shy as wild animals' and 'hide in the depths of our souls' (*AP* 191). It is a hesitation that will recur with the concept of the superobjective at the close of the book.

The unsystematic nature of what is proposed as a system is apparent from the faltering steps with which Stanislavski–Tortsov proceeds to the third section of the book, which nonetheless contains the summation of the theory. After chapters on communion with self and a partner on stage, and the adjustments or adaptations that an actor needs to realize in the path of performance, Tortsov announces the end of 'our study of the internal elements necessary to the creative process in an actor' (*AP* 243). This announcement, as I have mentioned, is accompanied by placards indicating other elements that Tortsov chooses to postpone. It is then followed, without explanation, by a celebratory recapitulation of the three vital 'inner motive forces': feeling, the mind or imagination, and the will. These are apparently the 'masters' that play upon the elements and methods of psycho-technique, but Tortsov faces a complaint that he has concentrated the attention of his students largely on feeling, which he answers by claiming that he is compensating for a general tendency to discount feeling in acting (*AP* 247–8). There is a short silence at the end of this lesson, as if Stanislavski is willing to admit the inadequacy of his exposition as Tortsov. The subsequent chapters prepare the line of the actor towards the goal, which will not be clear until the line is established.

The 'unbroken line' is a principle of continuity for the actor in performance, and it has two facets. The playwright offers only what the characters say and do on stage, and this is inadequate for the actor: according to Tortsov, 'we have to fill out what he leaves unsaid' in the lives and experience of the characters (*AP* 257). The second facet of continuity, which would be less contentious, is that of the actor's attention on the stage, which must also be unbroken. This unbroken line in the life of a character will then have a direction, which must be sustained through the realization of objectives by the inner motive forces of feeling, mind, and will; if the objectives are vague, then this will adversely affect the inner creative mood (*AP* 270). The overall direction taken is guided by an awareness of the super-objective, about which Stanislavski is as uncertain as he was when it was introduced in the study of Griboyedov's *Woe from Wit* discussed above. The personal, spiritual motives of Dostoyevski and Tolstoy as authors are mentioned again, and in this case are linked with Chekhov, who, for his part, 'wrestled with the triviality of bourgeois life', a struggle which 'became the *leit motiv* of his literary productions' (*AP* 271). These authorial quests are, according to Tortsov, in some way to be associated with the superobjective of the given work, notably the play, but how we or the actors are to understand this subtle and obscure process is not explained. Instead, Tortsov chooses to equate the superobjective with the apparently simple but problematic concept of the 'main theme' of the play:

> The main theme must be firmly fixed in an actor's mind throughout the performance. It gave birth to the writing of the play. It should also be the fountain-head of the actor's artistic creation. (*AP* 273)

Once again, Stanislavski chooses to conclude with silence on the part of the students, and with the dissatisfaction with the system felt, on this occasion, by Kostya himself (*AP* 279–80).

Ultimately, the system is made to rely upon the subconscious, with which *An Actor Prepares* ends. It becomes apparent that the objectives, as steps towards a goal, 'will, to a large extent, be taken subconsciously' (*AP* 300). The through-line of action is made up of these objectives, large or small, and the through-line eventually realizes the superobjective. Even the 'main theme', which must be chosen to be 'in harmony with the intentions of the playwright', can only be found subconsciously by the actor, clothed in the person of the character (*AP* 301–2 and 306 respectively). So the whole process is subconscious, and appears as the initiation concludes to be rather like a mystical journey into the underworld, announced by a prophet: 'Then, as I have told you, truth and faith will lead you into the region of the subconscious and hand you over to the power of nature' (*AP* 295).

Building a Character represents, in its own account, the second year of the fictional course in the school run by Tortsov, which 'is devoted to the external aspect of acting, the building of our physical apparatus' (*Building a Character* = BC 275). Predictably, for this reason, the narrative includes references to a greater variety of classes apart from those led by the director, who introduces teachers and whose own role is more of an intervention in those classes. Apart from his assistant Rakhmanov's classes in 'drill', we read of 'regular daily exercises' in Swedish gymnastics (BC 37–8), of 'a famous circus clown' teaching tumbling (BC 39), of a dancing class (BC 41), of exercises in plastic movement led by Madame Sonova (BC 48), of voice classes led by Madame Zarembo (BC 92, 105, 108), and of classes on accentuation led by Sechenov (BC 171). The conclusion offers a picture of even more: gymnastics, acrobatics, fencing, wrestling, boxing and carriage or deportment are listed (BC 272). While these skills together provide one narrative framework of support for the physicality of the student-actor, the need for a discipline of acting is enhanced by analogy with other arts. This is first apparent in the curious exhibition assembled by Rakhmanov, which includes plaster casts of statues, paintings, photographs and books on costume, scene design, ballet and dance, and a list of the Moscow museums (BC 36). But the most insistent comparisons in the narrative, largely made by Tortsov himself, are with painting and then with dance and music. So a director may add a touch to the work of an actor rather as a master painter may improve the work of a pupil (BC 76), while the actor may make a painting with a word (BC 151), or use rhythms like a painter uses colours (BC 205–6). Musicians, singers and dancers are fortunate in the control of rhythm offered by metronomes, time and measure, conductors and choir masters, and these performers with the addition of writers and even a meticulous surgeon are later all examples of skilled practitioners who keep in daily training (BC 214 and 259–60). In conclusion, the actor must have control of his instrument, that is 'of all the spiritual and physical aspects of a human being', and actors should study 'the laws, the theory of their art' just as musicians do. It is this which constitutes 'the programme of work' which is the 'system' (BC 294).

Of the theoretical ideas elaborated in *Building a Character* possibly the most significant is that of 'subtext', that which 'lies behind and beneath the actual words of a part', as Tortsov formulates it in ch. VIII. The subtext runs towards the ultimate super-objective as an equivalent, in its relation to speech, to the through line of action. More precisely:

> It is the manifest, the inwardly felt expression of a human being in a part, which flows uninterruptedly beneath the words of the text, giving them life and a basis for existing... It is the subtext that makes us say the words we do in a play. (*BC* 113)

In this theory, the scripted word itself is empty or inert, 'not valuable in and of itself', like a musical score, until actors or musicians 'breathe the life of their own sentiment into the subtext' (*BC* 114). In order to illuminate his concept of the subtext, Tortsov draws on a picture-book theory of language which postulates that words (notably nouns) evoke mental pictures and 'visual images', which may then be communicated to an actor's partner on the stage (*BC* 115–18). These 'inner pictures' should be composed into 'a whole film, a running subtext', with the actor as 'author' of the subtext conveying the images and not just the words to a partner (*BC* 119). A reliance on this 'inner stream of images' which is 'like a moving picture constantly thrown on the screen of our inner vision' will also stimulate the emotion memory, just as physical actions had acted as 'lures' to the actor's feelings in the first part of the programme (*BC* 124–6). Curiously this theory reverses Stanislavski–Tortsov's insistence on the importance of verbs in realizing the objectives of a role, but it is not challenged by the students.

The demonstrations with the metronome that are meant to establish the value and validity of the concept of tempo-rhythm (in ch. XI) are extended, but provide little in the way of theoretical conviction, and fail absolutely to consider the cultural context and determinants of socially specific actions. The narrative relies on what Kostya feels to be the actions associated with different tempo-rhythms, with little sign of an accompanying systematic or disciplinary rigour. So, in the final stages, an agitated rhythm conjures up galloping to Kostya, but he himself becomes a fugitive in the mountains hiding from a pursuing horseman; when the melody tracing the tempo-rhythm turns 'tender', his thoughts turn to love, and it is his 'sweetheart' rather than a 'mounted bandit' in pursuit (*BC* 203). The power attributed to tempo-rhythm of suggesting 'not only images but also whole scenes' clearly extends to clichés of dubious systematic value, and the physical definition of the concept mutates into a metaphorical instrument for the analysis of roles. Not only are different tempo-rhythms found in the actors performing different characters in one scene, but they may also be found 'inside one of them.' In Hamlet's irresolute and doubting soul 'various rhythms in simultaneous conjunction are necessary', a contention which proves extremely hard to demonstrate successfully in the examples of a drunken pharmacist, an actor getting ready for performance, or a woman being led to execution (*BC* 206–7). The concept of tempo-rhythm is also applied to 'whole plays' and 'whole performances', in which it is achieved by 'a series of large and small conjunctions of varied and variegated rates of speed and measures', but the assertion rests largely in a description of success rather than a communication of means or method. Faced by scepticism from the students, Tortsov concludes that 'our great predecessors' in the art of acting 'may have had special ways of doing this about which we, unfortunately, have no information,' and the required exercises remain far from the students' grasp (*BC* 217–18 and 222–3 respectively).

The concluding chapters (XIII-XVI) of *Building a Character* concern themselves with various kinds of accomplishment, with ch. XIII dedicated to 'stage charm', but they also permit Stanislavski to emphasize some fundamental principles governing his view of acting. One of these is the authority of the director or régisseur, and failure to listen to this presiding figure is classified as 'a crime against all other workers in the theatre', in a sequence which castigates the lazy or inattentive actor (*BC* 254–67). A second principle sees the actor compared to a priest 'who is aware of the presence of the altar during every moment that he is conducting a service' (*BC* 252). But the most important principles are those which supposedly 'naturalize' the system itself. The method advocated by Stanislavski–Tortsov was not, the author makes Tortsov claim, 'concocted or invented by anyone', but is 'a part of our organic natures', and is 'based on the laws of nature'. After all, he adds, since we have 'an innate capacity for creativeness' which is to us a 'natural necessity', it is inevitable that we should express it 'in accordance with a natural system' (*BC* 287). Tortsov completes the argument by suggesting that nature would be enough – 'All we ask is that an actor on the stage live in accordance with natural laws' – but for the unfortunate 'tendency toward distortion' that working in the theatre occasions. It is this tendency that the system is called upon to correct, 'in destroying inevitable distortions and in directing the work of our inner natures to the right path', so doing no more – it is claimed – than returning the actor to 'the creative state of a normal human being' (*BC* 288–9). Theoretically, the system is merely a restoration of what is natural, but its ultimate promise is both ambitious and seductive: those wise enough to take advantage of it 'may grow into the class of those who are akin to the geniuses' (*BC* 289).

Primary Sources

Benedetti, J. (ed.) (1991) *The Moscow Art Theatre Letters* (London: Methuen).
Nemirovich–Danchenko, V. (1937) *My Life in the Russian Theatre*, trans. J. Cournos (London: Bles).
Stanislavski, C. (1990) *An Actor's Handbook*, ed. and trans. E. Reynolds (London: Methuen).
—(1924) *My Life in Art*, trans. J. Robbins (London: Bles).
—(1950) *Stanislavsky on the Art of the Stage*, trans. D. Magarshack (London: Faber).
—(1968) *Building a Character*, trans. E. Hapgood (London: Methuen).
—(1980) *An Actor Prepares*, trans. E. Hapgood (London: Methuen).
—(1981) *Creating a Role*, trans. E. Hapgood (London: Methuen).
—(1981) *Stanislavski's Legacy*, trans. E. Hapgood (London: Methuen).

Secondary Sources

Archer, W. (1957) *Masks or Faces?* (New York: Hill & Wang).
Balukhaty, S. (ed.) (1952) *'The Seagull' Produced by Stanislavsky*, trans. D. Magarshack (London: Dennis Dobson).
—(1989) *Stanislavski: An Introduction* (London: Methuen).
Benedetti, J. (1988) *Stanislavski: A Biography* (London: Methuen).
Boleslavsky, R. (1949) *Acting: The First Six Lessons* (London: Dennis Dobson).
Braun, E. (1982) *The Director and the Stage* (London: Methuen).
Carnicke, S. (1984) 'An Actor Prepares', *Theatre Journal*, 36, 4, pp. 481–94.
—(1993) 'Stanislavski: Uncensored and Unabridged', *Drama Review*, 37,1, pp. 22–42.
Counsell, C. (1996) *An Introduction to Twentieth-century Performance* (London: Routledge).
DeHart, S. (1981) *The Meininger Theater* (Ann Arbor: Michigan University Research Press).
Edwards, C. (1965) *The Stanislavski Heritage* (New York: New York University Press).
Gorchakov, N. (1954) *Stanislavski Directs*, trans. M. Goldina (New York: Funk & Wagnalls).

Jones, D. (1986) *Great Directors at Work* (Berkeley: University of California Press).

Krasner, D. (2000) 'Strasberg, Adler and Meisner: Method Acting', in A. Hodge (ed.), *Twentieth-Century Actor Training* (London: Routledge) pp.129–50.

Ley, G. (1999) *From Mimesis to Interculturalism: Readings of Theatrical Theory before and after 'Modernism'* (Exeter: University of Exeter Press).

Magarshack, D. (1950) *Stanislavsky: A Life* (London: MacGibbon & Kee).

Roberts, J. (1981) *Richard Boleslavsky: His Life and Work in the Theatre* (Ann Arbor: University of Michigan Research Press).

Strasberg, L. (1988) *A Dream of Passion*, ed. E. Morphos (London: Methuen).

Toporkov, V. (1979) *Stanislavski in Rehearsal: The Final Years*, trans. C. Edwards (New York: Theatre Arts Books).

Wilson, E. (1994) *Shostakovich: A Life Remembered* (London: Faber).

Worrall, N. (1996) *The Moscow Art Theatre* (London: Routledge).

2

Proposals for Reform: Appia and Craig

Edward Gordon Craig (1872–1966) and Adolphe Appia (1862–1928), roughly contemporaneous practitioners and theorists, have frequently been linked because of the affinities between their visions for a reformed stage design and *mise-en-scène*. They had followed very different routes into the theatre; Appia had been a student of music and a spectator of theatre before his fascination with Wagner led him to analyse and design for Wagnerian music-drama. Meanwhile, Craig had started as an actor, coming from a family of performers, before running his own troupe as an actor-manager and later operating as a freelance director. The theatrical environments in which they worked were also distinct, and yet their writings and illustrated stage designs, the primary way in which they disseminated their ideas, reveal striking similarities. Apologists have tried to claim preeminence for each, but it is a futile exercise to attempt to untangle the lines of influence between the two, as Appia commented in a letter to Craig in 1917:

> In the depths of our souls we have *the same vibration and the same desire*; only expressed differently, owing to our different temperaments and our very different circumstances. What matter! (Bablet 1981, 77)

The similarities between Appia's and Craig's work are part of a wider movement of change in the visual, music and literary spheres. Appia reflected in his criticism of Wagner's work:

> The influence of the age manifests itself in many ways; it can affect not only the making, but also the very conception of the

work, subjecting the artist to positive tyranny ... The theatre has always been bound strictly by the special conditions imposed by the age, and consequently, the dramatist has always been the least independent of artists, because he employs so many distinct elements, all of which must be properly united in his work. (*Music and the Art of Theatre = MT* 9)

The two men met in February 1914, at the International Theatre Exposition in Zurich, and maintained a correspondence for many years despite sharing no language. Their mutual admiration and acknowledgement of shared interests did not conceal the distinctions of ideas.

One area of shared agreement was their rejection of the notion of realism as an adequate expression of theatrical art. At the turn of the century, Europe thrilled with the new realistic drama and its demands for a new kind of staging and a new kind of acting. This came out of years when in England, at least, the commercial theatres had been largely dominated by melodrama or spectaculars. A rash of intimate theatres, such as Antoine's Théâtre Libre, Brahm's Freie Bühne or the somewhat larger scale Moscow Art Theatre, were experimenting with stage naturalism. Craig's writings for his journal, *The Mask*, and his three major texts all rail against the debased tyranny of realism for the actor and the limited vision that this quest for realism produced in the actor:

[The actors] must create for themselves a new form of acting, consisting for the main part of symbolical gesture. To-day they *impersonate* and interpret; to-morrow they must *represent* and interpret; and the third day they must create. By this means style may return. (*On the Art of the Theatre = OAT* 61)

For Appia a similar kind of debasement occurred in the staging of realistic theatre, particularly in realistic stage painting, where elements merely *indicated* rather than *expressed* the inner life of the drama. Nor were many of their scenographic reforms uniquely their own. For example, Craig heard Herkomer lecture in London on 'Scenic Art' in 1892 and Appia's visit to Anton Hiltl's Brunswick Court Theatre in the 1880s, renowned for its ensemble work, allowed him to see the impact of different platforms and stage levels on the performer. Less well-known to us today are those theatre workers who developed and used the potential of electric stage lighting or simplified stage pictures, but who did not attempt to integrate their work into a coherent theoretical premise, nor perhaps regarded their work with the kind of experimental rigour that both Craig and Appia applied.

There were some essential differences between Craig and Appia in their approaches to the art of theatre. For Craig, his sense of aesthetics was forged in English isolation, and for his English audience his desire to consider the stage as having its own aesthetics was a rather radical one. For Appia, living in the shadow of Nietzsche, Schiller, Schopenhauer, Goethe and Wagner, debate, analysis and theories of aesthetics were already a significant cultural force. His primary debt is to Wagner, whose language from theoretical texts like *The Art-Work of the Future*, seeps inexorably into Appia's prose.[1] Both Craig and Appia approached Wagner's call for an integrated work of art in the theatre with caution. Craig dismisses Wagner's attempts at *Gesamkunstwerk* in his article 'The Actor and the Übermarionette', which nevertheless betrays much unacknowledged Wagnerian influence (*OAT* 72–3). Even Appia, for whom Wagner was the Master, was to come to call this integrated art work, 'a dangerous theory' (*The Work of Living Art* = *WLA* 18).

Both men acknowledged that their theoretical writings were to be almost more significant than the rare occasions when collaboration and finance allowed the practical implementation of their ideas.[2] Craig's relentless search for a theatre of his own was only briefly to be realized in the Arena Goldini, Florence in 1913, before the privations of the First World War interrupted his work. As a result, his practical collaboration with other directors, actors and designers produced only piecemeal elements of the controlling theory of his visionary writing. However, he tackled head-on the implication that the lack of practical outcomes damaged the virtue and vigour of his theoretical writing:

> because I have not given you a text book called 'Craig's Ideas, and how to put each one of them into practice', do not misrepresent the book and me by saying that I am unpractical. If I haven't given you the whole of my Ideas the modern theatre holds proof that I've given you some, and that these are put into execution. (Craig 1979, lxxxv)

Appia's autobiographical *Theatrical Experiences and Personal Investigations*, also written in the 1920s but never published, ponders the purpose and limitations of his own theoretical writing:

> A theorist gains a thorough knowledge of the work he is studying; then he seeks a general principle to which it may be reduced. From this basis he develops a theory and applies it to lesser details of the work. Through that artificial procedure he, of course, obtains a unity, but this unity does not emanate from the work itself; hence it remains an illusion, and the real meaning of the work escapes; the theorist has not even touched it. A work of art comes to life only when in contact with an artist to whom alone it confides its secret. If the author of these lines has become a theorist, it was because of the impossibility of realizing his dream. (*Essays, Scenarios and Designs* = *ESD* 55)

As we shall see when we examine Appia's approach to interpreting Wagner's work and other music-drama and theatrical writing, he considered himself first and foremost as the artist to whom Wagner's work confided its secret. The passage above continues, 'First I obeyed the dictate of my vision, and only later did I discern the reasons that make it possible to establish a theory'. It is the visionary, sometimes spiritualized, always richly metaphorical nature of theses two practitioners' writing that rewards detailed study. There is not space here to ponder at length the relationship between the theoretical writing of these reformers and the achievement of their aims in the theatre.[3] Insightful biographical studies of both practitioners exist and chart the development and change of their thinking and practice. However, it is useful in understanding the rhetoric and form of the writings of Craig and Appia to have some notion of when in their career they were writing and to speculate on the audience they were hoping their work would reach.

Adolphe Appia

Of the two practitioners, Appia was the less well-known initially, and certainly he was less of a self-promotionalist than Craig. His writing is most readily accessible in collections of his articles and excerpts from his books gathered in Volbach and Beacham's edition

Essays, Scenarios and Designs (1989) and in Beacham, *Adolphe Appia: Texts on Theatre* (1993). Appia's earliest writing was a scholarly and detailed analysis of Wagnerian music-drama and his vision of the broader possibilities of the 'new' theatre seemed for some years restricted by his interest in Wagner. *Staging Wagnerian Drama (La Mise en scène du drame wagnérien*, 1895) had a limited print run of only 300 copies, paid for by Appia himself, and not all of those were distributed during his lifetime. Although published in Paris, the pamphlet was aimed at a German audience, specifically at Bayreuth, home of Wagner and his legacy. Unfortunately for Appia, the pamphlet received very little review or attention in Germany, but his work interested some in the symbolist movement in France. Appia expanded on the possibilities of staging Wagner in his second book, *Music and the Art of Theatre (Die Musik und die Inscenierung*, 1899). Once again this text initially received little notice, but by 1924 Appia claimed that, 'gradually it has become widely known and influential on the art of staging. It may be regarded as having been the first impetus towards all contemporary reform, and it contained the elements required to continue that movement and consolidate it' (*Essays, Scenarios and Designs* = ESD 61–2). Appended to the text of *Music and the Art of Theatre*, like his other books, were collections of designs and detailed scenarios for the staging of various of Wagner's works. These appendices are fascinating studies which reveal how radical Appia's practical vision was. Accessible, pragmatic and thought-provoking they had a great impact at the time and have continued to do so. There was a long break before his third book, the visionary and polemic *The Work of Living Art (L'Oeuvre d'Art Vivant*, 1921). During the intervening years Appia had developed his practical designs and solutions with collaborators, notably Jacques-Dalcroze, and published occasional articles outlining the principles he was employing, in journals across Europe.[4]

Music and the Art of the Theatre took many of the ideas Appia had touched on in his earlier book, and expanded them. The book is not an easy one to read, and part of its difficulty is suggested by a telling passage from his autobiography:

> I continued to rely upon the example of Wagner, for at that time his were the only works that could provide a point of departure. But in writing it I gradually grew aware of the extent to which my thinking had separated itself from Wagner's work, in order to

deal with the subject in all its complexity and implications. (*ESD*
61–2)

Not only has Appia been influenced by Wagner's convoluted
sentence construction, but Appia's ideas about Wagner were
themselves changing as he was writing, with the result that the
last section of the book envisages 'The Word-Tone Drama *without*
Richard Wagner' (his italics). The treatise uses the language of
densely argued logic, stock phrases; 'we have seen that' (*MT* 17),
'one might find it logical' (*MT* 18), and occasional lapses into the
third person, which give it a patina of pseudo-scientific enquiry. But
there is very little logic in the organization of his argument, particularly in parts II and III. Even the titles to the multiple sections in
the later parts are prone to repetition. Appia makes considerable
claims for the theoretical value of the text, as 'founded upon laws
and facts quite independent of the personal taste of the artist;
therefore, its theoretical value is absolute' (*MT* 17). The vigour
of his defence here is partly explained by the dual readership
he was anticipating. In the 1898 preface, he identifies two groups:
'the artists for whom I am writing', and the non-specialist reader
who will nevertheless 'contribute to the reading of this book
all the sensitivity to music he possesses' (*MT* 7). Essentially, Appia
was aware that his criticism of Wagner would meet with
considerable resistance, and he coyly concludes by asserting that
the study is 'in accord with the secret desires of many of my readers' (*MT* 9).

The book is broken into four sections, including an appendix of
designs and scene-by-scene analysis of *Tristan and Isolde* and *The
Ring*, which centre around the lighting possibilities: 'lighting reigns
supreme and determines everything else on stage' (*MT* 208). These
designs and his later practical experiments, combined with his
championing of the expressive properties of light in all his writing,
have contributed to his reputation as the architect of modern theatre
lighting. Appia undoubtedly offers for the first time a theoretical
approach to the function of light in theatre, in particular for the
recently available possibilities of electric lighting. He discusses how
electric light can produce a dual effect, both 'general illumination'
and 'exactly focused beams' which allow the designer to shape
space with shadow: 'we shall call them diffused light and living
light' (*MT* 74). He dubs the focused beam a 'living' light because it
was used directly to illuminate the actor, and was therefore con-

nected to both movement on stage and contributed to the audience's perception of the stage space as three-dimensional.

The first part of the treatise leaps straight in with a complex debate about stage aesthetics. Appia compares the art of theatre with painting, sculpture and poetry, art forms in which the 'content of their work is identical with its form, and so the object of expression and the means employed to communicate it to us are in a way equivalent' (*MT* 10). For the modern drama, by which he means Wagner, he identifies a disjunction between the 'idea' expressed in the dramatic text and production values. He had been bitterly disappointed by the half-hearted, realist attempts to stage Wagner's texts, even at Bayreuth. In effect he is suggesting that a far more abstract visual picture and mode of movement is in keeping with Wagner's intentions. Scene-painting, particularly attempts at realistic illusion, was derided by Appia, as it was in Craig's texts, as no more than 'signs with which to indicate the scene'; 'hieroglyphs' (*MT* 23). However, curiously, at the same time as they banish the scene-painter from the theatre both men value painting and the painter as artist in their use of analogy. This is linked to the status that the painter and easel painting occupied in Europe, where it seemed to be the epitome of 'new' art, fracturing and developing in many directions particularly the abstract, which was to the taste of both Craig and Appia as their own designs reveal. Yet for Appia, any criticism of Wagner's own staging, however poorly realized, was difficult to justify. The problem was to find '*a principle, deriving directly from the drama's original conception, without passing again through the will of the dramatist ... to prescribe the* mise-en-scène' (*MT* 13). Appia's solution was to elevate music to the position of controlling principle. In his text he suggests that an 'organically composed' hierarchy exists where 'music, the soul of the drama, gives life to the drama, and by its pulsations determines every motion of the organism, in proportion and sequence' (*MT* 26).[5] In this way he tries to argue that the will of the dramatist-cum-composer remains the artistic, unifying force which guides the *mise-en-scène*, in contrast to Craig's notion of the stage-director. However, later in the argument Appia also designates a role for the director as an artist who will 'examine the play of his own imagination in order to strip it as much as possible of convention ... and who must possess a kind of magnetic influence, much like that of a genial *conductor*' (*MT* 41). This role of genial conductor was one which Appia himself was eager to fill, but his ideas received short shrift from Cosima Wagner, who sought to preserve Wagner's legacy at Bayreuth in all its realist glory.

Indeed, Appia's writing takes a decidedly symbolist turn when he considers the 'hidden world of our inner life' which is to be expressed in art. It is not clear what this inner life comprises, but it is linked to 'the basic needs of our personality', 'our latent powers' and 'our most secret longings' which are revealed in our dreams (*MT* 98–9). For Appia, art must express this inner life directly to the audience, and 'this life *cannot be expressed* except through music, and music can express only that life' (*MT* 26). There is also an early appearance of an image which is to become central to all Appia's work, when he argues that the relationship between the musical score and the production should be organic: 'If one of the links of this organic chain breaks or is missing, the expressive power of the music is cut off there and cannot reach beyond it' (*MT* 26). The moral imperative of this kind of music-drama and its impact on an audience was to be developed more fully in his later writing. The interrelation between the actor and the audience was idealized as one of direct communication, through music. Appia discusses the need for a new use of stage space to facilitate this interrelation, which extends to the theatre building itself, where he envisages 'no permanent feature except an auditorium, on the other side of which a fairly large area will remain empty. In this space, the drama will come into existence, no longer in its usual impersonal form, but in its nonessential and provisional form' (*MT* 53). Written a decade before his collaboration with Dalcroze, this idea was to find an echo in both his rhythmic space constructed at Hellerau, and in his fondness for the festival, the temporary theatrical event. It was picked up in his *Work of Living Art* and elsewhere as 'a cathedral of the future', with all that that implies about the content of the event and its participants.[6]

Appia's hopes for the actor are paradoxical. He notes that the texts of spoken drama can only 'suggest to the actor his mime and his actions; they cannot dictate them precisely', and this encourages the actor to observe the 'external appearances of daily life' and of the 'hidden springs' of his own and others actions as source material (*MT* 18–19). But Appia does not clearly distinguish between the performer and the character when he goes on to suggest that allowing music 'to paint the images of his [i.e. the character's] suffering, can keep his [i.e. the actor's] pain buried in the depths of his soul and express emotions that have to do only with his [i.e. the actor's] present existence' (*MT* 19). Although Appia places the actor as the first element to be considered in the *mise-en-scène*, he immediately reduces the performer's status to 'but one medium. Neither more nor less important than the others, at the poet's disposal' (*MT* 21). Later, he reigns the actor in further, by demanding obedience to the music score:

> such an initiation gives a far greater value to the initiate's very subservience than any sort of highly original 'interpretation' could ever offer. For far from weakening the indispensable spontaneity of the actor, it confers that quality on him in the highest degree. Just as the music permits only the purest essence of the dramatist's personal conception to emerge, so it admits only the noblest elements of the actor's personality. (*MT* 43)

This limitation on the role of the actor is to be radically overhauled after Appia's encounter with Dalcroze, as we shall see in his later *The Work of Living Art*.

The second and third parts of the treatise are studies of Richard Wagner and German art. The nationalist tone is hardly surprizing in the light of the triumphs of the Franco-Prussian war, only recently concluded. Partly in response to the militaristic idealism that surrounded him at the time, and partly a result of the violence contained within Wagner's scenarios, Appia's language takes on an aggressive edge. Wagner was 'a violent revolution, a revolution similar to those instigated by the speeches of a social or political reformer' (*MT* 116). Indeed Wagner's work is pictured almost as a crusade:

> *Parsifal* may rightly be called a *Bühnenweihfestspiel* (holy festival of the theatre), for it consecrates the stage upon which it appears. Indeed, Wagner accomplished a miracle in his last work. He overcame the obstacle and problems of visual realization with weapons more powerful than any technical principle. (*MT* 127)

The redemptive and violent power of Wagner's work also appears in a later simile: 'like all messiahs he has come bringing not peace but a sword' (*MT* 133), and he found a 'weapon in modern music'. The idea of music as a weapon repeats like a motif throughout the work.

The second section is a study of Wagner's theoretical writings, particularly his *Art-Work of the Future*, which is criticized for its limited ideas about scenic painting and staging. Appia feels happier with Wagner's *Opera and Drama*, in which Wagner resists 'concrete ideas about staging' (*MT* 111) but concentrates on a history of opera. Then follows a study of *Tristan*, *Parsifal*, the *Ring* and *Die Meistersinger*. The third part of the book, entitled 'The Word-Tone Drama *without* Richard Wagner', returns to the creation of the drama itself rather than the *mise-en-scène* or production. Appia makes much play of the distinctions between the German and the Latin (by which he means, French) forms of opera, music-drama and word-tone drama. He provides a disclaimer about:

> the question of nationality (or, if one prefers, of race) which has so much bearing on the future of the word-tone drama... (It goes without saying that I attach not the slightest political notion to the word 'nationality'). (*MT* 147)

However, although it would be personally expedient to maintain good relations with both French and German readers, Appia constructs a history of cultural occupation.

> For a long time German culture has been stifled by the oppressive effects of French genius. Even today, this oppression is a serious obstacle to the realization of a national culture. (*MT* 150)

More disturbingly to our ears, Appia invokes images of disease and contamination. The purity of German blood 'has been weakened by the ill-advised introduction of certain foreign elements... his conscience seems to point to all those corruptive elements and to demand their rejection', in order to escape 'a state of sterility and symptom of sickness and perversion' (*MT* 153). However, reconciliation is personified in Bayreuth (Appia follows Nietzsche's view on Bayreuth), which was 'no longer a symbol of battle but a place for the exchange and blending of cultures' (*MT* 151). The financial nuances of exchange are not lost on Appia: 'only through exchange can wealth be created and increased' (*MT* 153).

Appia wrote a French preface in preparation for an intended English edition in 1918 which never materialized. In it Appia reflects on his interest in Wagnerian music-drama, with the hindsight of a decade of work with Dalcroze. Appia can express the conflict with which the whole book, like 'the Master', struggles:

> the conflict between music for which there was no suitable expression in the living body of the performer, music which *could not achieve such externalization* without the risk of having its own identity suppressed – and the necessity, nevertheless, of presenting the music and the human body *simultaneously*. (*MT* 3, his emphasis)

This was a conflict that finds theoretical resolution in his later texts through Dalcroze eurhythmics. Written during the First World War, the 1918 preface expresses most strongly the idea of the link between performer and audience in 'the *Salle*, cathedral of the future':

> There is no art form in which social solidarity can be better expressed than in the drama, particularly if it returns to its noble origins in the collective realization of great religious or patriotic feeling, or simply of human feeling, transforming them into our modern image. (*MT* 5)

Founded in the idealized understanding of ancient Greek art as essentially social, Appia predicts that:

> the dramatic art of tomorrow will be a *social act*, in which each of us will assist. And who knows, perhaps, one day we shall arrive, after a period of transition, at majestic festivals in which a whole people will participate, where each of us will express our feelings, our sorrows, our joys, no longer content to remain a passive onlooker. Then will the dramatist triumph! (*MT* 6)

A brief comparison between the 1898 and 1918 prefaces reveal how much more relaxed and casual, allusive and metaphorical Appia's language has become, or perhaps how much trouble the translator had in subjugating the earlier preface to the German turn of phrase.

Trained as a musician and with his early experience of theatre gained primarily as a critic and audience member, Appia's theoretical thinking was sparked by his experience in the auditorium. He presented his reforms as solutions to the sense of disappointment he felt as an audience member, and he builds scenarios expressing this disappointment into many of his works. For example, 'Comments on Theatre' begins with an anecdote about a boy's first visit to the theatre, and his disillusionment with scenic illusion and operatic convention:

> the child will never forget the deceptive words that chased him so cruelly from the forest of his dreams, to set him on a solid and clearly-marked road leading to theatrical aesthetics. (*ESD* 174)

Likewise *The Work of Living Art* offers a view of the modern audience member who is troubled by the presence of 'an unknown element that escapes our conscious thought at the very moment it is affecting our emotions', searches their memory '(now too fragmentary and too concerned with the intellectual content of the piece) for the elusive something ... each new experience finds us similarly distracted, until we completely abandon the search' (*WLA* 6). As a result the audience is always a factor in his theorizing. His suggested reforms for the *mise-en-scène* are to allow for artistic expression from the author to be perceived directly by the audience. The search for 'a theatre that requires each spectator to be personally involved in the performance – the very character of aesthetic pleasure – instead of delivering him to inertia' (*ESD* 182) begins early in his work, and he has nothing but disdain for productions that 'have forced us into a passivity so despicable that we have carefully concealed it in the darkness of the house'. More than simply offering a critique of the distance between auditorium and stage, Appia is moving towards a concept of a different kind of art, one of 'fraternal collaboration. We wish that we, ourselves, were the body we are observing: the social instinct is awakened in us' (*ESD* 185). This reaches its apogee in his *Work of Living Art*, where he ecstatically announces that the:

> *living* art is the only one that exists completely, without spectators (or listeners). It needs no audience, for it implicitly contains the audience within itself. Since it is a work *lived* throughout a determinate length of time, those who live it – both its creators and its participants – assure its complete existence through their activity alone ... from the moment it exists, we are with it, in it. (*ESD* 65)

This idealized role of art as social activity is based on his understanding of a nostalgic vision of ancient Greece, where he identifies a 'harmony' between people and their surroundings. For the ancient

Greek freeman, it was 'on the steps of the amphitheatre he realised the supreme fact of his social life...the work of art was the *environment* from which his whole life radiated' (*MT* 181). This homogeneity between art and life is, of course, nostalgic fantasy, but one taken up by, for example, post-Revolutionary Russian artists, who abandoned easel painting in favour of practical design and who opened schools for the 'workers' to be trained in the arts. This appeal to an idealized Greece is the one of the few moments when Appia employs history to support his argument. Unlike Craig he is not trying to place his work in an antique tradition, nor draw widely on earlier theatre styles; his focus is primarily on the future. His coinage, via Goethe, of the 'Word-Tone drama' is a new form, and his concern is to 'assure [its] posterity – for, without a tradition, mere isolated productions of the word-tone drama could hardly satisfy us' (*MT* 131). However, Appia finds in Richard Wagner, the Master, the kind of legitimating father of his theories, even if he criticizes or moves beyond his mentor's thinking.

His final book, the prophetic *The Work of Living Art*, summarizes and reformulates ideas that Appia had expounded in articles, often more lucidly, over the previous twenty years. In 'Comments on the Theatre' as early as 1908 he outlines all of the most important elements of *The Work of Living Art*, but without the complex rhetoric of the latter. In this last book the actor is foregrounded as never before, since its appendix suggests *Man Is The Measure Of All Things*. After years of work with Dalcroze, the actor and the plastic living body become the centre and source of all design; 'deep in my heart and before my drawing paper I knew that for me the *mise-en-scène* means the performer' (*ESD* 56).[7] Gone are any precepts about how the actor should perform and in their place is an idealist rhetoric which makes repeated use of the 'organic' as an authenticating and originating metaphor. Appia rejects all forms of realism on stage, since they are contradicted by the reality of the actor's body which determines the order of the *mise-en-scène*'s construction. It is the presence of, and contact with, the actor's body that makes all other elements of the stage 'living', the highest praise he can give. In fact, the body of the actor seems to have almost usurped the place of the newly-coined dramatist-director:

> The living body is thus the real creator of the supreme art, hold-ing as it does the secret of the hierarchical relations between the

conflicting elements, because it stands at their head...our point
of departure. (*WLA* 9)

Later he claims 'our body is the dramatic author' (*WLA* 54); Appia
pauses to take a side-swipe here at Craig and his marionettes, which
cannot provide that 'living' element. Appia revisits his calls for
altered staging and the significant place of light, but couches them
in terms of 'living space' and 'living time'. In *Music and the Art of the
Theatre* it was music that provided the connection between spatial
and temporal elements, following Wagner, who in *Parsifal* 'makes
Gurnemanz say, "Here, time becomes space"' (*MT* 126).[8] In *The
Work of Living Art*, it is movement and particularly the movement of
the actor that reconciles these elements.

The final sections draw on image systems of adventurer 'Robin-
son Crusoe' and exotic 'Tahiti', incidentally a destination favoured
by the group of symbolist painters, the Nabis, to take the reader into
the 'Great Unknown'. There is much expressly religious reference to
Christianity, and the underlying philosophy of the whole is con-
trived by religious metaphors of 'communion', 'renunciation', the
hall as 'cathedral' and 'the Presence' of 'divine light'. The final image
of the artist as 'bearer of the flame' shares much with the iconography
of the Olympic Institute, with its ideas of refinement through communal activity and the redemptive power of sport! Yet Appia concedes that this communal art is an idealized one, only to be striven for
in the future, while 'in our day *living* art is a personal *attitude* which
should be shared in common by all men' (*WLA* 81). This retreat to
interior space is in keeping with the movement of many elements of
Modernist work. Appia here takes into the theatre and the question
of the *mise-en-scène* the Nietzschean affirmation that it is only as
conscious dream, or 'aesthetic phenomenon', that we find 'human
existence and the world eternally *justified*' (Nietzsche 1967, 52).

Edward Gordon Craig

Craig's first significant piece of writing was the pamphlet *The Art of
the Theatre* (= *AT*), which expounded his definition of the role of the
stage director and his vision of a kind of performance generated
from the essential elements of theatre. The booklet was first released
in a German translation by Maurice Magnus, Craig's financial manager, with a foreword from Craig's aristocratic and well-respected

patron, Count Kessler.[9] Few Europeans apart from Kessler had seen Craig's production work in England; rather, Craig was known in Europe primarily through his designs and illustrations, which had been widely exhibited.[10] Not only did Craig exhibit actual production designs, but also his explorations in staging and light that were unconnected to particular plays, theatres or performers. Unfortunately, this led collaborators like Otto Brahm and Max Reinhardt to view Craig principally as a stage designer, a role he was unhappy to play. After the breakdown of work with Brahm at the Lessing Theatre, Berlin, Craig complained in an open letter to the papers:

> I was expecting to conduct rehearsals of this play, as I have always done in England with plays for which I have made designs. It was preferred at the last moment to put on a perform-ance that was all shreds and patches... (Bablet 1981, 72)

The Art of the Theatre was published after abortive attempts to work with several practitioners, and was in part Craig's attempt to explain the role of stage director he wanted to inhabit in these collaborations, and in part a bid for the establishment of a theatre of his own.[11] He wanted to reach a Europe-wide audience of theatre specialists with this theoretical work, as he had done with his exhibitions of designs.

Dictated between 22 April and 4 May, *The Art of the Theatre* was a dialogue between the 'expert' stage-director and the playgoer. The dialogue form had been used by writers of theatrical theory since Plato, whose *Symposium* Craig suggested should be performed for public edification.[12] As a rhetorical tool the dialogue gives imme-diacy to a debate, framing it in the present tense, and allows the writer to inhabit many postures within the text. The questioning 'character' in the dialogue represents the role of the ideal reader, critically engaged with the thesis presented. The actual reader is persuasively absorbed into the fiction of the dialogue and cast in the role of questioner, becoming the object of the teacher's direct address. The dialogue form allowed Craig to appear to admit both challenge and contradiction to his argument, while proceeding triumphantly to defeat all critical voices. The internal logic of the dialogue seems to suggest that the ordinary playgoer is the audi-ence Craig imagined for his pamphlet, yet the playgoer is powerless to effect the changes Craig calls for. In effect, the rhetoric of the dialogue envisages a reader who also works in the theatre, and who is able to answer Craig's call for a 'systematic progression' of reform. The dialogue of *The Art of the Theatre* is set in the auditorium, the province of the stage-director and audience. The voices of the playgoer and the expert are not fully differentiated. They share a vocabulary and a style, but the interplay of the dialogue functions to control the pace of the reader's progress through the piece. Longer sections of explanation by the stage-director are interspersed with moments of rapid question and answer, as in the banter about stage directions, or the staccato exchange which uses the simile of the theatre as a ship. In these two moments, and at the opening and closing of the dialogue, the stage-director takes over the asking of questions. This heuristic mechanism guides the playgoer, and by implication the reader, to deductive conclusions which seem logical and natural.

The content of the dialogue falls broadly into three parts, beginning with an aesthetic debate and an attempt to define the art of theatre. The central section offers a model description of the interpretative craft of the stage director, and the piece ends with a vision of the future work of the stage director as originator of a creative art. This was a dazzling and new suggestion from Craig. All over Europe exponents of 'new' theatre movements were championing some kind of reformation of the theatre through realism, symbolism, or the reform of single elements like acting or stage lighting. Many of Craig's practical suggestions for reform, like the removal of footlights, were not original, as he acknowledged in the dialogues.[13] Craig's distinctive contribution to the debate was two-fold. Firstly, he established a theoretical legitimacy for the stage-director as a visionary figure, through whom the integration of all the elements of a piece of theatre was to occur. Secondly, he looked forward to a kind of performance which was generated, not from the playtext, but through an alternative:

ACTION, SCENE and VOICE... when I say *action*, I mean both gesture and dancing, the prose and poetry of action.

When I say *scene*, I mean all which comes before the eye, such as lighting, costume, as well as the scenery.

When I say *voice*, I mean the spoken word or the word which is sung, in contradiction to the word which is read... (*AT* 180–1)

The suggestion that these three elements would give form and structure to an idea, rather than a written text, was a remarkable departure in 1905.

The text's opening attempt to define theatre as an art form was part of a wider discussion of aesthetics and the place of élite art within national culture, which was more familiar in mainland Europe than Britain at this time. Craig was attempting to 'rescue' theatre from what he perceived to be its degenerated form as 'merely' commercial or popular entertainment. The difficulty Craig encounters is philosophical, in that 'if unity, the one thing vital to a work of art, is to be obtained' (*AT* 157), he must banish the notion of theatre as merely a composite form, pieced together by craftsmen. If theatre is an Art, like poetry or painting, it raises its cultural significance and re-opens the way for patronage by private individuals and the state, and concomitantly raises the status of stage-director to that of an artist. To suggest a simile for this integration of elements in the theatre he draws on images from other arts, particularly music and painting. He insists repeatedly upon the need for 'harmony' between elements in the art of the theatre, a harmony he argues that can only be produced by a stage-director. An actor-manager would be stranded like 'the conductor of a small orchestra playing the part of the first violin, but not from choice, and not to a satisfactory issue' (*AT* 174). Craig considers that not even the best actors could work together and 'be harmonious, without following the directions of the stage-manager' (*AT* 166). The comparison between the conductor or painter and the stage-director is forced, as the director is struggling with elements far more diverse in nature than an orchestra. The painter, likewise, is an obvious but misleading model for the stage-director who, in his bid to be an artist; 'in his mind's eye mixes his palette (to use a painter's expression) with the colour which the impression of the play has called up' (*AT* 155) and 'weaves into a pattern certain objects ... as the centre of his design' (*AT* 157). Yet, the actor in this metaphor is relegated to the role of a pictorial figure, which although 'the very heart of the emotional design' (*AT* 166), is only part of the greater whole. How much simpler for the painter who has only to deal with inanimate paints, than the director who must tussle with living actors. What stands out from the use of these similes is that only the director is granted the sobriquet 'artist' and, instead of being collaborators, the other theatre workers are relegated to the place of tools.

The imagery of the harmonious weaving of elements in the theatre clashes awkwardly with violently authoritarian models of unity. Undoubtedly these images were linked to Craig's frustration at being sidelined within other people's theatre institutions. He has no time for 'this same powerful usurper of the theatrical throne – the box-office' (*AT* 165), dismissing all commercial theatre as treacherous. Ideas of monarchical absolutism recur as the playgoer wonders whether the stage-manager is 'to rule on the stage', and Wagner is praised because he 'was careful to possess himself of his theatre, and become a sort of feudal baron in his castle' (*AT* 174). Craig's vision of a fully integrated theatre art requires a clear line of command and discipline from crafts-people and actors:

> Mutiny has been well anticipated in the navy, but not in the theatre. The navy has taken care to define, in clear and unmistakable voice, that the captain of the vessel is the king, and a despotic ruler into the bargain. Mutiny on a ship is dealt with by a court-martial, and is put down by very severe punishment, by imprisonment, or by dismissal from the service. (*AT* 171)

He continues with ironic humour that 'the theatre, unlike the ship, is not made for purposes of war, and so for some unaccountable reason discipline is not held to be of such vital importance' (*AT* 172). Yet he does imagine the theatre at war, and he casts his reform as a battle against 'our enemies ... vulgar display, the lower public opinion, and ignorance' (*AT* 172). This justifies his call for discipline among the crafts-people of the theatre. The two image systems of harmonious artistry and of militaristic zeal jostle uncomfortably together, but are linked in the way Craig employs them, to support hierarchical structures dependent upon an authoritarian leader.

Craig uses the voice of the stage-director to call for reform of the theatre; 'ENTIRE, not PART reform' (*AT* 177). In his later writing he was to abandon the implicit conservatism of a call for reform, but here he makes use of the simple rhetorical strategy of many reformers, that is he dresses his innovation as a return to earlier glory, a restoration. He makes a beginning at the beginning, with a search for origins. The attempt to establish a genealogy, even metaphorically, is a way of naturalizing a version of theatrical development in the mind of the reader. The first challenge to the unity of theatrical art is that drama is only a bastardized form of Literature or Poetry. So Craig's opening gambit is to claim 'the father of the dramatist was the dancer' (*AT* 140), which he reiterated later in a stronger definition: 'the first dramatist was the dancer's son, that is to say, the child of the theatre, not the child of the poet' (*AT* 142). By excluding the poet from the family picture, this image assumes the dancer is the originator of theatre. Although reluctantly granting the dramatist's 'birth-claim to the theatre' (*AT* 142) Craig subordinates the written word to the visual representation of theatre, and suggests the Art of theatre will soon be self-reliant and dispense with the 'assistance of the playwright' (*AT* 148). The dialogue ends with a projection of the play-less theatre of the future.

Craig does not often employ the terms 'new' or 'modern' in his writing, except pejoratively, but rather uses ideas of genealogy and restoration.[14] It is the stage-director who is to 'recover the ground lost to the theatre, and finally... restore the Art of the Theatre to its home by means of his own creative genius' (*AT* 147). This is also subtly implied in Craig's fondness for the image of renaissance, summoning up an earlier spectacular flowering of European culture. The playgoer asks, somewhat unexpectedly, 'Is your belief in a Renaissance of the art based on your belief in the Renaissance of the stage director?' (*AT* 148), a phrase picked up and used by the expert later in the dialogue. The director, as Craig pictures him, is a polymath and ideal Renaissance man, but the role of the director itself is an innovation. Rhetorical flourish and the satisfaction of balance in the phrase carries the reader over this glitch. The piece continually assumes a falling-off in modern theatre, with the suggestion that 'it is not only the art which has degenerated, but that a proportion of the audience has degenerated also', a complaint that is capped by Craig's simile of the musical delights of the 'barrel organ' (*AT* 146). There is a sense of continuity implied in the return to a previously glorious past, from which theatre has now degenerated, but there is hint of the pseudo-religious in this language of 'degeneration' and 'belief'. The expert prophesies that theatre 'in the West is on its last legs. But I look for a Renaissance'. 'How will it come?' the playgoer asks, and the reply is with 'the advent of a man who shall contain in him all the qualities which go to make up a master of the theatre' (*AT* 176). Craig pictures the director of the future in messianic terms, with disciples:

The advent of this artist in the theatre world will change all this. He will slowly but surely gather around him these better crafts-

men of whom I speak, and together they will give new life to the
art of the theatre. (*AT* 146)

There are many echoes of Craig's rhetoric here in Copeau's early
writing, as Chapter 3 discusses. Most notably, Copeau takes up the
debate about reform or renaissance in the theatre, and he takes even
further the tendency to clothe the theatre artist in religious imagery.

The pamphlet was circulated through theatre-literate circles
across Europe, and raised Craig's profile as a serious theorist of
theatre. Isadora Duncan was on tour in Russia and gave Stanislavski
the German version of the pamphlet. Duncan was romantically
involved with Craig and the influence of her ideas on movement
and gesture have been seen in Craig's identification of action as the
first motor of theatre. On the basis of *The Art of Theatre* and Craig's
further writing in his journal, *The Mask*, Stanislavski invited him to
see his work in Moscow and initiated a collaboration which was to
culminate in the 1912 *Hamlet* at the Moscow Arts Theatre. Craig
writes admiringly of Stanislavski's work and his school in *The Art of
the Theatre: The Second Dialogue*, which was written during his collaboration and first appeared in *The Mask*. This dialogue begins as if
it is a sequel to the first, but its tone and structure are quite different.
The setting for this dialogue is unspecified, but we are in England
and the piece is clearly aimed at an English audience. Craig con-
trasts theatre in England and 'its collection of dry skulls' with
theatre 'abroad', which he finds 'dancing'. Rather than an exposition of Craig's belief, the dialogue is a bid for sponsorship for a
school. The overarching image is one of quest, with Craig out
hunting 'an absurd monster called The Theatrical' and including
an extended metaphor equating Nansen's search for the North Pole
with Craig's search for the unknown future of theatre. The bulk
of the text is a detailed description of the structure and financing of
the Moscow Arts Theatre and school, followed by what amounts to
a prospectus for Craig's school. His biting critique of the financing
of British theatre is linked to an unashamed bid for £25 000
funding from the State or a private individual for the establishment
of his school in England.[15]

The imagery in this dialogue is linked to the movement for the
establishment of a 'national theatre' in Britain, a topic of serious
debate at the time. Craig discounted the idea of the proposed
scheme (*OAT* 218) and instead attempted to demonstrate in the
dialogue that his school would provide trained staff for an 'ideal'

theatre, in essence a national theatre, in order to garner financial support from the state. He uses the metaphor of the House of Parliament to imply that he would offer a kind of theatre that transcended partisan affiliation:

> We have the equivalent of the Conservatives, Liberals, Progressives, Radicals, Socialists, the Labour Party, and even the Suffragettes are an established part of our institution... But above and beyond all parties there are the Imperialists... the best name I can apply to that universal party, or brotherhood, which is composed of people holding or tolerating many different, and opposite, views. (*OAT* 191–2)

The mention of suffragettes is, of course, deliberately misleading and an attempt to pacify the new woman within Craig's brotherhood. Women were not yet voting in the Parliamentary institution, nor does Craig envisage a place for them in his school. The overall tone of his discussion of actresses in the dialogue, even of Eleanora Duse, is dismissive, centred around their ability to appear beautiful. Indeed the whole metaphor is deeply disingenuous. In the contemporary ear, the use of 'Imperialist' and the expansionist imagery of the polar expedition summon grim echoes of the cost and subjugations implicit in the establishment of the 'universal' party. There is little doubt about the exclusive quality of Craig's theatre vision.

The Mask extended Craig's influence still further allowing him, under the guise of multiple pseudonyms, to 'bring before an intelligent public many ancient and modern aspects of the Theatre's Art which have too long been disregarded or forgotten. Not to attempt to assist in the so-called reform of the modern Theatre – for reform is now too late' (Bablet 1981, 102). Subscribers included artists, writers and theatre-makers such as Copeau, Louis Jouvet, George Bernard Shaw and Strindberg. The article or journal concerned with matters of aesthetics was a familiar way of circulating ideas at the end of the nineteenth century. Journals like the *Yellow Book* or *Harper's New Monthly Magazine* carried theatre criticism and analysis, and some, were dedicated to specific movements in art or theatre, like the French symbolists' *La Revue Blanche* (Eynat-Confino 1987, 30). Craig himself had been particularly cutting about two English theatre journals, *The Era* and *The Stage*. Despite the best efforts of Magnus and Craig, no commercial publisher could be found for *The Mask*, so from his base in Florence Craig produced the journal almost single-handed and with capital of £5. Five hundred copies, and 16 deluxe editions, of the first issue were printed in March 1908 and sent free to leading directors in Europe.[16] Craig hoped that:

> through that publication I might in time come to change the whole theatre – not plays alone, but playing, sceneries, construction of theatres – the whole thing. (Craig 1957, 268)

Craig's writing about *The Mask* in the prospectus employs again those rhetorical strategies already familiar from his earlier dialogue. He authenticates his ideas for a theatre of the future by asserting they are 'based upon an ancient and noble tradition', and so they borrow the legitimation of that tradition, establish themselves as mainstream and imply an inevitable continuation rather than rupture (Bablet 1981, 102). Articles in the first issue included the important, 'The Artists of the Theatre of the Future' and 'Motion'. The second issue, which came out in April 1908, contained one of the most significant and unsettling of Craig's works, 'The Actor and Übermarionette' (=*AU*).[17]

Admiration for the puppet and puppet theatre had been a vogue in Paris in 1880s and 1890s, and writers connected to the symbolist movement, like Maeterlinck and Jarry, had written plays for marionette theatres, and Craig was to do so in later years. Anatole France, a symbolist admirer, had written in praise of the new Paris puppet theatre of 1888. His vision of the potential of the marionette was more limited than Craig's. France thought 'these artless images to be symbols; I should like these simple forms to be animated by magic; I want them to be enchanted toys...' (Segel 1995, 81).[18] Craig had no time for the modern puppet with its reduced dimensions and limited movement, he wanted something much more magnificent, the Übermarionette. The marionette offered Craig an alternative to the personality cult of the 'artless' actor. A 1912 edition of *The Mask* included an article by Anatole France which echoed this criticism of the actor in contrast to the puppet:

> I am infinitely thankful to them for having replaced living actors...actors spoil comedy for me. I mean good actors... Their talent is too great; it overwhelms everything. There is nothing but them. Their personality effaces the work they represent.[19]

Even Wagner had complained that acting was 'a very dubious trade, which seems plied with the exclusive object of displaying the actor's *persona* to the best advantage. All concealment of the actor's personality, an illusion alike aesthetically pleasing and conducive to the most sublime effect, we here see dropped entirely out of count' (Wagner 1995, 191).[20] But here Wagner is urging the actor towards the illusion of becoming one with the part, the exact opposite of Craig's call, which was to 'get out of the skin of the part' (*AU* 64). Craig returns to the idea that 'the great personality has triumphed both over us and the art' (*AU* 76), by distracting audiences from the paucity of the modern theatre. Yet he also asserted at the very time he was writing this essay, in a letter to his mother, the actress Ellen Terry:

> I believe that the great actors possess the power of creating pieces of work without assistance from anyone else... by movement, scene and voice [they] put before the audience all the different meanings of [a theme]. (Craig 1979, 255)

As an afterword to this letter in 1917, Craig reflected 'Always and now here, again, *I ask only for the liberation of the actor that he may develop his own powers,* and cease from being the marionnette [*sic*] of the playwright' (*ibid.*, 260; his emphasis). Can the contradictions of these statements be reconciled?

The essay opens with an echo of the ideas of *The Art of the Theatre,* where the playgoer begins the aesthetic debate by suggesting that acting is the Art of the theatre. Craig returns to debunk this theme fully in this essay, which for all its appearance of logical argument, contains various and conflicting thoughts on acting. The first half of the piece offers a critique of actors and idea of acting as an art, going as far as to recommend the removal of actors altogether, and the second section introduces the symbolic replacement for the performer, the Übermarionette. The tone of the two sections is quite different, moving from a cacophony of voices, brought in to decimate the pretensions of the modern performer, to the mythical history of the puppet, replete with exotic locations and reverential vocabulary. He begins his detailed rejection of acting as an art with a centuries-old argument. The battle for ascendancy between emotion and intellect in an actor was a cliché. The metaphor of emotion as wind, torrent or fire, heating the actor to disorder in movement, facial expression and voice, is a dated vision of acting, at odds with the burgeoning contemporary interest in the psychology and science of acting. Craig even suggests acting as a Dionysian activity, with the actor 'possessed' by emotion (*AU* 56). It is not clear what Craig means by 'acting' here, or whether the emotion of the character, experienced in the flesh by the actor, is at stake. Disorderly emotion results in accidents in the performer and allows Craig to deduce that the actor produces 'not a work of art; it is a series of accidental confessions' (*AU* 58). Craig then offers two pejorative illustrations of the origins of acting. Gone is the idea of *The Art of the Theatre* that the dancer was the father of theatre, or that the performer's body, even in its constituent elements of movement, gesture and voice, was at the root of theatre. The history Craig outlines in this debate, begins with 'the passionate tussle between the elephant and the tiger' (*AU* 58), and proceeds to the story of the handsome young man flattered into presenting someone else's ideas, 'a superb advertisement for the art of literature' (*AU* 60). This second example does not suggest impersonation or characterization, but rather a kind of oratory. Craig returns to the idea of the actor's internal battle by concluding, as if these illustrations have proved his point, that even if the actor presented 'none but the ideas which he himself should compose, his nature would still be in servitude; his body would have to become the slave of his mind' (*AU* 60–1). The battle is now presented as between the mind and the body, and again an antique metaphor of slavery is used. Yet at the same time the actor is useless as 'material' for the theatre since 'the whole nature of man tends towards freedom'. This 'bondage' has an apparent escape, much quoted in commentaries on his work:

> They must create for themselves a new form of acting, consisting for the main part of symbolical gesture. To-day they *impersonate* and interpret; to-morrow they must *represent* and interpret; and the third day they must create. By this means style may return. (*AU* 61)

Arthur Symonds, champion of symbolism in England, whose study was the source of Craig's headnote from Eleanora Duse, was keen to absorb Craig into the symbolist camp, and encourage this search for symbolical gesture.[21]

Central to understanding Craig's writing at this time is his disgust with the limitations of realism on stage. *The Mask* is full of denigrations of 'photographic' realism and its impulses. Here Craig disparages mimetic action and gesture, which contains no more artistry than the work of the animal-stuffer or ventriloquist. He sets up a dialogue in which the painter and musician discuss the nature of art, and convince the actor that he cannot produce adequate proof that his is an art. Craig changes tack and drafts in Flaubert, Lamb, Hazlitt, Dante, Duse and Napoleon to argue that the sign of art is the absence of the artist as a personality from that art. This clinches the point against the actor, for at root the actor can never remove his or her own body as material. Moreover, the actor is always drawn toward realism since their bodies are always involved in a mimetic activity; without the actor there 'would no longer be a living figure to confuse us into connecting actuality and art' (*AU* 81). Having attacked the inadequacies of the actor's body from several angles, Craig triumphantly introduces the alternative:

> The actor must go, and in his place comes the inanimate figure – the Über-marionette we may call him, until he has won for himself a better name. (*OAT* 81)

The name is reminiscent of Nietzsche's *Übermensch*, a superman who achieved the strength of will to overcome his own weaknesses and rise above the limitations of Judaeo-Christian morality, and certainly Craig talks of the marionette in religious terms. This Übermarionette figure is to take on mythic and almost divine proportions.

The imagery of the puppet for Craig is that of the little god or the idol. He deliberately takes the reader imaginatively to distant and spiritually-coded sites in his pictoral language – to ancient Greece and temple-theatre, to the Ganges, a sacred river and religious festivities. Much of this has a symbolist ring. For Anatole France the marionette was 'like Egyptian hieroglyphics, that is they have a certain pure and mysterious quality', and he venerated 'their divine innocence' (Segel 1995, 80). Craig also mixes a Judaeo-Christian imagery throughout the Übermarionette article. 'If we should laugh at and insult the memory of the puppet, we should be laughing at the fall that we have brought about in ourselves – laughing at the beliefs and images we have broken' (*AU* 92). Indeed the last section of the treatise is called The Fall, and Craig's reforms are to restore 'the symbol of godhead' as he 'pray[s] earnestly for the return of the image' (*AU* 94). The image is definitely the marionette, and yet Craig also leaves the door open for the actor's reform, who will begin a new way of working on the 'third' day. Yet ultimately the kind of theatre Craig hopes to regenerate with the Übermarionette draws its ritual sources from a non-Christian ideal, where the people will 'return to their ancient joy in ceremonies – once more will Creation be celebrated – homage rendered to existence – and divine and happy intercession made to Death' (*AU* 94).

Are there possibilities for actors within the argument for their abolition? Clearly Craig is talking about a certain kind of performance which is anti-realist in nature. His own work with performers continued throughout his life and his collaboration with Stanislavski at this time continued apace. In his later work, *Rearrangements* (1915), the marionette has become merely a metaphor for the actor, rather than a substitute. The influence Craig had on practitioners like Copeau and Decroux, for whom the performer was central, might also give us pause. Decroux acknowledged that there had been contradictions in what Craig had written on actors and acting, but concluded:

> if the marionette is, at least, the image of the ideal actor, we must consequently try to acquire the virtues of the ideal marionette. We can only acquire these by practising a specially applied form of gymnastics, and this leads us to the mine known as corporeal. (Decroux 1985, 7)

Decroux's choice of Craig as a key inspiration is surprizing, but what it reveals is the powerful influence that Craig's writing had on many European practitioners. With its rich allusive language and its visionary rhetoric, Craig's treatises and his journal offered a rigorous aesthetic debate which chimed with the aspirations of many theatre practitioners in the first decades of the century.

Primary Sources

Appia, A. (1960) *The Work of Living Art & Man Is the Measure of All Things*, trans. H. Albright and B. Hewitt (Coral Gables, Florida: University of Miami Press).

—(1962) *Music and the Art of Theatre*, trans. R. Corrigan and M. Dirks (Coral Gales, Florida: University of Miami Press)

—(1982) *Staging Wagnerian Drama*, trans. P. Loeffler (Basel: Birkhäuser Verlag).

—(1989) *Essays, Scenarios and Designs*, trans. W. Volbach and R. Beacham (Ann Arbor: UMI Research Press).
—(1993) *Adolphe Appia: Texts on Theatre*, trans. R. Beacham (London: Routledge).
Craig, E.G. (1905) *The Art of the Theatre* (Edinburgh: Foulis).
—(1908–29) *The Mask* (Florence).
—(1911) *On the Art of the Theatre* (London: Heinemann).
—(1913) *Towards a New Theatre: Forty Designs for Stage Scenes with Critical Notes by the Inventor* (London: Dent).
—(1957) *Index to the Story of my Days* (London: Hulton Press).
—(1979) *The Theatre Advancing* (New York: Blom).
Nietzsche, F. (1967) *The Birth of Tragedy out of the Spirit of Music*, trans. W. Kaufmann (New York: Random House).
Walton, M. (ed.) (1983) *Craig on Theatre* (London: Methuen).
Wagner, R. (1995) *Über Schauspieler und Sänger*, trans. W. Ellis (Lincoln, Nebraska: University of Nebraska Press).

Secondary Sources

Bablet, D. (1981) *The Theatre of Edward Gordon Craig* (London: Methuen).
Beacham, R. (1987) *Adolphe Appia: Theatre Artist* (Cambridge: Cambridge University Press).
Craig, E. (1968) *Gordon Craig: The Story of his Life* (London: Victor Gollancz).
Decroux, E. (1985) 'Words on Mime', trans. M. Piper, *Mime Journal*, 13.
Eliot, T.S. (1955) 'Gordon Craig's Socratic Dialogues', *Drama*, 36, pp. 16–21.
Eynat-Confino, I. (1987) *Beyond the Mask: Gordon Craig, Movement and the Actor* (Carbondale: Southern Illinois University Press).
Fletcher, I. (1967) *Edward Gordon Craig: A Bibliography* (London: Society for Theatre Research).
Herkomer, H. (1908) *My School and My Gospel* (London: Constable).
Innes, C. (1983) *Edward Gordon Craig* (Cambridge: Cambridge University Press).
Levenson, M. (ed.) (1999) *Cambridge Companion to Modernism* (Cambridge: Cambridge University Press).
Lyons, C. (1969) 'Gordon Craig's Concept of the Actor', in E. Kirby (ed.), *Total Theatre* (New York: Dutton and Co.) pp. 58–77.
Segel, H. (1995) *Pinocchio's Progeny: Puppets, Marionettes, Automatons and Robots in Modernist and Avant-Garde Drama* (Baltimore: Johns Hopkins University Press).
Volbach, W. (1968) *Adolphe Appia: Prophet of the Modern Theatre* (Middletown, Connecticut: Wesleyan University Press).

3

The Popular Front:
Meyerhold and Copeau

A danger in attempting to study the theoretical writings of two practitioners in one chapter is the powerful compulsion to find thematic links which elide significant distinctions, or to read the works only for their own sake without adequate alertness to the immediate context and purpose of their penning. Yet there are significant shared contexts for Vsevolod Meyerhold (1874–1940) and Jacques Copeau (1879–1949) which influence, and find expression in, their theoretical thinking in different ways. The first observation might be that they both participated in a rejection of the hegemony of naturalism in their respective national theatrical cultures. Their anti-naturalism was not motivated by the same aesthetic concerns that drove Craig and Appia's work, with its atavistic homage to Wagner. This anti-naturalism considered art as an ideal realm, quite distinct from life; a place of transcendence, encouraging a different kind of illusionism to the grubby depiction of the everyday that was the alleged role of naturalism. Whilst both the practitioners under consideration here knew their Wagner and read articles by Craig, Appia and Fuchs, yet at the centre of Meyerhold and Copeau's writing was a sense of theatre as a social art and a social act. Their anti-naturalism came from an interest in 'the basic laws of theatricality' itself (*Meyerhold on Theatre* = *MT* 126).[1] The stage pictures that they created might appear similar to those of Craig and Appia, with their pared-down simplicity and use of geometric and architectonic forms, yet their theoretical writing indicates that this was produced by a philosophy of the theatre which refused illusion. Copeau reflected on the connection between his work and Meyerhold's in 1938:

> At the time we took over, naturalism was a dead weight on dramatic inspiration. It had made the stage uninhabitable for poetry by overloading it with properties and decors... We decongested the dramatic arena and denuded the stage. At about the same time, Meyerhold in Russia and myself in France were expressing the same unlimited dramatic ambition by asking for *a bare stage*. (*Copeau: Texts on Theatre* = *CTT* 111)[2]

This emphasis on theatricality as self-referential, deliberately revealing its workings for aesthetic or political purpose, might be considered a hallmark of modern thinking, although not modernist with all its connotations of elitist high culture.

The idea of theatre as a social art was connected to the burgeoning interest in popular culture. Populist movements and a championing of the importance of the people as an entity in government, industry, society and art, had been gathering force in different ways in Russia, France and Germany for at least half a century. Whilst national distinctions in tone are played out in the individual rhetoric of the writers, the overarching thrust of the popular movement, which incidentally also fuelled the rise of naturalism, was a pan-European one.[3] In the theatre it was marked by the reclamation of popular theatre traditions; a renaissance for *commedia dell'arte*, mystery plays, fairground entertainments and public festivals. The populist concerns which underlay this kind of artistic development were informed by two distinct political viewpoints. One which drew on a romanticized feudalism, in which festivals and publicly participatory events patronized by the élite, supposedly provided an outlet for the criticisms and frustrations of the disempowered, united the people and generated a sense of national identity. This kind of idea was developed in relation to other arts by thinkers like Mikhail Bakhtin, whose theories of the function of the carnivalesque and grotesque were influential in Meyerhold's work. The other political subtext to the championing of popular culture figured it as an empowerment of the worker and with the potential for effecting social change. This empowerment might take different forms, such as education. For some, educating the worker meant introducing a large working class audience to the best that élite culture could offer through cheap seat deals, large theatres and classical repertoires. For others, it meant education in issues of direct concern to the working-class audience, presented by either their peers or sympathetic intellectuals. There was also an economic element to this populist concern in the theatre. In a period when private patronage for the theatre was waning and government subsidy hard to come by, commercial producers had tapped into a lucrative market with music hall, variety shows and spectaculars. The practitioners under discussion may have denigrated the content or style of these enterprises, but they were impressed by their viability. In their writing, as much as in their practice, Meyerhold and Copeau engaged in the debates over the potential and place of popular theatre within their distinct national traditions.

In addition to the search for popular theatre forms, both practitioners were engaged in the search for new drama, that is new textual forms which would adequately answer their requirements and what they perceived to be society's requirements in a 'new' age. Early in the century Meyerhold and Copeau looked to the symbolists to provide a theatre of new conventions and forms. However, it was often necessary for them to develop text themselves, either original creative work or adaptations, and with varying degrees of success. Copeau's symbolist play *La Maison Natale* was a box-office flop for much the same reasons that it was praised by Antonin Artaud. He thought it an 'agonising play [that] stirs up questions which are too fundamental, its events present us with a mass of beauty which is too overwhelming and too total . . . for those that act it' (Rudlin 1986, 28). Rather more successful were Copeau's adaptations of *commedia* scenarios for his school troupe 'les Copiaus', which arose from workshop improvisation. Meyerhold's post-revolution work made such use of teams of adapters that critics joked that his posters should read '*The Marriage* by N.V.Gogol, Text by Schershelyafamova, Verses and prose by Antiokhiskovo, Author of the show, Nikolai Sestrin' (Symons 1971, 120). As Brecht quipped later 'Anyone can be creative, it's rewriting other people that's a challenge' (Thomson 1994, 25).

However, it is clear in both Meyerhold's and Copeau's theoretical writing that they did not always find the text of primary importance. As Copeau's interest in *commedia dell'arte* developed, fuelled by his study and staging of Molière, his ideas about the place of the written text in the theatrical hierarchy changed. In his notebooks he wondered whether an actor's propensity to *ad lib* or improvize around a text was 'an hereditary professional tendency. One could say he is protecting his territory, trying to win back the encroachments made on theatre by the *litterateur* and the writer' (*CTT* 152). The extension of this thinking was to use improvisation in the

training of actors which would 'give back to the actor the...true
spontaneous life of the word and the gesture...the true contact
with the public...the fire and daring of the jester. And what an
education for the poet; what a source of inspiration' (*CTT* 153). This
upended the traditional view, and one that he had earlier espoused,
that the actor should serve the dramatist, who was his inspiration.
Meyerhold, for his part, began with a theory of 'the theatre of the
straight line', where the dramatist's idea was to find uninterrupted
expression through the skilled actor. As his work continued,
although he rarely worked without a text, the actor and her skill
became the focus of his attention, to the extent that he felt a 'new'
dramatist would need training to understand his place:

> He will be permitted to put words into the actor's mouths, but
> first he must produce a scenario of movement. How long will it
> be before they inscribe in the theatrical tables the following law:
> words in the theatre are only embellishments on the design of
> movement? (*MT* 124)

The theoretical writings I shall explore below do not go so far as
to banish the dramatist from the process of making theatre. However, the ideal dramatist in this new theatrical world is a living
dramatist, who can work closely with the actors in the rehearsal
room.

Another element which Meyerhold and Copeau reveal through
this debate about text is a desire to place the actor at the centre of
their theorizing. Indeed with the benefit of hindsight it is clear that
naturalism had unleashed a new relationship between the body of
the performer and the audience. No longer content with the conventional signs of rhetorical or melodramatic performance the naturalistic tendency had demanded that the actor observe human
behaviour and reproduce it in its minutiae on stage, within fictional
structures that demanded increasingly understated playing. The
new theatricalism did not reverse this process of observation in
the actor, but transformed its purpose and the manner of the result-
ing performance. Moreover, audiences were accustomed to reading
the visual clues in the expressivity of the performer's body: a
tendency equally evident in the rise of expressive dance, or 'Dun-
canesque balleticism' as Meyerhold dubs it (*MT* 142), as in the
pathology of the body in psychoanalysis.[4] Symbolist drama, despite
its propensity for static portrayal, shared this sense that clues to the

inner dramas were played out in external form. The focus of interest moved to the performer, her skill, and her relationship with the audience. Both Meyerhold and Copeau's written texts contain plans for training actors in order to develop the skills and the correct attitude towards the audience that their work required.

Of course, not all of the theory of these practitioners was communicated in written form, nor was all their writing theoretical. Shared experience of other practitioners, reports of others work and theatrical criticism third-hand were also part of the way their own theoretical approaches were shaped by others' practice. Meyerhold imbibed much from Reinhardt, through his reading and his 1907 visit to the Munich Kammerspiele, which he writes about in *On the Theatre (O Teatra)*. His work also owed a debt to Piscator's practice and his vision in *The Political Theatre (Das Politische Theater)* published in 1929.[5] Meyerhold and Brecht were brought together through the good offices of Serge Tretiakov and Asya Lacis among others and, as has been extensively documented, the reciprocal influences were considerable.[6] After the closure of the Meyerhold Theatre in late 1938, Brecht, who was himself in exile, gloomily recorded in his journal a long list of those who had stopped writing, disappeared or been tried in Stalin's Russia, concluding:

> meyerhold has lost his theatre, but is supposed to be allowed to direct opera. literature and art are up the creek, political theory has gone to the dogs, what is left is a thin, bloodless, proletarian humanism propagated by officialdom.[7]

Likewise their awareness of each other's work came as much through reports of or visits to productions as from written theorizing. Copeau read about Meyerhold's production work in Alexander Bakshy's *The Path of the Modern Russian Stage* and noted his surprise at finding:

> all my own ideas, my central and most insistent preoccupation (the pre-eminence of the actor and of the actor's role) in Meyerhold, with all the consequences that that point of view entails...It is not therefore surprising that the word which is being passed to us from this new movement is: *Back to the booth and the commedia dell'arte*. One cannot imagine a greater coincidence of views. But how do we go about *getting* back? (Rudlin 1986, 92)[8]

It is useful to remember that where these practitioners found common ground was not always in the details of their theoretical thinking. It is also useful to reflect that their published theoretical writing stood at a critical distance from, and sometimes in contradiction to, their theatrical practice. Why they write and who they write for is intricately linked to the development of their practical experimentation at any given moment and the specific economic and social context of that practice.

Vsevolod Meyerhold

Meyerhold's writing was gathered, almost 30 years after his death and once he had been politically rehabilitated, in a two-volume edition of articles, letters, speeches and conversations *Stat'i, rechi, pis'ma, besedy* (Meyerhold 1968). Excerpts from his public writing and lectures, which also appear in the Russian collection, along with commentary from himself and others on his productions, are translated and grouped in Edward Braun's (1969) *Meyerhold on Theatre*. This remains the primary access to his material in English. The collected volume of his letters was published in Russian as *V.E. Meyerhold – Perepiska* (Korshunova and Sitkovetskaya 1976). One of these letters, Meyerhold's notes on 'Russian Dramatists' taken from a letter he wrote to the Englishman George Calderon, providing him with an overview of Russian drama, was printed in the Russian collected works and is reproduced in *Russian Dramatic Theory from Pushkin to the Symbolists* (Senelick 1981, 200–9). Paul Schmidt has published some letters and excerpts from Meyerhold along with commentary from his students and actors in *Meyerhold at Work* (Schmidt 1980). Jean Benedetti has included letters from, to and about Meyerhold in *Moscow Art Theatre Letters* (Benedetti 1991), and Marjorie Hoover translated 'The Actors Emploi' in her study, *Meyerhold: The Art of Conscious Theater* (Hoover 1974).

Using Braun's collection as a guide, I shall look at five significant pieces of writing that chart the transitions in Meyerhold's thinking and practice over his life. There is a concentration of published written work in the early part of his career; firstly his contributions to the anthology of symbolist theatre theory, *Theatre: A Book on the New Theatre* (Petersburg, 1908). These were reprinted in his collection of his writings on his work at the Moscow Art Theatre Studio, Komissarzhevskaya's company, the Alexandrinsky theatre, small-scale cabaret productions and his own school, *On the Theatre*, which appeared in 1913. It is interesting to note that he felt himself to be a unique enough and significant enough figure in the theatre by this time to publish a collection designed as much to record his production work for posterity, as to point the way for the future of theatre in Russia. His aspirations and experiments in actor-training were documented in the journal, *Love of Three Oranges*, in the years before the Revolution. Writing from the later part of his life is more dispersed, reflecting in part the urgency and privations of the immediate post-revolution period, and I shall look at two collections of lectures; one from the early 1920s on his great scheme for the October Revolution in the Theatre and the actor of the future, many of which were reproduced in the journal *Theatre Herald* (*Vestnik teatra*). The second collection of lectures was gathered and published as *The Reconstruction of the Theatre* in 1930. The tone of this last major work from Meyerhold is defensive and reflects the increasingly complex ideological environment, under Stalin's stricter cultural regime, that Meyerhold was having to negotiate.

Chapter 1 on Stanislavski in this volume indicates much of the initial context needed to ground a reading of Meyerhold's early theoretical writing. His first published essays are full of the Moscow Art Theatre (MAT) and its First Studio experiment. Five short essays were collected in the symbolist theatre polemic, *Theatre: A Book on the New Theatre* of 1908. He wrote a letter to Stanislavski apologising for the cruelty of his criticism in his essays, which was indeed very sharp (Schmidt 1980, 16). The context of the volume reveals his indebtedness to the symbolist movement in Russia. The volume itself owed its publication to the temporary relaxation of censorship of printed work, which was one of the few successful outcomes of the abortive 1905 Revolution. All of the contributors to the volume were members of a symbolist salon, hosted by Vyacheslav Ivanov at his home on Wednesday evenings, dubbed the Tower. Essays were included from poets and critics like Ivanov, Benois, Bely, Bryusov, Sologub and, surprisingly, Lunacharsky, who was to become that most materialist of officials, the first People's Commissar for Enlightenment after the Revolution.[9] Meyerhold had been involved with this group for some time and in January 1906, after his ousting from the Moscow Art Studio, the symbolists had suggested supplying Meyerhold with a theatre to use. In the end this came to nothing, but Meyerhold's connection with the actress Vera Komissarzhevskaya, who did find a theatre for him, was strengthened by their shared interest in staging the 'new drama'. The agenda for the volume had been set by Bryusov's 1902 article, 'Unnecessary Truth', published in *World of Art* (*Mir Iskusstva*), Benois and Diaghilev's Petersburg journal.[10] Bryusov, a literary man, not a playwright, had been damning in his criticism of the Art Theatre and its devotion to naturalism. Senelick attributes the founding of the Theatre Studio at the Moscow Art Theatre in part to his pressure (xlvi). Although the volume was dedicated to Stanislavski, the production work at the Moscow Art Theatre, particularly the attempt to stage non-realist texts, was stingingly mocked by all contributors.

'The Theatre Studio' headed the collection of essays.[11] In it Meyerhold reveals one of the reasons for his writing, which is 'to help the future theatre historian assess accurately the significance of the Theatre-Studio, to help directors who are painstakingly seeking fresh means of expression, to help the spectator fathom what it is that inspires the theatre of the New Drama' (*MT* 47). The 'New Drama' appears almost exclusively symbolist, and the first essay is largely an account of the abortive work of the Studio on Maeterlinck's *The Death of Tintagiles*. In all five essays, but most notably in 'The Naturalist Theatre and the Theatre of Mood' Meyerhold reiterated a commonplace of the symbolist critique of the Moscow Art Theatre; that it is in the thrall of the 'trifles of everyday life' (*MT* 25) and the dated hyper-realist style of Meiningen productions.[12] Unsurprisingly in a symbolist-inspired analysis, he made use of musical analogies to describe the success or shortcomings of the productions, an analogy he was to return to throughout his working and writing career. He described the director as responsible for the creation of harmony in the whole performance. By this he does not use harmony, as Craig did, as a metaphor for the way a director must synthesize staging elements and coordinate his team, but rather as a metaphor for the play's performance itself. His detailed and sensitive critique of *The Cherry Orchard* Act III, sees the performance as 'translated into musical terms, this is one movement of the symphony' (*MT* 28).[13] His criticism is of the direction, not of Chekhov whom he identifies as a fellow symbolist. Chekhov earns this epithet because of the importance of 'fate in the new mystical drama' and because he created characters who 'dance among the "philistines" in a costume familiar to the puppet theatre' (*MT* 28). Meyerhold even paid him the highest compliment by directly and favourably comparing him with Maeterlinck. The criticism of the Moscow Art Theatre's version of *The Cherry Orchard* was particularly pointed, as Meyerhold had persuaded Chekhov to release the play to his company simultaneously in 1904 and had directed his own version. All in all Meyerhold is broadening his criticism of the Moscow Art Theatre from its inability to stage symbolist drama to its inability to stage Chekhov, in many ways the defining playwright of the MAT.

Chekhov himself is one of the many past and present masters Meyerhold summons to his cause. He makes selective use of Schopenhauer, Tolstoy, Voltaire and Fuchs to support his argument that 'in the theatre the spectator's imagination is able to supply that which is left unsaid' (*MT* 25). Meyerhold's focus on the spectator was a powerful and fresh element to his rhetoric and work. Moreover, as he conceives it the spectator is more than simply interpreting, she is completing the creative task of the stage. In the third essay 'The New Theatre Foreshadowed in Literature' he rephrases arguments made by Bryusov and Ivanov, although he speaks as the only symbolist of the Petersburg circle who was actively involved in making theatre. It is from them that he borrows the notion of stylized theatre, and descriptions of the attempt to put these ideas into practice with Komissarzhevskaya fill the last two essays, 'First Attempts at a Stylized Theatre' and 'The Stylized Theatre'. The idea of the theatre of the straight line which offers actors creative independence within the collectively agreed framework of the play's interpretation, is surely a reaction to his personal frustrations when acting at MAT. With so much responsibility passed to the actor, the essay outlines the skills in diction and plasticity that the actor must possess adequately to communicate the essence of the drama to the audience. These were skills that he felt that the Moscow Art Theatre School was not able to offer its pupils (*MT* 45–6). The need for a new kind of actor-training is one which recurs frequently in his writing and his practice from this point onwards (*MT* 52). The final essay makes use of Ivanov's reading of Greek theatre and the power of the dithyramb to develop a new relationship between the audience and the stage-performers, where they 'participate in a *corporate* creative act' (*MT* 60). It draws together, and reiterates as a programme for future productions, the key points of Meyerhold's earlier analysis.[14]

On the Theatre is a curious book which gathers brief descriptions of the staging of certain plays Meyerhold had directed, alongside

lectures and articles in which he expounded the broader theoretical
issues in his work. In the introduction Meyerhold himself found a
coherence in the selections since 'all the threads of the different
themes in this book are drawn together in the question of the
forestage' (Leach 1989, 38). The tone of the whole book centres
around the pragmatic demands of working in the theatre. The
inclusion of the production descriptions and the use of specific
examples that litter the longer theoretical writing, ground the rhetoric. The book is less about vision and aspiration, and more about
experimentation and reported findings. In his writing, whether he is
documenting the process of making certain performances, describing elements of staging, arguing with his critics or providing his
version of theatre history, Meyerhold is primarily concerned with
stylistic matters. By the time the book appeared Meyerhold's manner of staging had become so widely recognized that Blok could
criticize the second production of *The Fairground Booth* for containing too much 'Meyerholdia' (*MT* 117). It is clear from the volume
that Meyerhold considered his work to be unique, needing a wider
dissemination beyond sometimes inaccessible venues, and worth
preserving for posterity, even if the work had never reached the
stage. In the longer pieces his tone is combative, his criticism and
analysis of others' work is unsparing. The collection begins with his
essays on symbolist theatre discussed above, followed by his study
of Wagner and Appia which had arisen from his production of
Wagner's *Tristan and Isolde* at the Marinsky Opera in Petersburg.
This essay had had its first outing as a lecture in November 1909
and was recorded in *The Yearbook of the Imperial Theatres*. It is written
as if for an academic audience and is deeply indebted in tone to
Appia's *Music and the Art of Theatre*, from which diagrams, examples, and phraseology are reproduced almost verbatim. For example, it focuses on dance which joins the concern with the human
body in motion and rhythm, with the actor as the means through
which 'the music translates the dimension of time into spatial terms'
(*MT* 86). He also quotes liberally from Wagner on the subject of the
actor as a living work of art, but like Appia comes to the conclusion
that Wagner did not find the appropriate staging to realize his
dreams for music-drama. The essay is so completely consumed by
the rhetoric of Appia, Wagner and Fuchs that at times it is difficult
to reconcile this esoteric concern with the art of the stage picture,
with any of Meyerhold's other writings. Ultimately what links his
work to theirs is a concern with an actor's movement on stage, and

he has to conveniently side-step the ideological underpinning of their work to assert this connection.

The next piece, a study of the preparation and staging of *Don Juan*, again concentrates on theatre history and reveals Meyerhold's awareness of the Japanese Noh stage and conventions. What he concentrates on here, as elsewhere in the collection, is the theatricality of these modes of theatrical production, one that recognizes the spectator's role. 'Bright light infects the spectators with a festive mood as they enter the theatre. When the actor sees a smile on the lips of a spectator he begins to admire himself, as though looking in a mirror' (*MT* 103). This attention to the actor-audience relationship, the exposure of staging techniques, the self-admiring actor as a far from morally superior being, and the focus of attention in the auditorium are all elements drawn from the popular theatre. The attitude to the audience implied here inverts traditional rhetoric and offers the audience as a mirror for the performer, who is altered through the input of the audience. As Copeau was discovering in France, a reexamination of Molière's work offered a fruitful starting point for this kind of self-alert theatre. *Don Juan* is used as an exemplary production here, as in the later essay 'The Fairground Booth'.

These concerns also resonate in the most significant piece of writing in *On the Theatre*, the essay 'The Fairground Booth', probably written in 1912. Although the essay shares the title of Blok's play, there is little reference within it to the production, which had premièred in December 1906 at Komissarzhevskaya's theatre. A short description of the 1906 staging, which made use of an actual fairground booth on stage, is included separately later in the book.[15] The fairground booth of the essay's title stands as a metonym for the style of theatrical performance and the process of making that performance that Meyerhold had been exploring. It was this style, or 'stylization', that had lost him his place at the Moscow Art Theatre Studio, at Komissarzhevskaya's theatre, and which was drawing criticism at the Alexandrinsky theatre as he was writing. The shape of the first half of the essay is guided by his criticism and response to Alexandr Benois's gushing review of Nemirovich-Danchenko's production of *The Brothers Karamazov* at the Moscow Art Theatre. Alongside their artistic differences, Meyerhold had personal reasons to resent this article: Benois had been the harshest critic of his work with Komissarzhevskaya's troupe, and Nemirovich-Danchenko had had a hand in removing Meyerhold from the Moscow Art

Theatre's acting company in 1902 and from his position as Studio director in 1905. The other production Meyerhold criticizes as counterblast to his own work is Remizov's *Devil's Play*. While Remizov was a fellow symbolist, the play had been staged at Komissarzhevskaya's theatre by her brother, Fyodor, immediately after Meyerhold had been asked to leave. The essay documents the abandonment of symbolist preoccupations and personnel in Meyerhold's work, a movement that had already had its day as the pressing demands of material reality increasingly impinged on theatre, performer and audience. The kind of theatre history that Meyerhold outlines in this essay, which charts an anti-illusionist tradition, shares much with the development of Russian formalism, as Leach has identified, in particular with the work of Victor Shlovsky. Walter Benjamin, who knew both Brecht and Meyerhold, reflected on Brecht's construction of an alternative theatre history similar to this one; ruled by theatricality itself, and charting the explosions of interest in popular forms through the ages:

> It is a European road, but it is a German one too. If, that is, one can speak of a road rather than a stalking-path along which the legacy of medieval and baroque drama has crept down to us. (Benjamin 1973, 18)

Although Meyerhold positions himself here as a champion of the popular theatre and calls for a revival of traditional modes which recognize the spectator, it is important to qualify what he means by popular entertainment. He is not thinking of attempting to draw a different audience to the theatre. When he set up his intimate cabaret, the Interlude House, in 1910 he wanted 'to create an artistic "balagan" [fairground booth]... a haven of rest for the cultured Petersburg theatregoer' (*MT* 111). The audience he has in mind within the essay is a literary public, that 'has formed an alliance with those so-called dramatists who turn literature for reading into literature for the theatre – as though the public's attitude to the theatre were not confused enough already' (*MT* 121). The theatre history that he creates in 'The Fairground Booth' draws extensively on examples from French theatre history, as Russian élite culture had done for many years. Molière is his role model for the artist who used popular forms in his work for the élite, in part to satirize his audience. Meyerhold also rejects popular or traditional theatre forms which use the paradigm of the religious. Indeed he argues that it is in the separation from the religious that 'theatre' was formed:

> Having sensed its own inadequacy, the mystery gradually began to absorb the elements of popular entertainment as personified by the mummers, and was forced to go from the ambo, through the parvis into the churchyard, and thence out on to the market-place...no sooner had it reached a compromise with the art of the actor than it was absorbed by this art and ceased to be a mystery-play. (*MT* 122–3)[16]

As Braun points out, Meyerhold was not alone in returning to 'traditional' forms; Yvreinov was exploring similar popular styles in greater historical detail at the Ancient Theatre in Petersburg. Even Stanislavski had addressed the first rehearsal of the Moscow Art Studio with a paean to the people.[17] Meyerhold used an awareness of the trend to place his work in the mainstream:

> Nowadays the majority of stage-directors are turning to pantomime and prefer this form to verbal drama. This strikes me as more than a coincidence. It is not a matter of taste. (*MT* 125)

In France and Russia, the development of mime and expressive movement training for performers was burgeoning. Yet at this point Meyerhold's interest in the audience does not extend as far as worrying about the bourgeoise's dominance of the auditorium. It is not until the socio-political environment changes so dramatically after the 1917 Revolution that Meyerhold's concern for the spectator becomes more explicitly a concern for the popular or proletarian audience.

A central element in 'The Fairground Booth' is an illumination of the task of the modern actor: to resurrect the cult of 'cabotinage'.[18] She must recreate the forgotten techniques using historical research, and rediscover 'the power of the mask, gesture, movement and plot'. These skills once acquired will force a change in the theatre as 'the actor may get bored with perfecting his craft in order to perform in outdated plays; soon he will want not only to act but to compose for himself as well. Then at last we shall see the rebirth of *the theatre of improvisation*' (*MT* 127). A metaphor that Meyerhold uses in the second part of the essay is that of the puppet theatre. Not only does this fit with his championship of popular forms, but the puppet had also been a favourite image of the symbolists. This was most passionately articulated by Craig's writing on the übermarion-ette, of which Meyerhold was aware, and the puppet theatre was of stylistic importance to many of the avant-garde theatres of France and Germany. Many critics thought Meyerhold's directorial work reduced the actor to little more than a puppet. After the staging of *The Fairground Booth* a cartoonist depicted Meyerhold in Pierrot costume manipulating Vera Komissarzhevskaya as a puppet (Leach 1989, 7), and her letter dismissing him from her theatre complained that 'the path we have been following the whole time is the path which leads to the puppet theatre' (Braun 1986, 83). However, in the essay Meyerhold uses the puppet as an example of a style of theatricalization that does not rely on the naturalistic attempt to reproduce life on stage, but one that develops its own 'make-believe' world and invites the audience in. Ironically the puppet is a metaphor for the empowerment of the actor. There are a great number of images of Meyerhold, both pejorative and posi-tive, from the pre-revolutionary period that depict him as a Pierrot or pantomime figure.[19] The iconography supports the emphasis he places on the skilled cabotin:

> if there is no cabotin, there is no theatre either; and, contrariwise, as soon as the theatre rejects the basic rules of theatricality it straight-way imagines that it can dispense with the cabotin. (*MT* 123)

The figure of the cabotin and the spirit of the fairground booth con-tinue to inhabit his writing for an initiated intellectual audience, as he moved further from sympathy with the poetic symbolists and to-wards more pragmatic, if splintered, groups who dubbed themselves Futurist, Aceist or Suprematist.[20] It was in his occasional perform-ances in the cabarets and intimate theatre clubs of Petersburg, while moonlighting from his serious job directing opera at the Alexandrin-sky Theatre, that Meyerhold was able to develop the skills of the cab-otin, in practice and in his training of young actors at his own studio.

Meyerhold made clear that the purpose of *The Love of Three Oranges: The Journal of Doctor Dapertutto*, produced between 1914 and 1916, was as 'an indispensable textbook' (*MT* 154) for the stu-dents at the Meyerhold Studio. The ideal reader implied in the rhetoric of the journal is the trainee theatre performer and many passages describe the experiments in performance of the studio members.[21] The course syllabus and the performance études are drawn from popular theatre movements in Western and Eastern theatre traditions. The programme for the 1916–17 year sets out not only the syllabus for the students, but the entrance and examination regulations and requirements. The articles on theatre history in the journal follow the syllabus of the school, looking at *commedia*, Gozzi, Spanish theatre, reviews of productions and translations of plays, and the overarching tone is instructive. Journals had often played a key role in supporting a theatre, providing a theoretical forum or generating new audience, as *Vesy*, the symbolist journal had done earlier in Meyerhold's career, or as *La Nouvelle Revue Française* was to do for Copeau and Artaud. However, Meyerhold was doing something distinctive in using the journal format explicitly as a teaching tool for a double audience; as a resource for initiated students and as a publicity tool for the wider, theatrically-initiated world.[22] The underlying philosophy of the school was that there are 'laws of theatricality' (*MT* 126) that can be studied and perfected. This was Meyerhold's contribution to the defeat of the fallacy of the 'inspirational' actor. The kind of training the school supplied was focused on 'forestage' acting, a presentational approach to the material. Meyerhold's students were required to experiment in front of a public, as apprentice performers, just as Copeau insisted upon performance as being of pedagogic value to the training performer.

When the Revolution occurred there was no avoiding the impact of external factors on the hallowed world of the theatre and the Meyerhold Studio. And yet, the early principles of the Bolsheviks seemed akin to Meyerhold's championing of popular styles. It is no coincidence that Meyerhold found enough to his taste to be part of the Commissariat for Education once Russia had embarked on its post-revolutionary reforms. Braun outlines Meyerhold's enthusiastic work in the first Commissariat workshops offering 'polytechnical education in the theatre arts' to anyone interested in Petrograd – a broadening of the catchment of his theatre training. Illness and the vicissitudes of the Civil War prevented Meyerhold from publishing much about his vision for future work post-revolution. It was not until he became head of the Moscow, and hence national Theatre Department of the Commissariat for Education (TEO) and editor of its journal *The Theatre Herald* (*Vestnik Teatra*) that he had the opportunity to publicize his point of view. The selection of articles Braun gathers for translation are transcripts of speeches concerning the production of Verhaeren's *Dawn*, a symbolist play from 1898 considerably reworked for the new production. The distance between Russian symbolism's focus on the individual's inner world and the Bolshevik's insistence on the social responsibility of the individual was not unbridgeable. Merezhkovsky, a leading symbolist of Meyerhold's Petersburg circle, had coined a neat formula: 'In politics, the fathers are "populists", the children "marxists", in art "realists" and "decadents", in philosophy "positivists" and "mystics"' (Pynam 1994, 114). It is difficult to assess the extent to which Meyerhold embraced Bolshevik ideology, but his writing from this period has a new vigour and denunciatory verve. He relished the rhetoric of the billboard, the slogan and the direct address of agitational propaganda.

Meyerhold's antipathy to 'professional theatre' companies, many of which were briefly under his jurisdiction as head of TEO, had been on stylistic grounds in the past, but was now translated into political terms. His complaint against them is that they were apolitical: 'No man (no actor) has ever been apolitical, a-social; man is always a product of the forces of his environment' (*MT* 168). The reluctance of many of the long-standing theatres in Moscow to adopt a Soviet repertoire, or to allow the apparently cataclysmic social and political changes outside their walls to affect their style of staging, is well-documented. Meyerhold took the opportunity, in the pages of *Theatre Herald*, to castigate the traditional theatre managements. Alone among the producers and directors he singles out Stanislavski for praise. His commendation is not for 'his notorious system for a whole army of actors, psychologically "experiencing" the parts of all those characters who do nothing but walk, eat, drink, make love and wear jackets.' Meyerhold dismisses this as a response to the demands for 'theoretical justification' from nervous theatre-managers, which had been bolstered by 'loathsome textbooks of French experimental psychology'. The time will come Meyerhold prophecies when Stanislavski-the-visionary will tire of the 'acute paradoxes tossed off at random' and 'hurl the oft-amended pages of his system; into the stove' (*MT* 177). Meyerhold's admiration of Stanislavski springs in the main from his performances as an actor which had had much of the theatrical, the pantomime and *commedia* about them. Although there was very little written by or on Stanislavski in circulation at this point, those moving in theatre circles were able to characterize Stanislavski's approach to acting as a 'system'. Moreover, friends and theatre initiates were aware of the developments at the Moscow Art Theatre, and of the changes which were emerging by 1921 in Stanislavski's studio practice. Meyerhold offers a glimpse of this in his parody of a Stanislavski lesson:

No 'authentic emotions'!...Walk theatrically! Suppleness! The eloquent gesture! Dance! Bow! Duel with rapiers! Rhythm! Rhythm! Rhythm! (*MT* 179)

This depiction of the convergence between Stanislavski's studio practice and Meyerhold's own acts as a valuable form of defence and justification for the latter's much more advanced experimentation.

Meyerhold's work was increasingly in need of defence, as the exchanges that Braun selects demonstrate. Most concern Meyerhold's justification of his radical staging of *The Dawn*, which seemed to some critics and leading party members to be still in thrall to élitist 'stylization' which was obscure and irrelevant to the worker. Meyerhold had experienced difficulty with the 'professional' actors that he had tried to work with. In his opening speech to his new company, the First Theatre of the RSFSR (Russian Soviet Federal Socialist Republic), he outlines plans for a new repertoire that will further the cause of Soviet reform:

We shall tackle the task of adaptation without fear, fully confident of its necessity. It is possible that we shall adapt texts in co-operation with the actors of the company, and it is a great pity that they were not able to help Valery Bebutov and me with *The Dawn*. Joint work on texts by the company is envisaged as an integral part of the theatre's function. (*MT* 170)

The need for the new repertoire was clear from 'the urgent demands of the modern spectator' (*MT* 171) and Meyerhold's defence against his detractors returns again and again to the 'new' spectator. These articles are also full of the rhetoric of nascent constructivism:

for us the art of manufacturing is more important than any tediously pretty patterns and colours...our artists will be delighted to throw away their brushes and take up axes, picks and hammers to hack stage sets out of the materials of raw nature. (*MT* 173)

However, while the rhetoric of the time extolled the virtues of the rule and the redemptive power of work, few of the leading administrators of artistic matters were convinced that these elements should find such bald expression in the theatre.

It was not until the establishment of the State Higher Theatre Work-shop that Meyerhold could work with a more stable company and develop once more the combination of training and experimental performance that was at the heart of his approach to theatre. There is little writing from him from this period in English translation, and most of the attention has been paid to the series of remarkable productions that he developed. One lecture 'On the Actor of the Future and Biomechanics' was recorded in the journal *Ermitazh* (1922). In it he expounds an acceptable version of biomechanics as the development of thinking of artistic performance as labour, where 'the work of the actor in an industrial society will be regarded as a means of production vital to the proper organisation of the labour of every citizen of that society' (*MT* 197). The focus on the citizen audience-member, and the assumption of the effective-ness of theatre in society, constitute a defence of theatrical investi-gation in the new society. This is a restatement of his old battle between the performance processes built on psychological founda-tions and those built on physiological and social processes. Leach explores the debt his formulation owes to older debates on perform-ing and to actors like Coquelin, and the links between this kind of thinking about performance and a widespread focus on mechanical and industrial advance (Leach 1994). Again, here, Meyerhold remarks on the shortcomings of acting guided by '"authentic emo-tion"; it is the system of my teacher Konstantin Stanislavski, who, by the way, will probably abandon it very shortly' (*MT* 200). The focus on the actor of the future in this lecture echoes a widespread transformation in public rhetoric. An aspirational positivism and romanticism about the future, rather than the past, was character-istic of much public writing and rhetoric in this period, which found ultimate expression in Stalin's Five-Year Plans.

Meyerhold's staging and training demonstrate a theoretical and stylistic coherence that found itself continually in need of justifica-tion within a changing world. During the late 1920s and beyond the governmental structures of the Soviet Union changed; party affilia-tion became the *sine qua non* of success, and the reduction of ideo-logical diversity echoed the imposition of a command economy, masterminded by Stalin. Written after being kicked out of the RSFSR First theatre, Meyerhold's justification of his work on the *Maganimous Cuckold* is worth quoting at length to provide an exam-ple of the ideological re-positioning that he continually had to perform. He asserted that:

the success of this production signified the success of the new theatrical philosophy on which it was based; now there is no doubt that the entire 'Left Theatre' not only dates from this production but to this day bears traces of its influence. The fact that the stylistic extremes displayed by this production – although they frightened a section of critical opinion – were greeted *with delight* by the widest possible audience, proved that an urgent desire for just such a theatrical style was felt by this new audience, which regarded the theatre as one of the many *cultural* conquests of the Revolution. With this production we hoped to lay the basis for a new form of theatrical presentation with no need for illusionistic setting or complicated props, making do with the simplest objects which came to hand and transforming a spectacle performed by specialists into an improvised performance which could be put on by workers in their leisure time. (*MT* 204–5)

There is an immodest attempt here to rewrite theatrical history with Meyerhold's work as the foundational moment of revolutionary theatre. The staging style makes a virtue of necessity with no need for expensive 'illusionistic' scenery or props. This is a mercy since no-one in the immediate aftermath of the Revolution, particularly in Meyerhold's run-down theatre building, had the money needed to produce theatrical illusion. The audience has become Meyerhold's defence against the conservative criticism of party *aparatchiks* and other theatre workers. Meyerhold's ideal audience is here constructed as the worker, who will find artistic inspiration in his theatre. This is an ironic, if logical, development of his championing of popular theatre forms within the new setting of Revolutionary Moscow. It also foreshadows what is to be his experience for the rest of his life; that while he was to continue to find an actual audience that contained a high proportion of workers, military conscripts and students, according to his own research (Kleberg 1990), the authorities were to find him increasingly 'alien'.[23] Yet this passage, if Meyerhold believed his own argument, is deeply self-deceiving, since the physical sophistication that his performers were able to achieve was the result of years of work. While Meyerhold's rhetoric during his 'October in the Theatre' phase may have championed the proletarian actor, his actual experiments with such non-professional groups were extremely limited. It is hard to imagine that what

Meyerhold might call improvisation here would be achievable by amateur workers in their lunchbreak.

The final piece of writing I want to look at is a collection of lectures from 1929, collated and printed as *The Reconstruction of the Theatre* (*Rekonstuktsia teatra*) the following year. In this Meyerhold's vision for the theatre broadens to an international scale and bears the traces of his company's recent visits abroad on tour for the first time, to Breslau, Berlin, Cologne and Paris. In Paris his work was seen by Louis Jouvet, Gaston Baty, Charles Dullin and Jean Cocteau among others and received rave reviews. Yet the rhetoric only too clearly reveals the immediate national context of the piece. In the first paragraph, Meyerhold sets out to answer the 'demands of both our Party and of the new spectator' (*MT* 253). As Russia's economic situation worsened and Stalin's Five-Year Plan gathered steam, there was a crackdown on divergent or unhelpful cultural and literary activity; consequently these lectures put on a conspicuous display of Party support. As collectivisation began, class war was declared against the *kulak* or middleclass farmer; Meyerhold parrots this enthusiastically (*MT* 268), calling for a new theatre which can address these ills. Meyerhold was also eager here to distance himself from his earlier support of Futurism. Marinetti's visit to the Meyerhold Studio in 1914, documented in *The Love of Three Oranges* that year, was now a dangerous example of collaboration with Rightist elements in the Arts that the Party was out to purge. Meyerhold makes much of the Fascist connections with the Catholic Church and denounces Marinetti's anarchic collaboration with Mussolini's dictatorship, although in the same breath he acknowledges that 'with their religious processions and their Fascist rallies, these two organizations are unrivalled in their restoration of the traditional devices of the street theatre' (*MT* 260). Meyerhold's links to Trotsky and his earlier connections to the upper echelons of the party might be construed as dangerous deviation by 1930, after Trotsky's exile and the beginning of the showtrials to eradicate saboteurs of the Revolution and the 'Left' opposition within the Party. Meyerhold treads a delicate line between quoting Comrade Stalin and resisting the full implications of the designation of this theatre as formalist.

Yet Meyerhold is taking the pulse of the theatrical nation when he identifies that agitational theatre was losing popularity. The Blue Blouse movement and other agit-prop groups had exhausted their enthusiasm and even the new hope that Meyerhold identifies as his

parting shot, the Theatre of Young Workers (TRAM), was reorgan-
ized by the Party in 1932 and disappeared (Leach 1994, 174). To
some extent the essay moves beyond what was politically expedient.
It was perhaps not wise to make such play about mass celebrations,
which had been frequent activities in the years immediately after the
Revolution but were mostly confined to the anniversary celebration
by the late twenties. Meyerhold's failure to mount a ten-year anniversary production (he argued there was no Soviet play worth
staging in his repertoire) was later held up as anti-Soviet by his
critics. Yet, here, Meyerhold calls for audiences of 'tens of thou-
sands'; aware that membership of an audience of that size itself
can generate a thrill, which much theatre had lost (*MT* 256). The
mass audience, of the kind that the cinema was able to generate,
seemed to offer fresh impetus to the theatre. But it needed a greatly
improved technological facility to match the excitement of the
cinema, technology that the Party was unwilling to fund. For all
this, Meyerhold is careful to distinguish between the kind of mass
celebrations he is advocating and those organized by the Catholic
Church and Mussolini in Italy, or those bourgeois boulevard festivals of the apolitical French, or the American masses delight in
saucy reviews and films. He concludes that in the cities of these
nations 'the street itself is a stage, the spectator – an actor; but both
lack the firm direction of an authoritative organization to transform
them into true theatre' (*MT* 265). Meyerhold whips up a nationalistic
defence of the theatrical training of amateur groups and the workers
in Russia. He advocates the Russian model of providing leisure for
the new man who battles with the forces of nature; leisure, a newly
psychologized term in the jargon of Taylorism and corporate industry, which trains a man in 'flexibility', a concept both metaphorical
and physical in Meyerhold's philosophy. There is a subtle suggestion that directly agitational theatre is no longer as socially effective,
and it is through the transformational power of participation in
theatre, that the worker is to be re-invigorated. Meyerhold does
not fully unpack this idea, and returns to the notion of the actor
and theatre as providers of complex stylized show to 'make the
theatre tremble with the sheer joy of living' (*MT* 272).

This essay also catalogues those practitioners Meyerhold came
into contact with through the writing of critics like Alexei Gvozdev,
incidentally a supporter of his work, who had written articles in his
defence. Meyerhold admires Piscator for his use of the cinema in
theatre, a modern technique, but argues with Gvozdev's interpreta-

tion of Piscator's production method as neglecting the actor. He was dismissive of the over-simplification in the work of Copeau's progeny, avowing that the French worker would 'gladly desert Louis Jouvet and Gaston Baty for a little boulevard theatre where he can see aspects of his own everyday life depicted in some ingenuous farce' (*MT* 264). In what he admits is a *volte-face*, Meyerhold asks why the worker should go to the theatre if he is not to be overwhelmed by the beauty of what he sees. He concedes that there was a time when he argued 'Down with beauty in the theatre', when beauty was an excuse to prolong bourgeois taste. However, now he was urging the State to continue to support the theatre so that it might continue to inspire the workers with its spectacle and 'powerful revolutionary content, dazzling in its variety and its complexity' (*MT* 273). Once more, as in much of his post-revolution writing, the demands of an audience of workers become the justification for his practice. The essay offers a theoretical exposition of the ideas that were finding physical expression in the actual reconstruction of the Meyerhold Theatre, with an enormous auditorium and multiple possible sites of interaction between performers and audience. The defensive tone of this work was carried through in several articles and lectures as the Party bureaucrats armed themselves against Meyerhold's work. When Socialist Realism was expressly established as the only acceptable form for theatre and fiction in the Soviet Union and its communist satellites, in 1934, Meyerhold's experiments were dangerously marginalized. Despite the international recognition of his work outside the USSR and his supporters, including Stanislavski, inside the country, Meyerhold was to fall prey to the blood-letting of Stalin's cultural orthodoxy.

Jacques Copeau

Although he had planned to collect his work for posterity, Copeau's writings were only gathered after his death. The French edition is a piecemeal affair, and students of his theoretical writings in English will encounter him primarily through Rudlin and Paul's *Copeau: Texts on Theatre* (1990) (=*CTT*), and through brief excerpts in two of Cole and Chinoy's anthologies, *Actors on Acting* (1970) and *Directors on Directing* (1963). Rudlin's study of Copeau (1986) also offers some textual sources. For those readers of French, many of Copeau's pieces are collected in *Registres* (1974), including the volume *Appels* (= *A*) which contains some of his shorter pieces, under the imprimatur of the *Nouvelle Revue Française*, the journal which Copeau co-founded in 1908. All of the collections conflate his lectures, theatre criticism, theoretical manifestos and essays, and his private journals and correspondence. It takes a careful eye from readers today if they are to attempt to distinguish public writing in its context from the previously unpublished musings in his journal. The public texts, which are in some ways less interesting than the journals, trace the changing nature of his work, from the early establishment of the Vieux Colombier Theatre, and later School, to writings and lectures connected to the school in Burgundy and the troupe 'les Copiaus'. Towards the end of his life, after this work with his own ensemble had for the most part come to an end in 1941, Copeau wrote another impassioned plea for theatrical development, *The Popular Theatre* (*Le Théâtre Populaire*).

The complex debate surrounding the theatrical stylistics of 'popular' theatre and the attitude to or involvement of a popular audience troubled Copeau throughout his career. Like Meyerhold, as social and politics circumstances changed, Copeau's ideas on the popular evolved and his influence helped to shape the flourishing of popular theatre forms in France after the Second World War. However, initially Copeau thought of the popular mainly in terms of theatrical style. A theatre critic in Paris in the first decade of the century he lambasted the 'populist' fare of the Boulevard Theatres, where ticket prices limited access for a working-class audience. He was dismissive of the stultifying reverence of the so-called national theatres, the Comédie Française and the Odeon. He remained sceptical of the rash of Little Theatres, which peppered Paris at the turn of the century, which he considered in the thrall of an élite whose revolutionary formulas 'are born and die every month in little artistic circles and whose boldness is mainly founded on ignorance' (*Appels* = *A* 20; my own translation). Although this dismissal of the little theatres came in an article publicising the opening of his own little theatre, the Vieux Colombier, he was keen to distinguish himself from those revolutionaries who were overturning received ideas in poetry, art and literature. As he was later to clarify in his 1926 lecture 'Is Dramatic Renovation possible?', he considered theatrical revolution as a short-lived chasing after '*nouveauté*', at which the modernist was well-practised (*A* 254). However, Copeau's own more modest aspirations for theatrical renovation still required that 'an enlightened élite plays the largest role' (*A* 255).

Copeau's first articulation of his creative work, 'An Attempt at Dramatic Renovation', was published in the same journal as much of his theatre criticism, the *Nouvelle Revue Française (NRF)*.[24] It was written in September 1913, as Copeau's company returned, for final rehearsals, to the restructured Vieux Colombier theatre on the Left Bank in Paris after their seclusion in rural Limon. It finished with a bold plea for support from the readers of the *NRF*. The connections between the *Nouvelle Revue Française* and its first theatrical enterprise at the Vieux Colombier were complex.[25] Several of the writers associated with the journal wrote plays for the new theatre company, and Copeau's co-editor Schlumberger oversaw its finances. Most significantly, Copeau already had in mind the kind of audience he was aiming at for his new theatre. He knew them because he had been addressing this theatre-going public through his critical work for this journal and others. Flattered as the 'leading section of the public', these readers were also to become audience members and financial patrons through the subscription system (*A* 32). Copeau makes much of his intention to limit expenditure in the running of the theatre in order to maximize its return (a clue to the kind of staging the spectator might expect). The self-supporting purity of the Vieux Colombier under its subscription scheme is contrasted with the corruption of state-subsidized theatre and the commercial boulevard theatres in France. With its detailed discussion of the theatre's financial foundations and the material necessity which conditioned its choice of repertoire and programming schedule, the article has something of a prospectus for investment, as much as a manifesto of ideas.

Copeau's work and writing always linked theatre with a moral and religious agenda, in a way which distinguished his thinking from Meyerhold. Meyerhold's writing grew increasingly virulent in its denunciation of the Church, particularly the Catholic Church and its institutional corruption, at the very moment that Copeau was reconverting to Catholicism. In 'An Attempt at Dramatic Renovation' the descriptions of the company's ethos and the future training of the student-actors are couched in a religious idiom; the actor is to be inspired with 'a sense of conscience' and the new theatre will 'initiate him into the morality of his art' (Cole and Chinoy 1970, 217). Copeau was later to offer a more realistic picture of company rehearsals, admitting that:

there was a lack of experience, clear ideas and methods on my part, of goodwill on the part of my unprepared pupils. They still did not have much confidence in me, and certain among them appeared reluctant and even hostile. (*CTT* 29)

So, not such devoted servants of art as he might have wished for. When the First World War broke out, the Vieux Colombier's experiment was dispersed by conscription after just one season. Copeau was dispatched as a cultural attaché to the United States to speak to and on the phenomenon of the Little Theatres.[26] His apostolic task was disseminate his work, and to play a part in the complex courtship by the Allies of their wealthy, well-armed cousin. Copeau propounded the Vieux Colombier's:

new spirit... I dare not say a religious spirit, yet I know it is a spirit of love. Love for beauty, for simplicity and for the modest task we wish to perform... banding together, under a leader worthy of that name, a 'brother-hood' of energetic and disinterested men, willing to work, willing to be led, willing to live and die for their art. Not a thing will be done until that new *spirit* has been infused into dramatic art. (*CTT* 79–80)

Because several of the actors who had formed the original company were at the front, the rhetoric coopts their heroism in war as a heroism in the theatrical battle, which is also characterized as a 'national inheritance' (*CTT* 80). However, the ideology of the hero is somewhat at odds with the ideology of ensemble work which Copeau espoused. Although a distinctly religious flavour was to haunt much of Copeau's rhetoric, the passage above might also usefully be set in the context of others' understanding of this of *l'esprit nouveau*. For example, Apollinaire's patriotic lecture delivered from the Vieux Colombier stage in 1917, *L'esprit nouveau et les poètes*, shared something of Copeau's moral concern for art (Shattuck 1958, 228). In contrast to the star-struck training of the major French Theatre school, the Conservatoire attached to the Comédie Française, Copeau insistently couches his aspirations for performers and performer training in the language of vocation, and resists the suggestion that it is a commercial or even a professional activity. Copeau's notebooks for the war years show his burgeoning interest in improvisation and popular theatre forms like *commedia dell'arte*. He demanded 'real actors, and, on a platform of plain rough-hewn boards, I will promise to produce real comedy', validating his 'real' work in contrast to the deceptions of naturalism (*CTT* 81). The logic of his rhetoric implies that real objects produce real performance, and yet the grand artifice of 'rough-hewn' boards is that they are cultivated to appear 'as they are', untainted by illusionism. What his essay cannot say, but becomes clear in his other work, is that more than anything the *treteau*, or 'bare boards', become the unifying factor of his Theatre and School's style (Rudlin 1986, 77). But for all his development of popular forms, inspired by Elizabethan staging, a detailed study of Molière and *commedia*, he did not have 'real' actors and he was not yet ready for a popular audience. In February 1920, with the impact of war beginning to subside, the Théâtre du Vieux Colombier could reopen, and later that year Copeau received a little government subsidy and opened the actor-training school that had been so much in his thoughts. The prospectuses for the various school seasons are ambitious, and it is hard to gauge how much of this schedule his pupils actually experienced. The financial support needed to maintain the two enterprises came partly through his lecture circuit and his dramatic readings, partly funds had to come from patrons and interested parties. The *Cahiers du Vieux Colombier* were designed as a series of pamphlets on the school and theatre's work that would appear six times a year, as 'a living bond between the artist and the public' (*CTT* 252). In the event Copeau only managed to produce two. The first *Cahier* was addressed to 'Les Amis du Vieux Colombier' and appeared in November 1920 through the *NRF*. A 'friend', it transpired, was a financial supporter. Both school and theatre operated a subscription system which Copeau characterizes here as a form of subsidy 'directly from the community and the audience, first from the élite and then one day from the general public' (*CTT* 134). There is a divergence between the actual and the aspirational. It was largely an élite that supported the enterprise. Even though Copeau characterizes the 'benevolent support' of three to five hundred subscribers as the public, he has to admit this is 'a restricted category of the public, the privileged class' (*CTT* 135). What he hopes to develop is the support of the general public, the new public, the entire public. The 'public' that Copeau is referring to here is a politicized term, almost consonant with a class, brought more strongly into focus by his celebration of the twenty franc subscribers, who 'mark the beginning of a popular membership' (*CTT* 135). This popular membership, which he envisages as 20–30 000 of the 'faithful', is not only to facilitate his 'creative independence' and his 'mission', but also to become his mission, 'they will proclaim our *raison d'être*' (*CTT* 136). This pamphlet marks the beginning of Copeau's interest in a 'popular' audience, which found rhetorical connections with other theatre movements developing in France during the twenties and thirties. Many of these movements were overtly political, sometimes founded on union membership, or who took their work to non-theatrical venues, streets and workplaces.[27] Even the 1907 plans for that most arty of art theatres, the Nouveau Théâtre d'Art, had articulated the need to 'educate the people and give it healthy fare and not intellectual hash... [and] to get in touch with the People's Universities and the Labour Exchanges and put a number of seats at their disposal, cheap' (Knowles 1967, 16). Copeau's staging had thus far centred and experimented with popular theatre styles and works, which the Art theatres certainly had not, but his interpretation of the popular audience at this stage in his writing had something of the quality of a religious revival.

A year later, the second *Cahier* argued for further government subsidy, since a theatre school should be 'a source of renewed inspiration for an entire epoch; it is up to the State, in a well-organized society, to assure its security and growth' (*CTT* 25). The result of maintaining a rotten Conservatoire connected to the Comédie Française was the deterioration of national theatre, where occasional flashes of life were the 'euphoria of the dying' (*CTT* 27). Copeau's ambitions for his school are no less than a renaissance of French theatre:

> I see no true transformation possible in the theatre except through and by a social transformation. New dramatic forms will come from new ways of living, thinking and feeling... our 'chapel', our laboratory, our School, whatever one calls it – could not honestly be described as anything but a renewal or, even better, a preparation. (*CTT* 27)

Copeau describes a circular and symbiotic relationship between the theatre and society, the theatre offers renewed inspiration to society and in the light of society's development, produces new forms which reflect its changes.

In a surprising move in 1924, Copeau closed the Vieux Colombier theatre and moved with the school to a tiny village in Burgundy. A major contribution to Copeau's decision to leave Paris was the search for a new audience. In 'Is Dramatic Renovation Possible', written after the migration to the country, he pays tribute to the work of Stanislavski, Appia and Craig (*A* 258) and finds much sympathy with Gordon Craig's rejection of all theatre life and his withdrawal to the Arena Goldoni to prepare for the overturning of the theatre. He asserts that 'in order to save the theatre we must leave it' (*CTT* 53).[28] In rejecting avant-garde and art theatre as simply tinkering with aesthetics, Copeau tackles the question of the function of theatre itself. Theatre regains its purpose when it 'ceases being an exploitation and becomes a ceremony' (*CTT* 53). The Parisian audience are identified as the reason that this ceremonial function of theatre was not achieved. He admits that his attempt to 'purify and renew the notion of dramatic art in people's minds' failed. The theatre became a commodity and their attempts at renewal were taken as a stylistic idiom, which 'speculators' wanted to 'popularize' to make money. In lectures he gave at the Laboratory Theatre in America in 1927, he addressed himself directly to the question of the new audience:

> There is a professional public (in the pejorative sense) in the same way that there are professional actors and professional authors. They have lost their sincerity. Theatre needs sincerity, authenticity on its stage. It needs it no less in the auditorium. A factitious public engenders factitious acting. We play with the public and the public plays with us ... (*CTT* 137)

The metaphor of play is extended from actor-training to the interaction between stage and audience. Copeau presents a romanticized picture of the audience member who can only afford a seat in the gallery, for whom a visit to the theatre is an occasion and requires sacrifice. He favourably compares his experience of a rural audience in Burgundy to the urban or standard theatre audience. Les Copiaus, the company formed by members of the Burgundian school, tended to perform on festival days:

> Thus our art rediscovers a little of its lost signification, it re-establishes its place in the city, its station in culture, its power and its nobility, each time it comes near to the primitive conditions which, in ancient Greece, at the time of the Great Dionysia, constituted a religious festival of theatre. (*CTT* 137)

Copeau's distinctive contribution to the renewed interest in the audience and the ordinary person as audience member is his resistance to the lure of mass spectacle which characterised much of the development of popular theatres elsewhere in France. Firmin Gémier was the arch apologist for the mass popular audience, and incidentally the first Ubu. He was instrumental in developing a series of mass spectacles and events, and in the establishment of the National Théâtre Populaire.[29] Les Copiaus work was on a smaller scale and developed from improvised comedy and scenes linked to the community who were to be its audience. Not that Copeau was completely dismissive of the power of the mass popular event. In the lecture to the American Laboratory theatre he makes a case for the quality of post-Revolutionary Russian theatre, despite its propaganda content, since:

an art which responds to the demands of millions of individuals, and art which unites all inclinations in a unanimity of need to which it responds, is a living art from which will come without doubt a great art. (*A* 137)

Copeau's theatre was never to express so coherent an ideology as this revolutionary mass spectacle, nor to involve ordinary people in the making of theatre, yet towards the end of his life Copeau's rhetoric about popular theatre takes on a more 'politicised' edge.

Le Théâtre Populaire (1941)[30] was written after Copeau had spent some years freelance directing and lecturing, and was a direct response to his sacking from the Comédie Française where, during the Occupation, he had been responsible for some distinctly anti-German plays. From the relative security of Vichy-controlled Burgundy, he delivered his riposte. The debate about popular theatre had been enlivened in France under the auspices of the briefly elected left-wing Popular Front government of 1936. Across Europe during the mid-1930s, as we have seen with Meyerhold, 'popular' came to signify a left-wing concern with mass, urban audiences. In the face of Nazi occupation the political significance of the popular took on a nationalistic tone in France. Copeau includes a sorrowful reflection on the Occupation and calls for the rebuilding of communal, national life through sincerity:

What we need is a Theatre of the Nation. It is not a class theatre, a theatre which makes claims for any particular group. It will be a theatre of reunion and regeneration. (*CTT* 190)

Here Copeau is able to side-step the party political overtones of a national theatre, and posit theatre as part of a cultural regeneration for a divided and temporarily defeated nation. This national theatre was to bear the hallmark of the popular. Copeau was not offering a new idea here. Indeed, he reflected on the difficulty exercises of this kind had run into in the past:

When you study the fortune of theatrical enterprises called 'popular' in France, one is astonished. Their intentions were lucid. Their expression eloquent. The French spirit seemed to have no trouble in conceiving of the necessity and the conditions for, as well as a vision of, a healthy theatre designed for the nation. But these projects ran aground. The idea never took root. (*A* 291)

He welcomes the decentralization of theatre that had been subsidized and encouraged by the Popular Front government, which echoed his own retreat to rural France. Interestingly, here he characterizes the dispersal of theatre as an invasion, able to 'conquer our cities and to spread out into the countryside' (*CTT* 192). There is also a reminder about how far he has come from a deification of the text, which characterized his first work at the Vieux Colombier, when he recommends to these companies the development of their own repertoire. He sees theatre now as an occasional ceremony, linked to local culture and events. He is careful to distinguish between the large-scale festival and the mass event of Hitler's National Socialists. Although much of this paper has made use of Gémier's work, he parts company from him, in the light of the new political circumstances and the new signification of 'mass', insisting that 'theatre *for* the masses is not necessarily theatre *of* the masses' (*CTT* 194). The pejorative sense of Copeau's view of the masses or popular audience is never diminished, but in his defence of local and community theatre he was opening the way for a new theatre in a changing and rapidly developing world. Undoubtedly one of Copeau's most lasting contributions to the theatre was through his training and influence on future practitioners like Jouvet, Dasté and Vilar who went on to develop the seeds of his work in France.

Primary Sources

Braun, E. (1969) *Meyerhold on Theatre* (London: Methuen).
Brecht, B. (1993) *Journals*, trans. J. Willett and R. Manheim (London: Methuen).
Cole, T. and Chinoy, H. (1970) *Actors on Acting* (New York: Crown).
—(1963) *Directors on Directing* (Indianapolis: Bobbs-Merrill).
Copeau, J. (1974) *Registres I: Appels* (Paris: Éditions Gallimard).
Gladkov, A. (1997) *Meyerhold Speaks/Meyerhold Rehearses*, trans. A. Law (Amsterdam: Harwood Academic Press).
Law, A. and Gordon, M. (1996) *Meyerhold, Eisenstein and Biomechanics: Actor Training in Revolutionary Russia* (Jefferson, N.C.: McFarland).
Rudlin, J. and Paul, N. (1990) *Copeau: Texts on Theatre* (London: Routledge).
Schmidt, P. (1980) *Meyerhold at Work* (Austin: University of Texas Press).
Senelick, L. (1981) *Russian Dramatic Theory from Pushkin to the Symbolists* (Austin: University of Texas Press).

Secondary Sources

Bakshy, A. (1916) *The Path of the Modern Russian Stage and Other Essays* (London: Cecil Palmer & Hayward).
Benedetti, J. (ed.) (1991) *The Moscow Art Theatre Letters* (London: Methuen).
Benjamin, W. (1973) *Understanding Brecht* (London: New Left Books).
Blanchart, P. (1954) *Firmin Gémier* (Paris: L'Arche) in French.
Bradby, D. and McCormick, J. (1978) *People's Theatre* (London: Croom Helm).
Braun, E. (1986) *Meyerhold: A Revolution in Theatre* (London: Methuen).
—(1982) *The Director and the Stage* (London: Methuen).
Eaton, K. (1985) *The Theater of Meyerhold and Brecht* (Westport, Conn.: Greenwood Press).
Hoover, M. (1974) *Meyerhold: The Art of Conscious Theatre* (Amherst: University of Massachusetts Press).
Kleberg, L. (1990) 'The Nature of the Soviet Audience', in Russell and Barratt, *op. cit.*, pp. 172–95.
Knowles, D. (1967) *French Theatre of the Inter-War Years* (London: Harrap).
Kolocotroni, V. and others (eds) (1998) *Modernism : An Anthology of Sources and Documents* (Edinburgh: Edinburgh University Press).
Korshunova, V. and Sitkovetskaya, M. (eds) (1976) *V.E.Meyerhold – Perepiska* (Moscow: Iskusstvo).
Kusler Leigh, B. (1979) 'Jacques Copeau's School for Actors', *Mime Journal*, 9 & 10.
Leach, R. (1989) *Vsevolod Meyerhold* (Cambridge: Cambridge University Press).
—(1994) *Revolutionary Theatre* (London: Routledge).
Meyerhold, V. (1968) *Stat'i, Rechi, Pis'ma, Besedy*, A. Fevralsky (ed.) (Moscow: Iskusstvo).

Pyman, A. (1994) *A History of Russian Symbolism* (Cambridge: Cambridge University Press).

Rudlin, J. (1986) *Jacques Copeau* (Cambridge: Cambridge University Press).

Russell, R. and Barratt, A. (eds) (1990) *Russian Theatre in the Age of Modernism* (London: Macmillan).

Senelick, L. (1990) 'Boris Geyer and Cabaretic Playwriting', in Russell and Barratt, *op. cit.*, pp.33–65.

Shattuck, R. (1958) *The Banquet Years* (London: Faber & Faber).

Willett, J. (1986) *The Theatre of Erwin Piscator* (London: Methuen).

Worrall, N. (1996) *The Moscow Art Theatre* (London: Routledge).

4

Artaud and the Manifesto

Antonin Artaud (1896–1948) is an artwork of the French theatre who has influenced other artworks. The periods concerned are, respectively, between the first and second major European wars of the twentieth century when Artaud was active, largely in Paris, and from 1960 onwards, when his influence has been active. That is perhaps the most concise description of a phenomenon. Further commentary is beset by difficulties.

Why is this? This question might apply as well to the description of the phenomenon as to the difficulties of commentary, and the answers are awkward and elusive. The best approach might be to phrase another description, and note that Artaud is a legend and an icon. The accounts of his existence are all uncertain in their bearings, but his posthumous reception has undoubtedly read him most consistently as a *mage*. So we receive his influence with something approaching awe, according his writings the respect due to revelation. In fact, the principal conclusion at the start of any review should probably be that Artaud is unique in providing the modern theatre with a sense of itself as something sacred. This conjunction of terms is interesting, because it recognizes that 'the theatre' has become something other than a place where plays are performed and actors act and money is made; it has become an entity in its own right, one whose very nature can be debated as one might debate over a soul. So that if Artaud, primarily and above all, has been used to establish this conception, it would seem to follow that the phenomenon that bears his name answers to a fear of its opposite: a producing system which does not have the dignity of being an entity, and which is secular or profane or mundane in the extreme. The construction of Artaud may be a necessity, at least for some, as much an act of continuing defiance and self-definition as a set of propositions for a particular practice.

It is conventional to call Artaud a theorist of the theatre, yet nothing less systematic than this discursive phenomenon can be imagined. For example, the connection between Artaud and Stanislavski is minimal, with the exception of a wonderfully distorted 'doubling' of the idea of 'a life in art', as fraught and tortured in Artaud's case as it was determined and productivist in the case of Stanislavski. This difference is an indicator, as much as my earlier use of the French term *mage*, of how deeply embedded Artaud is in a culture, an aspect of his phenomenon which criticism in English has curiously avoided. So, for example, in Braun's outstanding study of *The Director and the Stage* a relatively short account of Artaud's theatrical activity is separated by some chapters from the preceding account of symbolism in the theatre, which would explain or characterize many of Artaud's preconceptions (Braun 1982). This may be an accident of a design that is both European and chronological in its order, but it highlights a certain fixity in Braun's presentation: are his selected figures really most prominent as 'directors', or the most prominent directors, as his title would seem to imply? Is that why they form a canon, or were made to do so? According to his criteria Braun's inclusion of Artaud is puzzling, if not exactly paradoxical, and receives no commentary in a brief introduction. But the book is written within the legend, and Artaud is present because he is the anti-director, the double of the director for contemporary sensibility, perceived (perhaps) as the shadow for such figures as Antoine. Braun's provision of a context is evident in his spare and precise selection of detail. Yet despite the shadow of symbolism Artaud emerges as substantially self-made, although it is, perversely, the context that should be and mostly is the intricate subject of Braun's book.

This dilemma is at the heart of the legend, and it continues to have its effect on critical production. The most obvious example is Melzer's excellent study of dada and surrealism in the theatre, an enquiry which started from puzzlement over Artaud, specifically his early theatre-script *The Jet of Blood*, as Melzer states in the preface (Melzer 1980, xiii). The existence of Artaud as a contemporary icon is a precondition for the study, yet the study does not even aim to adduce the context it establishes to an interpretation of the originally fascinating figure. It is not that Melzer fails in an endeavour, or even refuses one; it is as if that endeavour is in some sense proscribed or deleted before one may think of it. To conjoin Artaud, even suggestively, with a context contravenes the prevailing ethos of critical reception, which is governed by something larger than the formidable powers, even the apparently constant rights, of academic enquiry. In a less direct manner, but no less noticeably, Deak's study of symbolism in the theatre (Deak 1993) keeps an invaluable context far from application to a figure who haunts its pages. The effect is as if Artaud may be thought in symbolism (or dada, or surrealism), but symbolism (or dada, or surrealism) must not be thought in Artaud. This is undoubtedly the immaterialism of legend or of iconic status and, for the record, it shows no sign of abating.[1]

Artaud is also distinctive because in place of a context we are offered a distraction, which is the theme of madness, most often posed as a question: was Artaud mad? The value of the question is not self-evident; after all, if there are worthwhile or sharp perceptions about the theatre, does it matter what we conclude about the mental or neural state of their inventor? It might be that the issue is an intrusion from what is strictly biographical, since Artaud was committed during his lifetime; but of what interest is biography in relation to theory?[2] Madness, unfortunately, is not just what it seems, and there are at least two aspects of its function in the overall legend. The first is one of guilt: was Artaud unjustly condemned as mad, persecuted as many have been for the disorientation or asociality of behaviour and speech? This is undoubtedly a 1960s topic for English-speaking countries, one that might be associated with the liberal questioning of psychology and its practices and assumptions carried out by R.D.Laing.[3] But its relevance to the study of theatre seems limited unless we consider what the social issue might offer the icon, which is plainly the status of a martyr. Artaud was imprisoned for his beliefs, the legend will run, condemned by society, and died in great pain professing his faith. An injustice has been done, and Artaud and his works stand in need of rehabilitation by the humanitarian and liberal conscience. Clearly if we are already inclined to believe in an entity called the theatre, and to cherish the thought that it may be sacred, then the existence of a martyr is thoroughly apposite.

The second aspect of madness is quite distinct in its function in the legend, although it is closely related in kind to the first. In this second function madness appears in an inverted form, not as the categorical and misplaced social stigma planted on an individual by society, but as the positive charge that attaches itself to the possibility of vision or revelation. As part of the cultural context for Artaud, this has at least four constituent strains. The first is Christian and biblical, one which needs no particular account except to say that it meets the renaissance humanism of letters in a scholar such as Erasmus and his *Praise of Folly*, in which 'the supreme reward for man is no other than a kind of madness' (Erasmus 1971, 206). The second strain is classical and Latinate, one that associates prophecy with poetry in the figure of the *vates*, and understands the inspiration or state of either prophecy or poetry as a kind of *furor*, in a translation of the Greek *mania*, or 'madness'. In this concept of the *vates*, the sacred and the secular are linked, producing the beliefs that 'the poet has a serious contribution to make to the progress of his society', and that 'through some form of inspiration, the poet has privileged access to eternal truths'.[4] The third strain is an inheritor of both of these in the immediacy, for Artaud and his peers, of the traditions of French poetic inspiration and quest from the mid-nineteenth century forwards. The magnitude of this context, and its intricate complexity, is not susceptible of a satisfactory summary, but its importance can be registered to some effect. The final strain composes itself in the 'alternativism' of the 1960s, in its own search through cult, mysticism, marginality and drugs for spirituality and enhanced experience, a quest or a lifestyle into which madness might well be drafted as an appropriate figure (of speech or behaviour) for that which was valid because it was not 'straight'.

Contexts

Artaud is a constituent of the French cultural tradition of *belles lettres*, and is inconceivable and incomprehensible without this culture. There is no place outside words for Artaud, nor is there any need for one in the amplitude of Parisian and French cultural discourse. From the mid-nineteenth century poetry in France had laid claim to the totality of experience, and had asserted its right and capacity to explore and extend experience. The most explicit and pertinent statement of this is the manifesto by Rimbaud, composed as a letter in 1871, in which he claims that the 'I' of the poet must be a 'visionary', a 'seer', a *voyant*: 'I say one must be a visionary, make oneself a visionary'.[5] To do so, Rimbaud insists, the poet must practise 'a long, gigantic and rational *derangement* of *all the senses*. All forms of love, of suffering, of madness'; this is the third strain of 'madness' mentioned above, and its relevance to Artaud is crucial. Rimbaud continues:

> he searches himself, he exhausts in himself all the poisons, to keep only the quintessences. Unspeakable torture in which he needs all his faith, all his superhuman strength, in which he becomes the great invalid among men, the great criminal, the great accursed – and the supreme man of learning! – Because he reaches the *unknown!* ... and when, maddened, he finishes by losing the understanding of his visions, he has seen them! Let him die bounding through things that are unheard of and unnameable: other horrible labourers will come; they will begin from the horizons where the other has fallen.[6]

The ambition, the endurance and the promise of status are all vast, and the end is death after exhilarating and poisonous madness. As Rimbaud remarks at the beginning of his letter, this is prose about poetry, and the prose poetry of *A Season in Hell* and *The Illuminations* was to follow. Rimbaud is a precursor of Artaud, in the assertions and aspirations which become part of the numerous topics of this cultured discourse. Here is one from *Night in Hell*, part of *A Season in Hell*:

> I am going to unveil all mysteries: religious or natural mysteries, death, birth, future, past, cosmogony, emptiness. I am a master of fantasmagorias.[7]

In his manifesto Rimbaud anticipates a universal language, one that will be 'of the soul for the soul, taking up everything, scents, sounds, colours, of thought taking hold of thought and pulling'.[8] So, in *Alchemy of the Word* from *A Season in Hell*, he refers to how he flattered himself 'on inventing a poetic language accessible, one day or another, to the senses', and finished by 'regarding the disorder of my mind as sacred'.[9]

There can be no doubt that Artaud was part of a cultural continuity of immense intricacy, but the most important quality of the vocation that French *poésie* became in the nineteenth century was that it was a pure and not an applied science. The role was lived, and the personality fused with the role. In theatrical history, this characteristic may seem to be most associated with Jarry, who became Ubu, and rolled through Paris in that form. But that is theatricality, and the role of poet was no impersonation. For the purposes here, it may be enough to mention the presence of mental instability and what might be termed breakdown, if not insanity; but in addition drugs, alcohol, hallucination, pain (neurological or otherwise) and the intoxications of sexuality were standard topics as well as constituents of a formidably intellectual experience. The aesthetic inheritance is also a vast accumulation of related, inverted, contrary positions and perceptions which fuse a sense of craft with a sense of being. Two examples may suffice as indications. Gérard de Nerval combines mental instability with the topics of alchemy, pagan mythology and metaphysics, the symbolism of the Tarot pack, and a fascination with the mystic potential of dream in his prose and poetry. For Stéphane Mallarmé poetry must participate in mystery as an act and expression of mind, a form of the sacred achieved with immense difficulty, disjunct from the mundane. Both are distinct and distinctive contributors to a continuity that embraces, incidentally, Eliot as well as Artaud, symbolism and the even more curious phenomenon of surrealism, giving rise to the belletrist prose born of the prose poem in which Artaud so often writes.

This is, if you like, the profound context for Artaud, without which he is, for all intents and purposes, unreadable as a writer. The more immediate context occurs in accessible documentation, and is in general theatrical. For Shattuck, in his study of the avant-garde in the *belle époque* from 1885 to the First World War, theatricality, performance and demonstration are cultural qualities of the era (Shattuck 1968, 3–28). To these he adds four characteristic 'traits': the cult of childhood, humour (modulating into the absurd), the eruption of the dream into waking consciousness, and ambiguity or equivocal interpretation applied to the artwork (Shattuck 1968, 29–42). All four traits are, according to Shattuck, subsumed in a fascination with the subconscious and the artistic logic required for its expression, which will combat 'traditional discourse' and the need for 'a single, explicit, discursive meaning' (Shattuck 1968, 37). His survey discusses the painter Rousseau, the composer Satie, the playwright Jarry, and Apollinaire, whom he titles 'the impresario of the avant-garde', a title which embraces criticism, poetry, the editing of pornographic texts, interventions and manifestos. His accounts of three major productions – Jarry's *Ubu Roi*, the Satie/

Cocteau/Picasso *Parade*, and Apollinaire's *The Breasts of Tiresias* – can all be supplemented by further documentation in English.[10] Braun concisely, and Deak and Melzer in considerable detail, provide a sophisticated and detailed impression of a theatrical background.

The significance certainly lies in the detail, which introduces what should be another component of our understanding of Artaud, that his sense of theatre and theatrical practice was unexceptional, and continued to be so. *The Cenci*, for example, effectively the last of Artaud's theatrical enterprises in 1935, had been produced by Paul Fort and the Théâtre d'Art in Paris in 1891, following a first production for Shelley's literary drama in London in 1886.[11] This apparently minor fact can clearly be linked to the choice of name for Artaud and Vitrac's Alfred Jarry Theatre, in an obvious preoccupation with the work of the small art theatres in the 1890s.[12] But Artaud is also holding to the homage set in place by the first Paris Dada demonstration, which was held in 1920 on the twenty-fifth anniversary of *Ubu Roi*, at the site of the play's first performance, the Théâtre de l'Oeuvre, as well as to the acknowledgement of Jarry's importance to them by the surrealists.[13] The first script, *The Jet of Blood*, is plainly indebted to symbolism, affected almost as one might expect by *coups de théâtre*: as Melzer comments almost in passing, 'the nurse with the big breasts which disappear echoed Apollinaire's Tiresias' (Melzer 1980, 197). A defining characteristic of Artaud's explosive sense of theatre might be assumed to be his advocacy and use of sound and noise; but as Melzer observes, noise had already been heavily and theoretically advanced by both futurists and dada, and so was hardly radical (Melzer 1980, 47). Artaud's theoretical obsession with the Balinese theatre is famous, and commentary tends to linger on his misinterpretation of it. But of greater interest, in terms of cultural continuity, is the information incidentally provided by Shattuck about the International Exposition of 1889, one of a series: 'The Javanese dancers became the rage of Paris, influenced music-hall routines for twenty years, and confirmed Debussy in his tendency towards Oriental harmonies' (Shattuck 1968, 17). There is, surely, nothing new in orientalism in the arts and intellectual life in France by 1930, and nothing new in the aspirational or metaphysical misinterpretation of the signs of the orient.[14] What is striking is that Artaud's theatricality is, if anything, conservative. His insistence on the theatre as a radical cultural force is nostalgic in the immediate postwar years, when performance was instrument of a larger disillusionment. Ironically, it has been this conservatism and nostalgia which have, to a great degree, ensured his later influence.

Artaud was, in theatrical terms, an actor of some ability and a director of some sensitivity and perception, as far as the evidence permits us to judge. He was also a surrealist, in so far as any person may ascribe to and be part of an artistic movement and then be rejected from it. So, indeed, was Roger Vitrac, his collaborator in the Alfred Jarry Theatre, who experienced a similar history with the group.[15] Artaud's surrealism is manifest and relatively ordinary, but it is decisive in our appreciation of his formation as an 'artwork' in two respects. The first is the fact of his quarrel with the surrealists, which participates in a long tradition of demonstration around performance. Controversy or *débat* is part of the essence of French dramaturgy and theatrical practice, associated historically with Corneille's *Le Cid* and Molière's *Le Tartuffe*; but the model for a disturbance at the first production of a play was, for the nineteenth century, Hugo's *Hernani* of 1830. It was to Jarry's enduring credit that he had prompted extravagant reactions with *Ubu Roi* in 1896, and the art of dada and surrealism was that of provocation and schism. The split between dada and the nascent surrealist group under Breton was enacted at performances, and surrealism gradually, under Breton's influence, turned more and more defiantly against the theatre (Melzer 1980, 153–60). Surrealism finally rejected theatre and theatrical aspirations as too contaminated by contact with a producing apparatus, and directly, in the case of Artaud's production of Strindberg's *A Dream Play* in 1928, with Swedish finance (Braun 1982, 182–3). What is significant here, apart from the fact of failure and our amusement at the details of the antics on the occasion, is Artaud's refusal to adjust or to 'leave' the theatre as a site of radical engagement. Artaud's programme of theatrical realization and provocation effectively looked back to the era before the First World War, one that had gradually disintegrated in the early 1920s, and with the desertion of the surrealists it was forced into the ideal state of theoretical existence.

But the fact of the schism with the surrealists also contains the fact of Artaud's refusal of the allegiance to Marxism expressed by Breton and the group under his influence. What is significant here is the lucidity of Artaud's objections to the surrealist stance, a lucidity which characterizes his later lectures in Mexico in 1936 quite as much as his reactions at the time.[16] In his response to the surrealist rejection in 1927, Artaud dismissed the supposed adherence of the surrealists to the revolution of Marxism as a form of 'fundamental bad faith', and insisted that 'all the exacerbation of our quarrel revolves around the word "Revolution"' (*Collected Works*, Vol. 1 = *CW* 1, 192; also in *Selected Works* = *SW* 139–45). Appropriately enough, Artaud's response was printed privately in a limited edition of 500 copies, and the closed circle of the controversy encourages a remarkably clear statement of Artaud's position, for which the justification is pain:

> For what does the entire world revolution mean to me when I know I am to remain in endless pain... No man should ever want to consider anything beyond his own deep sensitivity, his inmost ego. This is a completely Revolutionary standpoint to me. The only revolution that is any good is one I benefit from. Me and people like me. (*CW* 1, 193; cf. *SW* 140)

Artaud's allegiance is to 'a metamorphosis of inner states of the soul', and so any 'external metamorphosis... can only be something supplementary', since the 'social level, the materialistic level... is to me only a useless, implied show' (*CW* 1, 192 and 197, respectively; cf. *SW* 139 and 144). His position is absolute – 'I place the logical requirements of my own reality above all real needs. This seems the only valid logic to me...' (*CW* 1, 196; cf. *SW* 144) – and presents a total theoretical contradiction to the claims of materialism:

> as if, from the viewpoint of the absolute there could be the slightest interest in seeing the social armature change or in seeing power pass from the hands of the bourgeoisie into those of the proletariat. (*SW* 140; cf. *CW* 1, 193)

The intellectual controversy, for all its futility, carries serious implications for its participants, even if these are ultimately revealed as either bathos or pathos. Theory in conflict permits no compromise. At this juncture it is not simply a question of Artaud's right, for example, to continue a particular (theatrical) enterprise or activity. Artaud's practice is at the point of becoming 'absolutely' subordinated to the theoretical vision that emerges in the collection of his writings that he entitled *The Theatre and Its Double*. The controversy takes its significant place in the evolution of his position from the eclectic and subversive initiatives of the Theatre of Alfred

Jarry through to the hieratic imperatives of that collection. It by no means a case of an abrupt transfer from the empirical to the theoretical; but it is a case where a particular and partly theorized practice becomes envisaged as a theoretical model for the theatre, and not just for a theatre. This is fundamentally the difference between the Theatre of Cruelty and the Théâtre de l'Oeuvre or the Théâtre d'Art, between Jarry as a playwright and *persona* and Artaud as a practitioner and visionary. The conflict between the two versions/visions of revolution is not one between ideology and libertarianism, but between two theoretical positions which are absolute and total. With the controversy, Artaud splits from the dominant discursive community in which his own position had been conceived and fostered. The effect is that the surrealists are left with a supposedly collaborative enterprise, discursively and in practice, while Artaud is left with the paradox of discursive solitude. Ultimately and pragmatically, they are left with the concentration camp, the resistance or flight to the USA, while he is left with confinement to the asylum. It is, as so often, the schism itself which makes the 'madness', and the absolutism of theory that precludes the therapy of humane activity.[17]

Writing and the Manifesto

For us, Antonin Artaud exists primarily in writing, and this fact of reception is no accident. Artaud wrote constantly, and published widely and repeatedly, with considerable intent and purpose. The forms of his writing are diverse: poems, essays, lectures, manifestos, reviews, articles, prefaces, programme notes, open letters, professional letters, scenarios, production plans. The Anglo-Saxon tendency is to see writing as a form of expression, and to distinguish sharply between public and private, but for Artaud writing was an essential form of involvement in and engagement with a culture of letters. One direct consequence of this is that what is written can be both written and denied at the same time, can be registered as an essential involvement but denied as an effective expression. This is most readily apparent in the early correspondence with Jacques Rivière over Artaud's poems, which sets up a discursive model for much of Artaud's output. Artaud can, at one and the same time, press for the publication of his poems and deny their value, insist on the worthlessness of the form of expression achieved but on the value of the nervous experience and mental state that had to write them. In the letter of 5 June 1923, Artaud claims that the 'poorly written phrases' with which Rivière had reproached him are the result of 'the deep insecurity of my thoughts', yet they are at the same time 'manifestations of *mental* existence' (CW 1, 28; cf. SW 31–2). So what appear as stylistic infelicities are actually 'impurities' occasioned by 'a fearful mental disease', which is described bluntly by Artaud: 'My thought abandons me at every stage' (CW 1, 28 and 27 respectively; cf. SW 32 and 31). Writing cannot or does not express, but the record of that impossibility or failure can be read, as a record. The solution, eventually, is to publish the correspondence itself, by which the desired cultural involvement is guaranteed with one form of writing substituting for another.

Failure is obviously a major characteristic of the artwork that is Artaud, and in the legend it clearly has its appeal to our sense of the pathos of creative endeavour. But failure for Artaud has an important function in the complex dynamic that results in theory. The pattern is established, here in relation to poetry, of an actuality of words and expression which fails to represent a reality of mind, thought and anguish: 'I only want to feel my mind' (CW 1, 42; cf. SW 46). We might easily be tempted to call this duality 'poetry and its double'. It is also apparent, as Artaud acknowledges, that even the purer side of this double, the mind or soul, is impaired or disabled in its operations in some manner, that it too fails. The experience is of some kind of obstruction or weakness, what Artaud describes as a 'collapse of my soul' or a 'fugitive erosion in thought' (CW 1, 32; cf. SW 34–5). The consequence is that this duality of insufficiency must be expressed in another discursive form, in this case as the correspondence; it will finally, and most satisfactorily, appear as the theory of itself.

The discursive community sustains the artwork, even if the artwork can only exist as theory. The bulk of Artaud's writing is an engagement with that community, and the incentive is the right of a mind to a place in a culture. Even the activities exist as much in writing as they do in realization. This is manifest with the Alfred Jarry Theatre, but is plain in another way in the campaign Artaud waged by letter to found a theatre with the *Nouvelle Revue Française*, the journal of which Rivière and Paulhan were successive editors. This theatre fundamentally exists only as a space, not just a plan, but a discursive space in a literary journal which lies at the centre of that community:

I have a theatre project which I'm hoping to realize with the support of the NRF. They are giving me space to allow me to define the direction of this theatre objectively and from an ideological point of view. (*Artaud on Theatre = AT* 64)

The edited documentation gathered under this heading by Schumacher in his collection of translations is fascinating, precisely because it demonstrates the distinction between this kind of proposal or initiative and the formation of an absolute theory. As Schumacher notes, the theatre of cruelty came into being first in the matrix of this 'space', but its suggestion failed to gain the collective support that would have constituted a practical project. So the stage is gradually reached here where the notion of a specific initiative in theatre, and the writing that accompanies it, are functional only in relation to the conception of an absolute theatre that emerges from them. It is as if the manifesto is finally becoming self-sufficient, not as the demonstrative non-entity it was for dada, but as the only true form of the theatre that cannot otherwise exist.

The documents that were compiled into the publication *The Theatre and Its Double* consisted of essays, lectures, manifestos, letters and a preface. The significantly modern form amongst these is the manifesto. Manifestos are very often complex documents that make use of a bewildering variety of modes of address to the reader or listener, and they were deployed with great frequency by the futurists, dada, and the surrealists as well as (and largely in advance of) Artaud.[18] These modes of address would reward a fuller study, but in this context two may be of particular relevance. The first of them is immediately recognizable, and is the general mode of negation by which the speaker, writer or movement aims to define itself 'against' something else which is extremely familiar to the listener or reader. So we have 'X is against...', or 'X is for the abolition of...'. The most absolute version of this mode finds expression in 'No more...', and this version is instructive. In the catchphrase 'No more literature', for example, a wide range of linguistic possibilities, or indeed connotations, is included. The phrase may purport to be an announcement of fact (that is, there is no more literature any more, and that is a fact); it may be a prophecy (that there will be no more literature, whatever anyone may want); it may be a statement of intent or purpose by the speaker/writer (this writer will not engage in the production of literature); it may be an order (do not produce literature). This mode of address will occur or be most effective in situations where or when many of these possibilities may apply at the same time, in the judgement or apprehension of the reader/listener, and that would be in a situation of crisis or change or confusion, notably of extreme cultural uncertainty. Apart from denial, rejection and opposition, the mode of negation also includes contradiction, self-contradiction, arbitrariness and self-negation, as in a phrase such as 'anything that claims to be dada is not dada'.[19] Arbitrariness is the most deceptive of all, because it pertains only to the authorized speaker/writer, and its validation or verification is retained exclusively within her or his competence. So, for example, it is only Tristan Tzara who can declare:

> I write a manifesto...and in principle I am against manifestoes, as I am also against principles...I am against action; for continuous contradiction, for affirmation too, I am neither for nor against and I do not explain because I hate common sense.[20]

Arbitrariness combined with other aspects of negation in this mode is, of course, an elaborate cultural conceit: the published manifesto is nothing if not an assertion of status.

The negative mode is the most striking and memorable because the negative in the field of art or of intellectual activity is inherently alarming, and for that reason either shocking or exciting. But the promissory mode is no less common, and is a regular companion. So the manifesto may well promise more than it will or can perform, as in the formula 'the X theatre will release/ contain all the possibilities of...', where what is missing may be an artform, a (new) technology, the senses, or the mind. The restraints of contingency are not a problem for the manifesto in this expansive mode, and Futurist manifestos especially were inclined towards it. Futurism plainly combines a sense of political and social uncertainty, of flux and uncertainty, with the 'promise' implied in technological possibility. So futurism, in common with most of the movements in this era that deploy the manifesto, makes repeated use of the future-present, which is the logically incontrovertible ground or space of uncertainty. Both these modes, negation and the promissory, operate well in this field, and may well operate most successfully together. So, for example, 'The Futurist Synthetic Theatre' manifesto of 1915 declares that

IT IS STUPID TO RENOUNCE THE DYNAMIC LEAP IN THE
VOID OF TOTAL CREATION, BEYOND THE RANGE OF TER-
RITORY PREVIOUSLY EXPLORED[21]

This relatively typical assertion combines the negative ('no renunciation of total creation') with the promissory ('the futurist synthetic
theatre will leap dynamically into . . . '). With the prevalence of these
modes of address to the reader/listener, and its delight in an insistent disturbance occasioned by them, the manifesto rarely pauses to
be analytic or systematic. It is also questionable whether the manifesto is theoretical, or capable of supporting or sustaining theory.
This is a factor that affects Artaud's compilation, which combines
versions of the manifesto, and related writings, with other discursive forms arising from the lecture and the essay which advance,
more or less consistently, a theory of analogy.[22]

Artaud hesitated over the title of the compilation or collection for
a period of years, between the title of his major lecture 'Theatre and
the Plague' favoured early on in the conception in 1934, and the
final title of January 1936 (*AT* 87). The publication was dependent
on the contacts Artaud had established over a long period with the
editors of the influential journal, *Nouvelle Revue Française*, and in a
letter to Jean Paulhan, its editor, Artaud explained his choice. There
are at least several doubles of the theatre, which Artaud summarizes in the terms metaphysics, plague and cruelty. The theatre
is a 'figuration' which may become a 'transfiguration', and 'if the
theatre doubles life, life doubles the true theatre'.[23] Not much is
immediately clear from this, but it seems that two incarnations of
life and reality are to be understood, one everyday and manifest
and the other hidden: 'the Double of the Theatre is the reality
unutilized by human beings today'. Both myths and magic are constituents of this life and reality which is 'true theatre'.

The preface that Artaud wrote for the collection presents the idea
that culture does not match life but dictates to it, and the shadowy
something that might be 'life' finds expression as 'the mysterious
recesses of the self', while life as it is lacks 'fire and fervour, that is to
say continual magic', for which we cry out (*CW* 4, 1–3).[24] These
thoughts are a prelude to the introduction to the reader of the
'double': 'All true effigies have a double, a shadowed self' (*CW* 4,
5), a statement that may well connect with the earlier 'mysterious
recesses of the self'. Artaud continues: 'Like all magic cultures
displayed in appropriate hieroglyphics, true theatre has its own

shadows.' The theatre's shadows are stronger than those of 'all languages and all arts', because they have 'shattered their limitations'. The 'true theatre' stirs up shadows, and theatre 'is to be found precisely at the point where the mind needs a language to bring about its manifestations'. This formulation is plainly a kind of symbolist theory, but its configuration remains obscure. The problem is that there are clearly two types of theatre, 'our fossilised idea of theatre' which is 'shadowless' and true theatre, which is or has dominant shadows; but whether this 'true theatre' may manifest itself as actual theatre (practice) is uncertain. The Preface hesitates between presenting a theoretical entity or functioning as a manifesto, but the latter is Artaud's chosen conclusion, in a combination of the negative and promissory modes:

> To shatter language in order to contact life means creating or recreating theatre... This leads us to reject man's usual limitations and powers and infinitely extends the frontiers of what we call reality. (CW 4, 6)

The Theatre and Its Double, as a compilation, combines the character of the manifesto with components, cast in the discursive form of essays and lectures, which offer an extended theory of analogy to our understanding of 'the theatre'. The theory of analogy is, substantially, the theory of 'the theatre and its double', and the plague, metaphysics, alchemy, and 'the Oriental' all function in the first part of the collection as analogies, and in similar ways. This presentation leaves 'cruelty', as the last and possibly the crudest of the analogies, to the professed manifestos and their accompanying commentaries, which form the second part of the collection.[25] In the discussion that follows here I shall consider Artaud's theory of analogy as it is presented in the first part of the collection, and then refer some of the topics of Artaud's work to the context of related themes and topics in the manifestos of the futurists, dada, and the surrealists.

In a letter to Jean Paulhan Artaud suggested that the lecture on 'Theatre and the Plague' in its revised form as the essay should be understood as presenting a kind of 'Superior analogy'.[26] Schumacher's note on the lecture itself is also helpful, because it reveals in the account of Anais Nin who was in the audience the kind of performative lecture involved, intended to be a species of effective magic rather than a provocative demonstration. The lecture of 1933 seems to have been a failure, but Artaud wanted, according to Nin, to give the audience 'the experience itself' rather than talk about a subject.[27] The lecture/essay is lurid in its details and imaginings, and Artaud builds his argument from an incident of medical history into the strength of analogy he desires. A crucial contention is that the plague is a psychic entity, possibly 'the materialisation of a thinking power' (CW 4, 9), and he claims that this is apparent in the organs affected, notably the brain and lungs, which are understood to be dependent on the will (CW 4, 12). His intermediate conclusion is that the plague evolves out of a 'mental freedom', and is not resultant solely on a bacillus, which is 'a much smaller, infinitely smaller material factor' (CW 4, 12 and 13). The analogy begins to function once the plague is described as a 'spectacle', and 'theatre establishes itself' in those reacting to the presence of the plague:

> Theatre, that is to say, the sense of gratuitous urgency with which they are driven to perform useless acts of no present advantage. (CW 4, 14)

The analogy between plague and theatre is pursued by questioning 'the value of this pointlessness in relation to our whole personality' (ibid.), and it leads directly to a subordinate comparison of the actor with the plague victim. The actor is 'totally penetrated by feelings without any benefit or relation to reality' (CW 4, 15), and the uncontrollable qualities of performance and the inventive qualities of dramaturgy make theatre like an epidemic.

The purpose of the analogy becomes a great deal clearer only when the analogy begins to mutate into magic. Artaud first contends that the 'disturbed fluids' of the plague victim are an aspect of 'a disorder...equivalent to the clashes, struggles, disaster and devastation brought about by events', a theoretical contention that makes the plague itself an analogy of either cosmic chaos or human socio-political disorder (ibid.). This contention almost certainly relies on the earlier identification of the plague with 'mental freedom' and the will, rather than with the influence of a bacillus, and it prepares for a related but divergent contention about the theatre. This is that 'natural disasters' and political or military chaos,

> when they occur on a theatre level, are released into the audience's sensitivity with the strength of an epidemic.

The analogy is the argument, and theory is the process. There is no questioning of the problems of 'figuration' or what might be termed representation here, but the suggestion, by way of the analogy, of a total absence of obstructive mediation. The argument is not helped by a flawed reading of St Augustine's comparison of the plague and theatre, who is concerned with a contrast between physical and moral pestilence (*CW* 4, 16). If the onset of the plague results in an 'infectious madness', then 'we must agree stage acting is a delirium like the plague' and 'theatre is like the plague', with both the plague and theatre containing 'something victorious and vengeful' (*CW* 4, 16–17). The final proposition is, accordingly, that theatre is a kind of 'revelation':

> the exteriorisation of a latent undercurrent of cruelty through which all the perversity of which the mind is capable, whether in a person or a nation, becomes localised. (*CW* 4, 19)

The freedom of the theatre is like that of the plague: it is dark, like that of the 'great Myths', and tells of 'the original division of the sexes and the slaughter of essences that came with creation' (*CW* 4, 20). Life is to blame here, offering as it does 'a colossal abscess, ethical as much as social'; and, like the plague, the theatre is 'made to drain abscesses'.

'Production and Metaphysics' offers a second version or vision of theatre by way of an inventive discussion of a painting by Lucas van Leyden, and is based on a lecture.[28] The choice of painting rather than the plague makes the lecture more conventional, and the language is correspondingly more restrained, but the structure of the resultant essay is similar, with description in chosen terms followed by theoretical propositions. In 'Theatre and the Plague' Artaud contends that theatre depends on poetry creating 'symbols of full-blown powers held in bondage until that moment... exploding in the guise of incredible images' (*CW* 4, 17). In 'Production and Metaphysics' his advocacy for the theatre of languages other than dialogue insists on the primacy of the language of symbols and mimicry, 'which conjures up images of natural or mental poetry in the mind' (*CW* 4, 27). This is little more than a restatement of the tenets of symbolism in relation to the theatre, and it is linked to the uncontroversial claim that 'the present state of society is iniquitous' (*CW* 4, 29). To assert that music, dance, plastic art, mimicry, mime, gesture, voice inflection, architecture, lighting and decor are essential to the theatre is admirable but hardly revolutionary, and Artaud is less forthcoming about how the material becomes the immaterial, the physical metaphysical. The assertion is that the metaphysical must or will result, but that the creation of the appropriate images or symbols 'depends on production and can only be determined on stage' (CW 4, 32); objective examples cannot be given. Once again 'true theatre' is equated with the rediscovery of 'a religious, mystical meaning our theatre has forgotten' (CW 4, 33).[29]

If 'metaphysics' is a double which does not really manage to escape from the formulas of symbolism, then alchemy provides Artaud with a further analogy for his theatre, in the contention in 'Alchemist Theatre' that both alchemy and theatre are 'virtual arts' (CW 4, 34). In this doubling, the symbols of alchemy are understood to be 'chimeras just as theatre is a chimera', and alchemy 'is the mental Double of an act effective on the level of real matter alone'. The analogy is of two forms of 'virtual reality', of work done in 'the imaginary, mental field'. The 'theatre' is here quite theoretical, and Artaud confirms its profile by writing of a 'primal, archetypal theatre', which is connected to Artaud's sense of the 'metaphysical'. His description of this originative theatre combines the concepts of origin, foundation, base and principles with that of metaphysics in an extravaganza (CW 4, 35–6) of theoretical need: 'We feel this basic drama exists...', 'We must be led to think this fundamental drama...' (CW 4, 36). The concluding vision is of the Eleusinian Mysteries of ancient Greece, which theoretically 'must have' resolved 'the antagonism between mind and matter, ideas and forms, abstract and concrete...in one single expression that must have resembled distilled gold' (CW 4, 37).

The last of Artaud's major analogies for his theatre is composed of an intense reaction to a performance of Balinese theatre and more general speculations about a concept of 'Oriental theatre'. The Balinese theatre in his theoretical vision stands for a 'pure' theatre, 'whose products are hallucination and terror', which communicates 'the idea of a metaphysics', and is theoretically opposed to western 'entertainment' or 'an evening's amusement' (CW 4, 38 and 43–4). The 'pure theatre' offers 'something of the state of mind of a magic act', but has been regarded in the West 'as merely theoretical' (CW 4, 44); so, for Artaud, the Balinese theatre that he construes is purportedly the material evidence of a possibility. In this theatre, the actors are hieroglyphs, signs or symbols not dependent on words, and so may be understood as metaphysical, while the producer becomes 'an organizer of magic, a master of holy ceremonies' (*CW* 4, 43). The Balinese theatre is inscribed with all the positive terms of Artaud's theoretical discourse, and the Balinese 'have a far more inborn sense than us of nature's total, occult symbolism' and express a 'mental alchemy' (*CW* 4, 45 and 49). Through Artaud's intense experience of Balinese theatre a theoretical possibility passes briefly through materialization into a greater theoretical certainty, which is that of 'Oriental Theatre'. In the essay 'Oriental and Western Theatre' Artaud claims finally that Oriental theatre 'shares in the intense poetry of nature and preserves its magical relationship with all the objective stages of universal mesmerism' (*CW* 4, 55), which is to offer 'it' the greatest accolade. If the theatre is to be returned to 'its original purpose', which is 'a religious, metaphysical position' (*CW* 4, 52), the psychological drama of the west must acknowledge, by means of an acceptance of the powers of analogy, the resonant qualities of a virtual theatre.

The genre of the manifesto has recurrent topics, which undergo adaptation in a cultural continuity of radical change, and that of madness, which confronts us more prominently in the Artaud legend than in his writings themselves, is advanced by Futurism. It is, in this instance, a semi-allegorical figure which sweeps Marinetti, the founder of the movement, and his friends forwards in their motor car:

> The raging broom of madness swept us out of ourselves and drove us through streets as rough and deep as the beds of torrents. Here and there, sick lamplight through window glass taught us to distrust the deceitful mathematics of our perishing eyes. (Apollonio *Futurist Manifestos* = *FM* 20)

In later manifestos, madness is a 'smear' placed on 'innovators' by their detractors, which 'futurist' painters (Boccioni, Carrà, Severini, and others) in 1910 will 'bear bravely and proudly', and in the 'Technical Manifesto' of 'Futurist Painting' of the same year it is 'a title of honour' (*FM* 26 and 30). But the prelude to the 'Manifesto of Futurism' and the 'Manifesto' itself, published in *Le Figaro* in Paris in 1909, contain topics which are reworked and repeated by successive avant-garde movements and by Artaud himself, in his theatrical writings and elsewhere. 'No work without an aggressive character can be a masterpiece' is an prescription from the 'Manifesto', which is consonant with the more ambitious assertion that

'Art, in fact, can be nothing but violence, cruelty, and injustice' (*FM* 21 and 23). The 'futurists' are 'gay incendiaries', who will 'destroy the museums, libraries, academies of every kind' and will fight 'utilitarian cowardice', as they give themselves 'utterly to the Unknown' (*FM* 20–22). Technically, 'futurism' entails the creation of new musical instruments and the '*substitution of noises for sounds*', which is analogous to the 'destruction' of syntax and the self-expression of the 'gifted lyrical narrator' by means of 'essential *free* words', or 'words-in-freedom': 'Fistfuls of essential words in no conventional order' (*FM* 86–7 and 98–9). In exercising an 'imagination without strings', the 'gifted lyrical narrator' or 'futurist' will also develop an 'absolute freedom of images or analogies', reaching 'deeper and more solid affinities' than those apparent in conventional comparison or metaphor. As so often, the promissory mode of the manifesto is relatively weak on examples; supposedly inspiring offerings here are comparisons of a 'trembling fox terrier to a little Morse Code machine' or, with less obvious radicalism, to 'gurgling water' (*ibid.*).

The futurists were 'disgusted' with 'the contemporary theatre', preferring 'incessantly to invent new elements of astonishment', and their chosen model was that of 'The Variety Theatre', on which Marinetti wrote in 1913.[30] The emphasis on the theatrical resource of 'astonishment' or amazement is an interesting anticipation of the importance Brecht attached to that concept, and Marinetti was equally attracted by the fact that the 'Variety Theatre uses the smoke of cigars and cigarettes to join the atmosphere of the theatre to that of the stage' (*FM* 126–7). In a sequence of justifications for the choice of the 'Variety Theatre' as his model, Marinetti referred to 'the Futurist destruction of immortal masterworks', and to the opposition by the 'Variety Theatre' of 'body-madness' to the 'psychology' of the 'conventional theatre', which tediously

> exalts the inner life, professorial meditation, libraries, museums, monotonous crises of conscience, stupid analyses of feelings, in other words (dirty thing and dirty word), *psychology* ... (*FM* 129)

In a further manifesto on 'The Futurist Synthetic Theatre' of 1915 the theatre was identified as the most effective instrument in a summons to war: 'THE ONLY WAY TO INSPIRE ITALY WITH THE WAR-LIKE SPIRIT TODAY IS THROUGH THE THEATRE' (*FM* 183). (The manifesto is also translated in Kirby (1971, 196–202).) The manifesto also included an assertion of the 'autonomy' of the 'Futurist theatrical synthesis' and of a 'very modern cerebral definition of art', which recalled a previous tract on 'Weights, Measures, and Prices of Artistic Genius'. In that document, 'art' was 'a cerebral secretion', and the activity of intellect was that of 'smearing' and 'sticking':

THE WORK OF ART IS NOTHING BUT AN ACCUMULATOR OF CEREBRAL ENERGY; CREATING A SYMPHONY OR POEM MEANS TAKING A CERTAIN NUMBER OF SOUNDS OR WORDS, SMEARING THEM WITH INTELLECT AND STICKING THEM TOGETHER. (*FM* 149)

The conclusions to the manifesto on 'The Futurist Synthetic Theatre' juxtaposed this emphasis to a number of others:

THE DISCOVERIES THAT OUR TALENT IS DISCOVERING IN THE SUBCONSCIOUS, IN ILL-DEFINED FORCES, IN PURE ABSTRACTION, IN THE PURELY CEREBRAL, THE PURELY FANTASTIC, IN RECORD-SETTING AND BODY-MADNESS. (*FM* 196)

What was required was that 'DYNAMIC LEAP IN THE VOID OF TOTAL CREATION', and a further manifesto by Prampolini later in the same year, 'The Futurist Stage', called for the replacement of 'realism' by 'equivalents which interpret these realities, that is to say *abstractions*' (*FM* 194 and 201). (Prampolini's manifesto is also translated, with the title 'Futurist Scenography', in Kirby 1971, 203–6)

The 'much prayed-for great war' of 1914–18 proved terminal for the largest energies of 'futurism', as it did for many of its more bellicose advocates. But the genre of the manifesto flourished in dada and surrealism, most expansively in Breton's 'Manifesto of Surrealism' of 1924. Breton had a greater inclination to discursive argument than the 'futurists', and he was writing after the experience of mechanized war, rather than before it. But the opposition in the 'Manifesto of Surrealism' to 'an arbitrary utility' which regulated the 'imagination', and to 'the realistic attitude' which Breton found in the novel was consistent, while the 'imagination' itself was appreciated for its 'unsparing quality' (Breton *Manifestoes of Surrealism* = *MS* 4, 6).[31] In particular, madness attained an elevated status as the only obvious alternative to an uninhibited exercise of the 'imagination which knows no bounds': the mad were, accordingly, 'honest to a fault' and 'to some degree, victims of their imagination' (*MS* 5). For its part, 'surrealism' aimed to draw on upon the resource of dreams in a compromise with 'reality', to achieve 'the future resolution of these two states, dream and reality...into a kind of absolute reality, a *surreality*' (*MS* 14). The surrealists were to be 'the masters of ourselves, the masters of women, and of love too', and what for the 'futurists' had been 'the cerebral secretion' of 'art' became for surrealism 'spoken thought' and 'pure expression', notably that of 'automatic writing':

> one proposes to express – verbally, by means of the written word, or in any other manner – the actual functioning of thought. (*MS* 17, 23–4, and 26)

In particular, imagery in surrealist work was to be the juxtaposition of 'two realities', more valuable for 'the beauty of the spark obtained' than for any subordinating discursive function (*MS* 37). So 'the Surrealist atmosphere created by automatic writing...is especially conducive to the production of the most beautiful images', and imagery becomes a 'vehicle' for the 'rapture' and progress of the mind:

> By slow degrees the mind becomes convinced of the supreme reality of these images...It goes forward, borne by these images which enrapture it, which scarcely leave it any time to blow upon the fire in its fingers. (*MS* 37–8)

Violence and aggression were also features of surrealism, figuratively and in manifestation, and after the rupture between Artaud and the surrealists Breton described Artaud in the 'Second Manifesto' as one who 'had claimed to be a man of thought, of anger, of blood' (*MS* 130). The extreme importance attached to imagery, and to its capacity to 'enrapture' the mind, is perhaps the most impressive of all Artaud's legacies to the theoretical writing on the theatre that acknowledges his influence; but it is not, of course, original to Artaud. Nor, obviously, is the form of the manifesto, which Artaud deployed for the foundation and the 'abortive' operations of the Alfred Jarry Theatre from 1926 forwards. As Melzer has explained, surrealism 'had not sought to develop an aesthetic for the theatre', nor 'a unified program for the stage', and indeed proved regularly hostile to the theatre (Melzer 1980, 187). But Artaud's language and conception, despite the breach, remained nonetheless consistent with surrealism in its theoretical ambitions:

> We are not creating a theatre so as to present plays, but to succeed in showing the mind's obscure, hidden, and unrevealed aspects, by a sort of real, physical projection. (*CW* 2, 23)

A theoretical 'success' might only be possible after the acceptance of material failure, and the 'Manifesto for an Abortive Theatre' ironically advanced the surrealist project in uncompromising terms:

> What we would like to see sparkle and triumph on stage is whatever is a part of the mystery and magnetic fascination of dreams, the dark layers of consciousness, all that obsesses us within our minds. (*ibid.*)

The emphasis on the mind and on dreams was later accompanied by a reference to 'the stench and excreta of unadulterated cruelty', considered appropriate to 'encounters between things and sensations which strike us primarily by their physical density' (*CW* 2, 26). These 'encounters' were to be presented '*just as the mind remembered them*'; so the theatre, unsurprisingly, was not to be 'a museum for masterpieces', and any work 'which does not obey the *principle of actuality*' would be 'of no use to us whatsoever' (*CW* 2, 31).

As I have noted, the modes of address favoured in the manifesto result in an emphasis on the future-present set against the past. So for Artaud, in 'No More Masterpieces' from *The Theatre and Its Double*, the present must first of all assert its right to language:

> Past masterpieces are fit for the past, they are no good to us. We have the right to say what has been said and even what has not been said in a way that belongs to us, responding in a direct and straightforward manner to present day feelings everybody can understand. (*CW* 4, 56)

This declaration of rights is little more than a rephrasing of Stendhal's ironic contrast of the classical to the 'romantic' from the 1820s, and Artaud states his firm belief that there has been no 'worth-while show' since 'the last great Romantic melodramas' of 'a hundred years ago' (*CW* 4, 57).[32] In 'No More Masterpieces', poetry retains its cultural rank, but not its standard associations. 'Charm-poetry' is 'a decadent notion, an unmistakeable symptom of the emasculatory force within us', and there are to be 'No more personal poems benefiting those who write them more than those who read them' (*CW* 4, 59 and 60). What is envisaged is a transcendent poetry, which makes contact with what might be perhaps be best understood as its 'double': 'Poetry plain and simple, unformed and unwritten, underlies textual poetry' (*CW* 4, 59). This can also be expressed as a 'higher idea of poetry', which has access to 'certain predominant powers, certain ideas governing everything', and against the themes of decadence and emasculation is placed, by way of contrast, 'that energy which in the last analysis creates order' (*CW* 4, 61). In this formulation, the theatre actually appears as an incidental means to 'order' through poetry:

> Either we will be able to revert through theatre...to the higher idea of poetry...or else...we are fit only for chaos, famine, bloodshed, war and epidemics. (*CW* 4, 60).

But the violence of challenge must also be registered on the person of the writer: 'a *"theatre of cruelty"* means theatre that is difficult and cruel for myself first of all' (*ibid.*) The commitment to violence must be justified, and Artaud at the close of 'No More Masterpieces' insists that all 'depends on the manner and purity with which things are done', with the disclaimer that 'theatre teaches us just how useless action is since once it is done it is over' (*CW* 4, 63). In 'Theatre and Cruelty' violence offers a relatively facile contrast to the placidity of everyday life: so if 'everyday love, personal ambition and daily worries are worthless', it can follow that 'famous personalities, horrible crimes and superhuman self-sacrifices' are obvious subjects (*CW* 4, 65). But the propositions of surrealism also suggest two further means to the justification of violence, through reference to dreams and the mind, 'the omnipotence of dream' and 'the disinterested play of thought' in Breton's *Manifesto*. In Artaud's 'Theatre and Cruelty', the association of 'mental pictures' with 'dreams' achieved by the theatre will make them 'effective' on one stated condition, that is 'in so far as they are projected with the required violence' (*CW* 4, 65). Similarly, the assertion is made that 'the picture of a crime' is 'infinitely more dangerous to the mind' than a crime really committed. The mind is explicitly the object of the violence of the 'theatre of cruelty', and this is the 'true meaning' of that theatre, one in which 'life stands to lose everything and the mind to gain everything' (*CW* 4, 66). Breton had established this objective for 'surrealism' in his 'First Manifesto', in the 'expression', verbally or 'in any other manner', of 'the actual functioning of thought', and Artaud formulates the problem for the theatre.

In 'The Theatre of Cruelty: First Manifesto' the prescription for cruelty in 'every show' is justified by the sunderance of the present state of human beings from a participation in 'metaphysics': 'In our present degenerative state, metaphysics must be made to enter the mind through the body' (*CW* 4, 76). So it is that 'word, gesture and expressive metaphysics' must actually take the form of a 'tangible, objective theatre language', and the mind itself must be carefully defined (*CW* 4, 69). The appeal of 'a truly Oriental concept of expression' is immediately to the senses, and its 'lyricism of gestures' will surpass 'the lyricism of words'. This kind of language is Artaud's 'double' of poetry as it has been and is normally understood, and it is ultimately a form of redemptive magic:

> Finally it breaks away from language's intellectual subjugation by conveying the sense of a new, deeper intellectualism hidden under these gestures and signs and raised to the dignity of special exorcisms. (*ibid.*)

Language and the intellect also have their 'doubles' in this formulation, and Artaud is prepared to move away from the mind because it is so regularly understood to be just intellect in its ordinary definition:

> What matters is that our sensibility is put into a deeper, subtler state of perception by assured means, the very object of magic and ritual, of which theatre is only a reflection. (*CW* 4, 70)

We might find it easier to translate 'object' as 'objective' here, but the last phrase is instructive, because it subordinates 'theatre' firmly and unequivocally to 'magic and ritual'. In fact, the leading imperative of the manifesto makes that subordination absolutely clear:

> We cannot continue to prostitute the idea of theatre whose only value lies in its agonising magic relationship to reality and danger. (*CW* 4, 68)

The 'Letters on Language' return insistently to this essential characteristic of the 'language' that will constitute the theatre of cruelty. This is predominantly a 'physical' language but one that, like magic, is effective:

> I have added another language to speech and am attempting to restore its ancient magic effectiveness, its spellbinding effectiveness... (CW 4, 85)

In the 'doubling' of the west that is the 'Orient',

> this sign language is valued more than the other, ascribing direct magic powers to it. It is called on to address not only the mind but also the senses, and through the senses to reach even richer and more fruitful areas of sensibility in full flight. (CW 4, 91–2)

In 'The Theatre of Cruelty: Second Manifesto' Artaud conceives of the mind being 'affected by direct sensual pressure', and the theatre directing its magical means towards the 'nerves':

> If the nerves, that is to say a certain physiological sensitivity, are deliberately omitted from today's after-dinner theatre... the Theatre of Cruelty intends to return to all the tried and tested means of affecting sensitivity. (CW 4, 96)

The variety of expressions combines in a theory of analogy, of correspondence between the physical and the transcendent, of 'doubles' in a theatre which, at its best, can only be a 'reflection' of magic, the ultimate mediator.

The 'Letters on Cruelty' include one which refers obliquely to Gnosticism, and this connection forms the basis of a study by Goodall. The Artaud of legend has been persistently presented as a martyr and heretic, and the dignity of heresy gains immensely from the association with a specific sect:

> Artaud, as the most extravagant of heretics, may appropriately find himself in company with the Gnostics whose speculations served to *define* heresy for the Church Fathers. (Goodall 1994, 6)

The difficulties facing Goodall in her task of comparison are in part those of fact:

One of the curious aspects of the often remarked upon analogies between Artaud's ideas and the ideas of the Gnostics is the lack of evidence that he was influenced by any concentrated reading of Gnostic literature. (*ibid.*)

This undoubtedly complicates the problem of what Goodall intends to make of the connection, but it is not in itself insuperable. As Goodall observes, there are allusions to many 'occult and esoteric literatures' in his writing, and what Goodall describes as the 'common domain of heretical logic' may achieve a congruence which is not simply one of direct inheritance.

Although Goodall does not completely resolve the relationship between the two instances of cosmic heresy, the connection she explores encourages a close reading of much in Artaud's writings that might otherwise remain obscure. In particular, Goodall contends that 'the cruelty of theatrical performance has an anti-cosmocratic purpose' for its originator, one that is quite possibly irrespective of its comprehension by an audience. So the heresy of 'lifting the veil' may not require applause or even appreciation:

> The Theatre of Cruelty is to lift the veil of appearances which conceals the violence of creation, itself a violence begun in disastrous conjunctions but perpetuated as the disguised cruelty of a world of fixed forms. (*ibid.*, 106)

According to this analysis, association with the creed of Gnosticism releases Artaud from any responsibility for the introduction and advocacy of 'cruelty', since the violence and cruelty are those of the act(s) of creation. This is a claim that Artaud repeatedly makes in his writings, notably the second and third of the apologetic 'Letters on Cruelty', in which he apportions a rather ineffectual role to 'good', in opposition to an 'evil' which is 'continuous' and 'the paramount rule' (*CW* 4, 78–9). The connection that Goodall makes encourages a benign and therapeutic interpretation of the constitution of Artaud's theatre, because only a cruelty of an alternative creation can match that of the original:

> the logic of setting the theatre as plague and as cruelty in opposition to a fatality which can also be defined in these terms is homeopathic . . . (Goodall 1994, 107)

It is a thesis which reconstitutes the legend in appropriately contemporary terms, attributing by implication a spiritual status to Artaud's engagement with mysticism, but allowing the construction and validity of his theory of a theatre of magic to remain unexamined.

Primary Sources

Apollonio, U. (ed.) (1973) *Futurist Manifestos* (London: Thames & Hudson).
Artaud, A. (1974) *Collected Works*, trans. V. Corti (London: Calder & Boyars).
—(1970) *The Theatre and Its Double*, trans. V. Corti (London: Calder & Boyars).
—(1976) *Selected Writings*, trans. H. Weaver (New York: Farrar, Straus & Giroux).
—and others (1972) 'Antonin Artaud's "Les Cenci": Preperformance, Blocking Diagrams, Reviews', *Drama Review*, 16, 2, 90–145.
—(1956–) *Oeuvres Complètes* (Paris: Gallimard).
Benedikt, M. and Wellwarth, G. (eds) (1964) *Modern French Plays: An Anthology from Jarry to Ionesco* (London: Faber).
Breton, A. (1969) *Manifestoes of Surrealism*, trans. R. Seaver and H. Lane (Ann Arbor: Michigan University Press).
Erasmus (1971) *Praise of Folly*, trans. B. Radice (Harmondsworth: Penguin).
Gordon, M. (ed.) (1987) *Dada Performance* (New York: PAJ Publications).
Jarry, A. (1965) *Selected Works*, ed. R. Shattuck and S. Watson Taylor (London: Methuen).
Motherwell, R. (ed.) (1951) *The Dada Painters and Poets: An Anthology* (New York: Wittenborn, Schultz).
Rimbaud, A. (1966) *Complete Works, Selected Letters*, trans. W. Fowlie (Chicago: University of Chicago Press).
Schumacher, C. (1989) (ed.) *Artaud on Theatre* (London: Methuen).
Tzara, T. (1977) *Seven Dada Manifestos and Lampisteries*, trans. B. Wright (London: Calder).

Secondary Sources

Barber, S. (1993) *Antonin Artaud: Blows and Bombs* (London: Faber).
Bigsby, C. (1972) *Dada and Surrealism* (London: Methuen).
Braun, E. (1982) *The Director and the Stage* (London: Methuen).
Deak, F. (1993) *Symbolist Theatre: The Formation of an Avant-Garde* (Baltimore: Johns Hopkins University Press).
—(1976) 'Symbolist Staging at the Théâtre d'Art', *Drama Review*, 20, 3, 117–22.
Derrida, J. (1978) *Writing and Difference*, trans. A. Bass (London: Routledge).

Derrida, J. and Thévenin, P. (1998) *The Secret Art of Antonin Artaud*, trans. M. Caws (Cambridge, Mass.: MIT Press).

Finter, H. (1997) 'Antonin Artaud and the Impossible Theatre: The Legacy of the Theatre of Cruelty', *Drama Review*, 41, 4, 15–40.

Goodall, J. (1994) *Artaud and the Gnostic Drama* (Oxford: Clarendon Press).

Kirby, M. (1971) *Futurist Performance* (New York: Dutton).

Matthews, J. (1974) *Theatre in Dada and Surrealism* (Syracuse, NY: Syracuse University Press).

Melzer, A. (1980) *Latest Rage the Big Drum: Dada and Surrealist Performance* (Ann Arbor: Michigan University Press).

—(1977) 'The Premiere of Apollinaire's *The Breasts of Tiresias* in Paris', *Theatre Quarterly*, 27, 3–13.

Nadeau, M. (1968) *History of Surrealism*, trans. R. Howard (London: Cape).

Shattuck, R. (1968) *The Banquet Years: The Origins of the Avant-Garde in France, 1885 to World War I* (New York: Random House).

5

Grotowski and Theoretical Training

Jerzy Grotowski (1933–99) occupies an unusual place in an account of theoretical practitioners. His engagement with theatre productions as such only lasted for the first decade of his working life. Between 1957 and 1968 he established an ensemble at the Theatre of Thirteen Rows, later the Laboratory Theatre or Laboratory Institute, in Opole and Wroclaw. After this period he retreated from theatre performances and developed work which he called paratheatrical in that it was linked to the performer's craft but outside conventional theatre. Because of the limited opportunities to see his theatre work, or to participate in his training courses or post-theatrical work, written material by or about Grotowski has been the primary source of access to his practice. Grotowski himself wrote very little, producing only short articles for theatre magazines, occasional interviews and transcriptions of talks delivered at conferences or on courses. In particular, writing about the 'paratheatrical' projects became disproportionately significant, since only a small number of students and practitioners participated and witnesses were limited in number. Written accounts from short-term participants and occasional reflective articles from Grotowski form the only access to this work for the majority of those interested in tracing the development of his thought.

Grotowski's writing echoes the parabola of his career. As a young director working within the Polish theatre in the late 1950s, Grotowski's early articles were written primarily to publicize his work in Poland, and to earn himself an appointment to a small state-subsidized theatre at Opole. After 1962, when the Theatre of Thirteen Rows had developed a distinctive way of working, the frequency of his published output increased and was aimed more

117

often at an international audience, to be delivered at conferences or to accompany work and productions on tour around the world. The garnering of international significance undoubtedly aided his position within the Polish theatre hierarchy. Some of these talks and interviews from the most prolific period of his life were collected and published as *Towards a Poor Theatre* in 1968 in English, via the Denmark base of his Italian collaborator, Eugenio Barba. After this time the Laboratory Theatre produced no new productions, but toured with existing pieces as they developed paratheatrical work, about which Grotowski wrote far less frequently.

After Grotowski's decision to leave Poland in early 1982, when martial law was imposed, a trickle of writings was printed in the *Drama Review* and other international theatre journals connected to his work in America on Objective Drama and the Theatre of Sources. This pattern of occasional publication of reflective articles continued after the establishment of his Workcentre at Pontedera, Italy. A second book dealing with his experiments, *At Work with Grotowski on Physical Actions*, was produced in 1995. This offers an account of the last phases of Grotowski's work, although it was written in the main by Thomas Richards, whom Schechner identifies as Grotowski's heir.[1] The *Grotowski Sourcebook* (1997) reprints six interviews with and essays by Grotowski, as well as reflective articles from collaborators, participants and commentators, which span the whole range Grotowski's life. Schechner and Wolford's editorial choices display their own interests. Wolford was a participant in the Objective Drama project at Irvine, and although the selection of articles offers intriguing insight into this three-year project it is given a disproportionately large amount of coverage. Schechner's career has been strongly influenced by Grotowski and Barba's activities and their interests have shaped much of his writing. There are no critical voices in the volume, an absence felt particularly strongly with regard to the Theatre of Sources and intercultural aspects of Grotowski's work.

Much of Grotowski's writing, particularly the early material, is transcribed from encounters in the workshop, talks or interviews. These primarily oral texts have a casual format, but that does not necessarily mean a casual style. Grotowski was insistent that final editorial power lay with him. Barba, who put together *Towards a Poor Theatre* (*TPT*) and Schechner and Wolford, who collated *The Grotowski Sourcebook* (*GS*) attest to his rigorous editorializing, 'even if it went against standard grammar and word usage' (*GS* 471). In this strategy of authorization, Grotowski was surely recognizing the differing rhetoric of dissemination through the written word and the changed audience for his work, once it moved beyond the encounter in the studio or seminar. When approaching these texts several of his apologists find a darker undertone to this editorial concern. 'Has Grotowski absorbed the Polish and Soviet penchant for controlled history? Or the opposite, having experienced what can happen in a totalitarian state, will he always be fearful of the damage information can do, how fragile his reputation and situation?' Schechner asks, in a manner which reveals how deeply the language of the Cold War has seeped into the reception of this Eastern European practitioner (*GS* 471). Filipowicz, talking of later manifestations of Grotowski, counts him one of 'those artists who, deliberately or not, use an official language to conceal rather than reveal their ideas' (*GS* 403). Readers of Grotowski interpret his writings as an exercise in political obfuscation, self-preservation, or self-mythologizing. There is perhaps a little of all this in the early writings.

Schechner links Grotowski's 'need for control' editorially with his controlling presence in workshops. Although he floats the idea of Soviet controlled history as a model for this behaviour, he also situates this 'control' within a sort of tradition which was at odds with the totalitarian materialist state, the spiritual. The analogies that Schechner draws are various: 'the hierarchical Roman Catholic Church (Polish edition), the Indian guru–shishya relationship, the Hasidic rebbe, surrounded by adherents hanging on his every word, arguing and interpreting, guarding him from intrusions' (*GS* 471). These very distinct spiritual fields all find some mention within the content if not the *modus operandi* of Grotowski's work over his lifetime. I will explore later in this chapter how spiritual analogy is employed by Grotowski in his writing at different stages of his career. However, it is undoubtedly true that Grotowski's writing repays some knowledge of context. As Filopowicz notes, 'his language as a public figure and as an artist are two quite different things, often at odds with one another' (*GS* 403). Grotowski and his collaborators are quite explicit about the kind of language they need to employ to avoid the censor or cajole money from the Rockefeller Foundation and other international funding bodies. This in some way explains the names given to periods of Grotowski's post-theatre work, which remain very theatre orientated: Paratheatre, Theatre of Sources, Active Culture, Objective

Drama, Art as Vehicle. The economic context of Grotowski's work conditions his writing and the outlet he seeks for his published work. It was largely by maintaining a high level of international attention that he preserved the Theatre Laboratory's funding from the Polish state, although the reports in his local Wroclaw paper, *Odra*, complain about the low level of this subsidy.

In order to assess the significance of *Towards a Poor Theatre* and its reception worldwide, some idea of the context of its creation are useful. Firstly, an understanding of the place of theatre and theatre training in Poland. The role of the Catholic Church within Poland and its links to Polish theatre in general will aid an assessment of the specific significance of Catholicism and spirituality within Grotowski's early work. Finally, the rhetoric of the Cold War within the Polish state and the view from the other side of the Iron Curtain conditioned both Grotowski's work, writing and reception abroad. Plainly these elements also had an impact on his work beyond theatrical production (the paratheatrical and later projects), although Grotowski wrote much less about these research experiments. Once he left Poland in 1982, the immediate context of his writing and research changed. His writing about his work at Irvine and Pontedera is flavoured by and set within a cultural and political context greatly altered in time and significance. The later writing displays a preoccupation with pedagogy in various forms, not least because during this period it was educational establishments in the main that hosted him and found him funding.

Grotowski's theatrical ensemble, and the work which was documented in *Towards a Poor Theatre*, owe much to the influence of Polish theatre traditions. Osinski's study of Grotowski's Laboratory work identifies his debt to the Reduta Theatre Institution (Osinski 1979, 85–6). Reduta was a theatre and an actor-training institute, run by Juliusz Osterwa, which operated during Poland's period of national independence between the World Wars. The institute in its early years operated as a collective ensemble, concentrating on specifically Polish theatre writing, the study of Polish methods of acting and employing images drawn from national myths and art. The Reduta came to be a symbol of national independence and its theatre buildings were an early casualty of the hostilities in 1939. In March 1966 Grotowski appropriated the symbol of the Reduta, which had not been operational since its closure in 1939, replacing R for Reduta, with L for Laboratorium. He defended the 'monastic habits' of Reduta and 'its attempts to initiate long-term research concerning the actor's craft...its ethical premises... I would say that Reduta is, in our aspirations, our moral tradition' (Osinski 1979, 86). In adopting the mantle of Reduta he was seen to be situating the Laboratory Theatre at the heart of a specifically Polish tradition. He indeed makes reference to Osterwa more than once within the text of *Towards a Poor Theatre*, particularly in picking up Osterwa's dismissal of 'publicotropism' or a kind of acting orientated towards the public (*TPT* 181, 198).

The Laboratory Theatre was happy to situate itself within a tradition of radical, ensemble theatre from a golden age of Polish independent theatre. The Laboratory's choice of repertoire also situated itself centrally in the theatre of its immediate contemporaries. During the late 1950s and 1960s the canonical works of Polish romanticism were being performed all over Poland. Kazimierz Braun identifies the political component of this new-found interest in Polish romanticism, which had been made possible by a brief period of post-Stalin relaxation in censorship. The insistence on socialist realism in the state theatres was lifted for a short period after the October 1956 revolution in Poland, when Soviet influence in Poland was temporarily in abeyance. For the first time, national masterpieces could be revived in the state theatres like *Forefather's Eve*, *Kordian* or *Acropolis*, and it was possible to stage plays from Witkiewicz, Gombrowicz and Slowacki, as well as foreign writers.[2] Many of these pieces needed a different kind of acting and staging to the stolid banality of socialist realism. Grotowski was part of an almost nation-wide movement of celebration of these Polish classics and re-examination of the myths the plays supported. A sister theatre, the Teatr Rapsodyczny, Cracow, run by Kotlarczyk, performed works based on Byron and Mickiewicz's poem *Forefather's Eve* (1961), Goethe's *Faust* (1965), and *Acropolis* (1966); all works or writers tackled by Grotowski during this same period. Kotlarczyk invited the Archbishop of Cracow, who had once been an actor, to the première of his *Acropolis*. The Archbishop was outspoken in his praise of the theatre for its preservation of national culture and spiritual life. This explicit collaboration between theatre and church was not to the authorities' taste and the Theatre Rapsodyczny was closed in 1967.

Grotowski walked a careful line on the right side of the authorities and had taken advantage, during the 1960s, of the more relaxed attitude towards foreign tours and the reception of visitors from abroad. His *Acropolis* of 1966 was even allowed to visit Holland,

Belgium, Italy, the UK, France and the Cultural Olympics in Mexico City in 1968. It is difficult for us to assess the level of political impact Grotowski's use of religious iconography and of national classics had, but certainly he was not interested in expressing political comment.[3] When in 1965 the Theatre of Thirteen Rows relocated to Wroclaw, the theatre was moving to the capital of Polish experimental theatre, joining Tomaszewsk's Pantomime theatre (with its demanding physical training and emphasis on expressive mime) and a town which regularly played host to an international festival of avant-garde theatres. Both in its repertoire and in its search for experimental methods of performance, Grotowski's Laboratory was replicating developments in theatre across Poland at this time. What was unique about his approach was the particular kind of interrogation of classic texts he proposed and the development of actor-training.

The role of the Catholic church in the defence of Polish national identity should not be underestimated. During the partition of Poland into territories under Russian, Austrian and German rule, only the theatre and the church were allowed to use the Polish language. The Catholic church was a site of resistance to Soviet influence after the Second World War and after the imposition of martial law in 1980 was deeply implicated in the underground movement and Solidarity. Plays were often presented in churches during these years, since they needed no censors' licence there. There is also a strongly religious flavour to much of the writing of the Polish romantics whose work was so triumphantly restored to the repertoire during the 1950s and 1960s. Not only was the content of the work often a meditation on morality, but the figure of the suffering man whose individual battle is fought on behalf of his country or community found many echoes in the Christian mythology. In staging the plays of the Polish romantic writers, religious imagery recurs again and again. Grotowski was not alone in returning to this iconography in his confrontation with collective myths of Polish culture. An example of the kind of popular use he made of this iconography is given by Kumiega, who recounts that there was a moment in *The Constant Prince* when Fernando, the eponymous prince, sits with head to one side, eyes closed, drained but patiently listening to Fenixana's confession, in the image of the Little Polish Christ found everywhere in roadside shrines (Kumiega 1987, 82).

Curiosity about the countries behind the Iron Curtain added to the exotic appeal of Grotowski's production work once he travelled internationally. His visit to the World Youth and Student Festival in Helsinki in 1962 established his first foothold on the international circuit. On the basis of this talk and later visits from foreigners to watch the work, his cause was championed by several Western Europeans, notably French critic Raymonde Temkine who was to write the first book about Grotowski, and Eugenio Barba, who went to work with Grotowski, and then to edit *Towards a Poor Theatre*, and who has done more than anyone to disseminate information about 'the Master'. The idea of an ensemble who both work and *train* together was a relatively unusual one in Western theatre terms, but chimed with the increasing number of individuals who were interested in collective activity, counter-cultural communities and a deeper examination of spiritual experience. In stating that his aim was to shock or influence the audience and thus provide a kind of social therapy and provoke a vicarious self-examination, Grotowski's writing was at one and the same time palatable to the Soviet censor in Poland and in tune with the aspirations of those counter-culturalists in an increasingly individuated, alienated and self-doubting West.

'Towards a Poor Theatre'

This text is a collection of essays, notably the eponymous 'Towards a Poor Theatre', interviews, talks given after courses abroad and responses to questions at seminars, conversations with intimates like Barba, production and programme notes, descriptions of training sessions and prescriptions for students at the Laboratorium. Not all of the work was Grotowski's; Barba was the other major contributor, and the company's dramaturg and critic, Ludwik Flazsen, wrote on the treatment of texts. The collation of texts produces a collection of voices and pieces with quite differing dynamics. However, since the overall aim seems to be to proselytize on behalf of Grotowski's work, there is much repetition and overlap in the volume. Reading Grotowski is never straightforward, as over the period of his work inside and outside theatre he developed contradictory positions, and his pronouncements were often filtered through or complemented by the voices of his collaborators. Both this book and the later *At Work with Grotowski* contain a great deal of writing from his co-workers. The focus of these writers is conditioned by their relation to the work and to Grotowski himself. The two descriptions of the actor-training activities are from very different points of view; the first, 'Actor's Training (1959–1962)', is a record by Barba, who was an observer and collaborator with Grotowski's ensemble for around three years, of a day's training for members of the ensemble. The second description of training, 'Actor's Training (1966)', comes from notes made by a Belgium director who watched a brief training course given by Grotowski and Cieslak. Rather than just the bare outline of exercises, the account illustrates almost as fully Grotowski's interaction with students, the experience of being in the studio with him and Cieslak, as it does the actor-training itself. Likewise, the questions which shape the interviews of *Towards a Poor Theatre* reveal much about the preoccupations of the questioners, and the responses they elicit sometimes have an emphasis not shared by work authored solely by Grotowski elsewhere. So Barba's interview, which he entitled 'Theatre's New Testament' follows his interest in the 'holy' actor and the ritual elements of Grotowski's work, while Naim Kattan's Canadian interview 'Theatre is an Encounter' is predominantly concerned with work with texts. Grotowski also alters the register of his rhetoric according to his audience. 'Towards a Poor Theatre' began life as a polemic presentation of the Laboratory Theatre's research remit for a Wroclaw paper. It covers much the same ground as 'Statement of Principles', but the latter is a condensed statement for potential students at the Laboratorium, where the tone is far more dogmatic, and addresses the reader directly as a participant, adding many guidelines on the working methods and attitudes required in studio sessions and in the Laboratorium in general. When Grotowski addresses students from elsewhere, as in his address to the Swedish Skara Drama School, his tone is cajoling, and what was previously asserted as law is here offered simply as a suggestion. Grotowski softens his demands, taking into account the realities of the commercial theatrical environment that the Skara students would be entering.

Almost all of the texts collected for *Towards a Poor Theatre* were already in the public domain, published in journals, newspapers or recorded at public events. They appeared between 1964 and the end of 1967. In the book the writings are not arranged chronologically, and in attempting to follow the logic of their compilation, they seem to fall roughly into three phases: introduction to the principles of the Theatre Laboratory, textual concerns and actor training. Grotowski himself talked of the book as a 'kind of logbook' or 'only a travel diary, which – telling about the experience of past years – describes my searches. But they are past travels.' (Osinski 1979, 87; Kumiega 1987, 145). Indeed, by the time the book appeared in 1968, Grotowski had largely come to the end of his primary interest in theatre performance, and was already in transition to paratheatrical activities, although *Apocalypsis cum Figuris* continued to tour internationally until 1980. The notion of travel is also clearly encompassed in texts, all of which were written during the period when the Laboratorium was touring internationally, and three-quarters of which were originally aimed at an international audience. The only productions discussed are those that toured to festivals and universities, where most of the interview material was collected. The volume as a whole records the international dissemination of Grotowski's work, and as a collection has never been translated into Polish.

The title of the volume is taken from an article Grotowski wrote defining his company's work when they transferred to Wroclaw in 1965. In calling his Theatre Laboratory 'poor', Grotowski was marking out the distinctiveness of his work from the spectacular displays of scenic or visual theatre which were proliferating at the time. However, in moving to Wroclaw, the centre of much experimental theatre, he also needed to establish his theatre's unique contribution to more experimental work. As he admits, and Kumiega records, his own early productions made bold use of costume, mask and scenery. But Grotowski dismisses that work with a phrase replete with the ideology of the 1960s counter-culturalist: 'I know that scene: I used to be part of it'. He also dismisses Rich theatre, which he firstly interprets in terms of *mise-en-scène*, as 'total theatre' using all the artistic disciplines in 'synthetic theatre'. 'Synthetic' is intended to carry both the sense of a synthesis of forms and the sense of a manufactured material (*TPT* 19). By contrast, then, 'poor' theatre is generated by a process which eliminates and strips away, but this principle is extended far beyond the removal of unnecessary scenic decoration or the rejection of other art forms like literature or architecture. The elimination of unnecessary elements even extends beyond the acting techniques of the performers to their behaviour and personalities. In the later essays of *Towards a Poor Theatre* this concept of the *via negativa* is introduced, where the actor even strips away intention in movement. Rather than straining or setting out to achieve an exercise or state, the actor 'resigns from not doing it' (*TPT* 17). Poor theatre is therefore presented as a purer form, unsullied by non-theatrical elements and also as a morally better form, since

> poverty in theatre, stripped of all that is not essential to it, revealed to us not only the backbone of the medium, but also the deep riches which lie in the very nature of the art-form. (*TPT* 21)

Grotowski uses 'backbone' here to indicate the moral integrity of the poor form as well as implying that it lies as an essential skeleton under the fleshy accretion of total, rich theatre. And poor theatre is of course rich, but in a deeper way. In the earlier interview with Barba and in his many discussions of the kind of actor he seeks, Grotowski uses the metaphor of rich theatre in a second way, as one which is driven by commercial imperatives, where the actor sells him or herself into 'artistic prostitution' (*TPT* 214). As a result, 'poor' also comes to mean an ascetic approach which refuses the ideology of the marketplace and the actor as object of exchange. He makes this even more explicit in the 'Theatre's New Testament', where he asserts that the poor theatre 'defies the bourgeois concept of a standard of living. It proposes the substitution of material wealth by moral wealth' (see also section 10 of the 'Statement of Principles'). 'Rich' is also applied to other forms than theatre, to the mass, populist forms of cinema and television, whose technical resources create a *mise-en-scène* that no theatre could match. 'Poor' theatre is resistant to the lure of a mass market and restricts itself to an élite audience who are looking for neither entertainment nor cultural commodity; 'thus we are left with a "holy" actor in a poor theatre' (*TPT* 41). This rejection of mass media chimed with American and Western European theatre-makers, who were developing similar kinds of theatre as encounter, a phrase which recurs within this volume.[4] The rejection of consumerist ideology had much to recommend it in cultures which had spent the decade experimenting with 'dropping out'.

How did Grotowski define his own role within the ensemble? He was not an actor-manager, nor dramaturg, nor particularly interested in scenography. The term he most often uses about his role is 'producer'. In the earliest piece, 'The Theatre's New Testament', in interview with Barba, he uses producer to mean director. Grotowski is scathing about traditional theatre organization, and the kind of person who becomes a producer in order to sit 'enthroned on top of all the arts, although in reality he feeds off them all without himself being tied to the creative work which is carried out for him by others' (*TPT* 32). This links to his rejection of total theatre and therefore of the work of the director in integrating disparate elements into the *mise-en-scène*. More disturbingly, later in the article he suggests that what is creative in the producer is 'a sadistic component'. He acknowledges that some elements of the traditional role of the director are essential to this 'the art of leading', including 'learning how to handle people...a gift for diplomacy, a cold and inhuman talent for dealing with intrigues' (*TPT* 48). It seems that rather than the integration of scenic elements, the producer's role is the integration of the members of the troupe. Throughout the volume in all the texts it is clear that his primary interest as a producer is the relationship with the actor. This relationship is characterized in many ways, but always with the producer as dominant, 'a tyrant', while the actor reacts to him 'like a pupil does against his teacher, a patient against his doctor or a soldier against his superiors' (*TPT* 44) or as a younger family member: 'One must be strict but like a father or older brother' (*TPT* 48).

However, it is this producer's function as pedagogue that underscores all his work, within and without the theatre and this ensemble. It even crystallizes the way he thinks about his relationship to the audience – 'Even though we cannot educate the audience – not systematically, at least – we **can** educate the actor' (*TPT* 33) – and about the texts he works with and the wider role of theatre in society. The phrase 'the education of the actor' repeats endlessly, and it is within this context that actor-training becomes so important. It is not just a way of establishing a sense of ensemble, or extending an individual actor's technical range of expression, or offering the audience a more extraordinary form of theatre (although all of these elements are byproducts of this in the work). Primarily, the education and training of the actor is an end in itself. It functions as a therapeutic medium for actor and producer and by extension for the audience; it is an active form of self-improvement (*TPT* 213).

In the early 'Theatre's New Testament', Grotowski fantasizes about the possibilities of a theatre school, training pupils from younger than fourteen, before they are 'psychically formed', in a series of practical exercises and a humanistic education designed as a stimulus to awaken their sensibility. This school would use the services of 'a psycho-analyst and a social anthropologist' (*TPT* 51). Yet in texts produced after this time, such as 'Towards a Poor Theatre', he rejects the teacher/pupil dynamic, and redefines his pedagogy:

I hold a peculiar position of leadership in the Polish Theatre Laboratory. I am not simply the director or producer or 'spiritual instructor'. In the first place, my relation to the work is certainly not one-way or didactic... [The actor's] growth is attended by observation, astonishment, and desire to help; my growth is projected onto him, or rather, is **found in him** – and our common growth becomes revelation. This is not instruction of a pupil but utter opening to another person, in which the phenomenon of 'shared or double birth' becomes possible. (*TPT* 25)

Grotowski does not reject the titles of director, producer and spiritual instructor, but his method of instruction is heuristic. He sees his role as pedagogue as a passive one, not actively teaching but observing and reacting. This is very similar in nature to the concept of the *via negativa* for the actor; resigning from not doing something. The other side to the role of producer is Grotowski's presentation of himself as an active researcher. The actor is reduced to the status of experimental matter, and Grotowski the researcher can unearth and reveal what is 'found' in the actor.[5] Clearly the nature of the 'utter openness' between producer and actor does not involve a change in the relation of power. He also summons another role as analyst, when he describes his activity through the metaphor of 'projection'; a kind of counter-transference is implied, where the analyst lives vicariously through the analysand.

Despite Grotowski's group changing its name from Theatre of Thirteen Rows to Theatre Laboratory, and the Polish authorities granting it the status of 'Institute of Research into Acting Method' (1965), Grotowski is at pains in his writing to try and control the meaning of 'method'. The article 'Methodical Exploration' emphasizes the way in which the search for the 'objective laws' of creative process should be undertaken, 'obliging the actor who wishes to be creative to master a method' (*TPT* 96). However, Grotowski resists writing a 'recipe' or 'how to' instruction (*TPT* 97). He takes pains to distinguish his 'method' from the kind of working popularized as Stanislavski's method. What is difficult to grasp in the book, and which explains the frustrating lack of detail in a rhetoric which works largely by analogy, is that this process is not a method as such and later he repudiates the word altogether.[6] The essence of all Grotowski presents in these articles is that his 'method' is an attitude that actors should bring to their work. This attitude must be in place prior to any physical activity, whether exercise or performance. This places the physical discipline and exercises in a secondary place to the internal attitude. This understanding of 'method' exposes a paradox within much of his writing in *Towards a Poor Theatre*. Grotowski attempts to refute the Cartesian split of mind and body and purports to offer a way of working which eliminates the dichotomy.[7] However, his language is entirely constructed around the nexus of inner/outer, mind and body, attitude and expression. For example, he talks of 'the impulse is already an outer reaction' (*TPT* 16); 'if we strip ourselves and touch an extraordinarily intimate layer, exposing it' (*TPT* 23); 'to study what is hidden behind our everyday mask – the innermost core of our personality – in order to sacrifice it, expose it' (*TPT* 37); 'the sculptor takes away what is concealing the form which, as it were, already exists within the block of stone, thus revealing it' (*TPT* 39); 'the author's text is a sort of scalpel enabling us to open ourselves' (*TPT* 57); and '[the actor's] search must be directed from within himself to the outside' (*TPT* 203). These metaphors posit the body as resistance, as an obstacle, and as deceitful within an ideology which is Catholic at source. The abasement of the body is practised through the training, not just as an image within productions. This rhetoric also summons a complex hermeneutics for the audience, since the body is both deceiving and concealing, and at the same time reactive and expressive in performance signs.

Throughout Grotowski's writing there is a repeated use of spiritual analogy. Perhaps as much because of the context in which he was writing, as of his personal convictions, he is at pains to point out that this spiritual frame of reference is metaphoric:

> Don't get me wrong. I speak about 'holiness' as an unbeliever. I mean a 'secular holiness'. (*TPT* 34)... One must resort to a metaphorical language to say that the decisive factor in this process is humility, a spiritual predisposition. (*TPT* 37)

He dubs Stanislavski a 'secular saint' (*TPT* 50) and relishes Artaud's mystical suggestiveness. He defends this use of metaphor in materialist terms as:

> suggestion, aiming at an ideoplastic realization. Personally, I must admit that we do not shrink from using these 'quack' formulas. Anything that has an unusual or magical ring stimulates the imagination of both actor and producer. (*TPT* 38)

When he suggests that actors can '"illuminate" through personal technique, becoming a source of "spiritual light" ' (*TPT* 20) his use of quotation marks is intended to bracket the reference as metaphor, and a page later he explains how this can be achieved technically using a fixed facial expression and the actor's 'inner impulses' to produce 'the effect of a strikingly theatrical transubstantiation' (*TPT* 21). The analogy is extended to the experience for the audience who receive 'atonement' through the actor's performance of extraordinary acts in front of them (*TPT* 34), and for whom theatre still has some of the old religious force which 'liberated the spiritual energy of the congregation of the tribe by incorporating myth and profaning or rather transcending it . . . [as] sacral parody' (*TPT* 22–3). And yet the cumulative force of these analogies and metaphors, coupled with the content of the texts and images in performance, only reinforces the reader's sense of the ideology which underlies all Grotowski's writing. With regard to the spiritual, Grotowski's attitude to Artaud is intriguing. In 'He wasn't Entirely Himself' Grotowski argues that Artaud learnt 'the true lesson of sacred theatre', which is that spontaneity and discipline are mutually reinforcing (*TPT* 89). Conveniently, this is an approach that Grotowski shared. In fact Grotowski's article is almost entirely critical of Artaud's writing and thinking about theatre, but what does interest him is Artaud the man. To this extent Grotowski is writing very much of the late 1960s when the Artaud myth was being generated, as discussed in Chapter 4. For Grotowski, it is Artaud's personal suffering and illness which make him a significant figure and his martyrdom becomes 'a shining proof of the theatre as therapy' (*TPT* 93).

Rather than following Artaud's metaphoric raptures, in *Towards a Poor Theatre* Grotowski continually returns to acting and his engagement with actors. He positions himself as part of a continuum of actor-trainers which stretches forwards from Stanislavski, Dullin and Meyerhold amongst others. He makes much reference to Stanislavski's training in physical actions and applauds his methodical approach towards preparing the actor, and yet Grotowski's demands on the actor are of an entirely different order. Where Stanislavski invites the actor to discover what she brings to the role, for Grotowski the actor is invited to use the role as 'an instrument with which to study what is hidden behind our everyday mask – the innermost core of our personality' (*TPT* 38). The logic of Grotowski's argument is that whatever character the actor is assigned, the role she plays is her 'self'. The physical score, which provided the disciplining structure for the associative impulses of the performer, made use of the physical facility in the actor that had been produced by the exercises. Despite avowals to contrary, the link between exercise and performance sign is very close, as illustrated by the photographs of performances and training sessions. When constructing the performance sign, Grotowski claimed to be looking for innate forms already contained in the body (*TPT* 39), yet as Innes points out these were often forms from classical or religious iconography (Innes 1993). Furthermore, the classic texts that Grotowski used were also treated as an encounter to 'suit his own nature' (*TPT* 58) and manipulated, as Flaszen outlines in the chapters on the plays themselves, so that the experience is 'like looking at oneself in a mirror, at our ideas and traditions, and not merely the description of what men of past ages thought and felt' (*TPT* 52). As a result of these three elements Grotowski's production work undoubtedly had a characteristic style, one which was a function of the personalities of the ensemble, particularly Grotowski's own, rather than the 'discovery and use of the rules of theatre' (*TPT* 18).[8] Although Grotowski asserts throughout *Towards a Poor Theatre* that the practice reveals the theory, and that illumination of the rules of theatre, ideas and traditions is received directly through the expression of the body, he thus denies, dismisses or refuses to consider the ideological implications of the practical techniques he employs.

Towards a Poor Theatre assumes a homogenous audience for Grotowski's work. An audience of participants who come with a correct attitude, as the actor is expected to have the right attitude, and who will be able to recognize collective myths, and will be prepared for an act of self-analysis, which can be prompted in all of them by the performances of a limited number of actors (*TPT* 42). The volume includes idealist diagrams of the actor and audience configurations, which echo the aspirations of Grotowski's theorizing. Some diagrams use arrows between audience groups indicating their 'relationship' to each other, and describing the 'osmosis' of actor and spectator (*TPT* 126). Both ideas show how the theatre experience is designed to be one of presence for the audience as much as the actor. There is no room for illusionism here. The volume also captures actual audience members in the photographs of performances, whose various reactions, postures and interrelations demonstrate a more complex group than Grotowski's rhetoric allows for. The impact of the performers' proximity and their need for a precise score is clear, and the inactivity of the spectators reinforced. The audience's presence profoundly affects the *mise-en-scène*. In 1964 in 'Theatre's New Testament' Grotowski was advocating ways to 'abolish the distance between actor and audience' in both the physical and philosophical sense, through physical proximity. However, physical proximity does not always lessen the gap between actor and spectator.[9] By 1967, Grotowski had developed a variety of actor–audience constellations, and the audience had been cast in a variety of roles. The idea of characterizing an audience, for example as mental patients for Kordian, was gradually refused as it requires the adoption of masks, at the same moment as the performers were attempting to unmask themselves and prompt a sympathetic self-revelation in the audience member. What connected audience members to each other was their role as spectator, or witness, as Grotowski coined it, coupled with the attitude towards them of the performer. Each performer developed a combative mode of challenge or 'a kind of provocation' (*TPT* 99), in 'confrontation with the spectators', fulfilling 'an authentic act in place of the spectators' (*TPT* 182), but never 'for' the spectator. By the latest text in the volume, 'American Encounter' in December 1967, Grotowski is advocating the actor's development of an internal audience, a 'secure partner' (*TPT* 203). This foreshadows the abandonment of the audience altogether in favour of the participant of paratheatrical experiments.

Post-Production Writing and Theorizing

Grotowski's own documentation of the later developments of his work are almost without exception drawn from talks or interviews, which were later worked over prior to publication. His reluctance to offer written material that could be regarded as definitive makes much sense in the light of his avowed championing of the body as site of memory and knowledge. *The Drama Review* continued to publish his findings when he chose to clarify elements of the work. *The Grotowski Sourcebook* contains some key texts, which are really no more than fragments or a compilation from each phase of his work, but the great majority of the articles it contains are reflections from participants. Indeed as the later phases of Grotowski's work expanded to encompass more and more participants, many international, it was primarily through their record of experience that his ideas and experiments were promulgated. As Lisa Wolford notes in her introduction to the *Grotowski Sourcebook*, these were often short-term or peripheral participants whose understanding of the principles of the investigations were necessarily limited. So the reader of his writing from this period is faced with interpreting often highly allusive fragments, delivered as lecture or verbal instruction.

The first indications that Grotowski's research was leading him outside the bounds of traditional theatre are found in *Towards a Poor Theatre*, and Kumiega's account of the paratheatrical work is illuminating in the drawing together of threads from Grotowski's theatrical work. He crystallized many thoughts over two days at conferences in New York, 12/13 December 1970; *Holiday* is the written record of these interview sessions, which did not appear in the *Drama Review* until 1973. A revamped version is included in the *Grotowski Sourcebook*, where passages from a Wroclaw lecture in October 1971 and a seminar in France in October 1972 are added. The questions which prompted these responses from Grotowski are not included, in a departure from the editorial policy of *Towards a Poor Theatre*. To add to the frustration of trying to read as a logical whole diffuse responses to disparate questions, the reader is also left trying to figure out what the question was. Alternatively, we might read this as a dynamic of the conference room, where the questions were merely pretexts, in an apparent two-way communication, for a monologue with pauses. Some of the metaphoric language of the exchange hints at the Cold War context of 1970, where the 'disarmament' of the actor seems to have been raised by the questioner, but it is followed by Grotowski through several responses; the debilitating fear, the world as less permanent, the need to abandon force (*GS* 214). Grotowski begins by announcing the death of theatre, for him at least, and demonstrates an anti-theatricalism on two levels: firstly that it is 'dishonest', 'barren' and the actor must 'pretend', echoing a familiar anti-mimesis critique of theatre itself; and, secondly, that it forces the actor to put himself in 'a false position' and 'push oneself into the limelight', which is detrimental to the actor as person. And yet, the questioners and Grotowski are reluctant to abandon the discussion of theatre, theatrical sign, creative material and techniques.

Grotowski offers a brief elucidation of the difference between the theatrical realism that Stanislavski was striving for and his own appeal to the actor: 'what do you want to do with your life; and so – do you want to hide, or to reveal yourself?' (*GS* 216). The ideology of 'appearance' and depth, which has characterized his thinking about the performer in *Towards a Poor Theatre* resurfaces here, but now the rejection of 'hiding' (*GS* 215) and the need to 'discover oneself... uncover... to unveil' (*GS* 217) are placed outside the engagement of actor and spectator. Despite the withdrawal from theatrical conventions, much of his language still uses these parameters, just as the personnel for the paratheatrical work were often drawn from audiences of *Apocalypsis cum Figuris*. Indeed many of the concerns of *Holiday* are similar to the theatrical writing of *Towards a Poor Theatre*. For example, in place of the actor's confrontation with the audience, providing a shock to force self-examination, in *Holiday* the phrase 'face to' is used repeatedly to stress the importance of confrontation within the participants themselves, as a method of creative development. The same is true of the idea of the total act, as that which channels an impulse into a performative sign. In *Holiday* the total act is no longer about filling a theatrical sign, but rather about the quality a participant should bring to 'real-time' actions (*GS* 217). The idea of the *via negativa* has been refined into the metaphor of the river and flowing water: 'I am water, pure, which flows; and then the source is *he, she* and not *I*' (*GS* 215), 'a living stream' (*GS* 220), although 'order still remains, however, as a bed of the stream' (*GS* 222). The title *Holiday*, which the *Grotowski Sourcebook* carefully helps the non-Polish reader to interpret, summons some idea of the religious context for the work, as does Grotowski's audacious equating of his quest with the New Testament wilderness wanderers. However, there is also a broadening of the religious frame of reference from the Judaeo- Christian. This is accompanied by a concomitant broadening of approach in practice, as Grotowski departs from what Auslander has called, after Derrida, 'theological' theatre, with an absent creator who is represented in regulated signs (Auslander 1997). Grotowski's writing in *Holiday* continues to espouse the idea of an authenticating 'living presence' in his work, although the signs are no longer theatrical as such.

The paratheatrical work that was developed at the Laboratory by members, old and new, during the early 1970s can be sensed here, but more clearly visible is the through-line to Grotowski's individual work in Theatre of Sources. The paratheatrical work, although it involved an increased engagement of members of the group as leaders, was not 'collective creation' as one questioner implies. The phrase 'collective creation' alluded to those groups, like the Living Theatre, who chose to devise work collaboratively. Grotowski is scathing about the idea that a group can have a 'collective director', and dismisses this way of working as merely 'dictatorship exercised by the group' (*TPT* 222). This epithet, the dictatorial director, echoes the darker suspicions he harboured about his role as director in *Towards a Poor Theatre* and implies the degree of change he envisages in his work of meeting 'our kind'. There is also a new idea, at least a newly-formed assumption, that of shared physical origin. This assumption underlies the research that Grotowski undertook for the next 20 years through Theatre of Sources, Objective Drama, and Art as a Vehicle:

> If one carries one's sincerity to the limit, crossing the barriers of the possible, or admissible, and if that sincerity does not confine itself to words, but reveals the human being totally, it – paradoxically – becomes the incarnation of the total man with all his past and future history. It is then superfluous to go to the trouble of analysing whether – and how – there exists a collective area of myth, an archetype. That area exists naturally, when our revelation, our act, reaches far enough, and if it is concrete. (*GS* 222)

Here is the familiar call for revelation of the self, but now not for the benefit of, or on behalf of, an audience. Grotowski also indicates the end of his confrontation with the collective myths of Polish culture. The predication of the realm of archetype as naturally preexistent, rather than a construct of a social order, and of its accessibility through concrete physical action are the two assumptions that all further process is to be based upon.

The next significant phase of work on the Theatre of Sources demonstrates these assumptions and the quest built upon them. The text, 'Theatre of Sources', is one of the most manipulated in the *Grotowski Sourcebook* version. Gathered from selected fragments written before and after the project, both in planning and in experience, the text was generated for the book in 1997. It is not possible, therefore, to attempt to follow the minutiae of developments in the work.[10] Grotowski is at pains to point out that the intercultural phase which began with Theatre of Sources, was not a search for the sources of theatre, but that he was using the word theatre as a metaphor:

Our whole space, both indoor and outdoor, became the 'theatre of events,' in the same way it is said about a 'theatre of war.' In this sense, we can speak about Theatre of Sources. (*GS* 264)

This was somewhat disingenuous since the various international foundations, the Rockefeller, the National University of Mexico and the Theatre Research Center in Milan, were not funding anthropological work. Grotowski himself muddied the waters by acknowledging that he was not interested in forms from the meditative traditions, but rather active forms and 'persons who have a natural inclination toward performative behaviour in the work, englobing the impulses of the body and accepting the awake senses' (*GS* 259). The press release on Theatre of Sources calls it an 'elementary dramatic phenomenon' (Grotowski 1980, 19). The conflict between the insistence that 'theatre' is used here only as a metaphor, and Grotowski's abiding concern with performance, is insoluble. The choice of participants, including Haitian voodoo practitioners, a Bengal Baul yogin-bard, and a Huichol Mexican reflect this paradox. They are not just exponents of traditions of ritual, religious or ceremonial activity in which they are active themselves. Grotowski redefines 'dramatic' and 'performative', arguing that his interest extends to their activity only within a limited definition of the dramatic as 'related to the organism in action, to the drive, to the organicity; we can say they are performative' (*GS* 257). This sense of 'performative' is made to mean only 'active'. Yet in their 'traditional' culture their activity, to be a full or total act, requires witnesses or participants who are less active, and so these practitioners are also 'performative' in the sense of the word popularized by Schechner.[11] Theatre here is not merely a metaphor for the arena in which the activity occurs, but summons for the reader an associative context of the theatrical for interpreting the work Grotowski is describing. The distinction that Grotowski is trying to draw between a search for the sources of theatre and the sources of 'performative' behaviour common to all cultures appears to be almost too fine. Similarly he finds it difficult in his writing to keep clear the desire to find a unifying source of bodily knowledge –

There is a point which is anterior to differences, in other words the influence of social context; there are beginnings. These are ever present in us. They are like forgotten knowledge. They are 'knocking at the gates' (Grotowski 1980, 5)

– from his assertion that the practical research does not offer 'solutions which are either global or for all . . . if it is to be fertile, culture must be diverse and that a uniform culture is moribund' (*ibid*. 5).

Although Grotowski's work is the search for actions which precede difference, rather than a process of creating hybrid forms, and despite his ascetic approach (of which lack of published results is part and parcel – the absence of saleable commodity from the research), there is still the tinge of political and cultural appropriation to the work. This arises partly because of the sources of funding for the projects are primarily Euro-American: Grotowski makes no secret that this is his research and the participants function as resource material. He even suggests that they make regular trips home so that they can maintain 'some kind of autonomy face to me . . face to the person who is programming this work in a firm way' (*GS* 256). The sense of appropriation also occurs because of the ideology that, in the very choice of participants, constructs these traditions of ritual as closer to the 'origin' and the primal. There is a fetishization of the work of these practitioners as 'pure', as opposed to corrupted for show to others like tourists, and not subject to its own history and the contingencies of cultural development.[12] Grotowski also fails to acknowledge that this kind of interchange and intervention is exactly the sort of cultural event that moulds tradition and will form part of the history of the 'source' and its development. That he suspects this is hinted at by his insistence that specialists work with the group for short periods only to prevent their corruption into 'some kind of professional of Theatre of Sources' (*GS* 256).

When Grotowski helped to compile the texts generated before and during the project into the chapter in the *Grotowski Sourcebook*, he structured the whole to begin and end with autobiography. This is a rare glimpse into his personal world of reference, which concentrates on childhood anecdotes. He carries an interest in young people in all of his work, both in production and outside. His rhetoric in this chapter equates the non-habitual way of behaving and being in the world with the simplicity of the child, who discovers everything for the first time (*GS* 259/263). There was a developing idea of pedagogy in the Theatre of Sources work, when the primary, childlike elements that the intercultural staff had discovered were tested on the uninitiated. The students were 'confronted' with the work, in an echo of the spectator position from the theatre of productions period and they were taught the actions by imitation (*GS* 264). The cynical observer might want to question the designation of the actions of the visiting specialists as 'childlike' or 'infantile preferences' (*GS* 263). When this work was interrupted at the beginning of 1982 by the imposition of martial law in Poland and Grotowski went into exile in America, he was forced even further into a pedagogic role in his retreat at University of California-Irvine. The application for funding purported to be aiming to find a type of performance 'before the separation between art and rite, and between the spectacular and the participatory' (*GS* 287). The search for anterior physical connections was put to one side and the training of groups of participants taken up through this imitative learning.

The centrality of pedagogy to Grotowski's later work is clear from the surprisingly titled, 'Performer'. This appeared in written form in May 1987 as one of the first booklets from the Grotowski Workcentre in Pontedera, Italy, where he relocated at the end of 1985. This performer was not an actor, but 'a man of action . . . a doer, a priest, a warrior' (*GS* 374). Grotowski uses the lure of the theatrical to set up paradoxical challenges to the reader. There is the surpassing of 'aesthetic genres' and a return to ritual. This overturns what Grotowski was most insistent about during the Theatre of Sources work, that there would be no recreation of ritual. And yet ritual is not really what this work is about. As the talk progresses, the fourth section discusses a way to rediscover 'an ancient corporality', not through ritual means but through the reconstruction of details, which leaves the performer neither 'in the character nor in the non-character' (*GS* 376).[13] This work sees the return of the body/essence split which requires osmosis, that osmosis the 'Performer' must search for. There is also the return of the idea of the 'secure partner' from the production work, which is here presented as the 'part of us who looks on'. The role of the pedagogue, Grotowski's role, is twofold: to be the 'looking presence', which mirrors the self-regard that the student needs to develop, and also to be the one who says 'Do it' to the apprentice.[14] However, there is a considerable difference in this development of the teacher and apprentice paradigm, from the pedagogy of the production work. In the latter, Grotowski was always in the role of the director, operating in a different sphere to the performer. In this manifestation of 'Performer' it is implied that, through the learning process, the apprentice will become of the same order as the teacher, and will learn the craft of teaching.

In this role of teacher, one of control but not dominance, Grotowski seems to have settled his tussle with the dark side of his nature as expressed in earlier writings. There is room for passivity, as indicated by the passive verbs of his definition:

> A teacher – as in the crafts – is someone through whom the teaching is passing; the teaching should be received, but the manner for the apprentice to rediscover it can only be personal. (*GS* 374)

There is also openness and wry humour, 'how does the teacher himself come to know the teaching? By initiation, or by theft' (*GS* 374). The whole chapter is addressed as though to an audience of students, with warnings, jokes and advice, in a tone that is quite different to the 'Statement of Principles' of *Towards a Poor Theatre*. There is a brief editorial comment at the end of the piece, most likely from Richards, that the phenomenon of 'Performer' should not be linked to actual Workcentre participants. 'The matter is rather of the case of apprenticeship which, in all the activity of "teacher of *Performer*" occurs very rarely' (*GS* 378). That apprenticeship is one that Richards himself pursued and which he documented in *At Work with Grotowski on Physical Actions*. At the end of this book there is a poignant chapter in which Grotowski reviews his life's work and reflects on what he considers to be, and indeed was, the last section of his work, 'the point of arrival' (Richards 1995, 121).

Grotowski returned to methods which might well offer much to the devizing or interpretative actor in rehearsal, and used them to operate independently as a form in themselves. The ultimate question I return to in this chapter is not Barba's 'what is the point of watching?' but 'what is the point of doing?'. In the Theatre of Sources there was a clear goal in pursuing 'movement which is repose', that of developing an altered consciousness: 'you feel as if everything is part of the great flow of things and your body begins to feel it . . . it is the flow of all things around that carries you, but at the same time you feel that something is coming out of you too' (*GS* 262). But that work was part of the cultural moment of the mid-1970s. By the 1990s, Grotowski's attention had turned again to the 'other extremity of the same chain' as productions. The Workcentre was simultaneously developing the 'formation (in the sense of permanent education) in the field of song, of text, of physical actions, of the "plastic" and "physical" exercises for actors', and Art as a Vehicle, where 'the impact on the doer is the result. But this result is not the content;

the content is the passage from the heavy to the subtle' in the performer's work (Richards 1995, 121,125). It seems quite appropriate that these two contradictory impulses lived side by side in Grotowski's work to the end, and that his rhetoric could never resolve them, moving terms back and forth, from theatre and an anti-theatricalism expressed as ritualized behaviour, and using each side of the equation as metaphor for the other until the end.

Primary Sources

Barba, E. (1999) *Land of Ashes and Diamonds* (Aberystwyth: Black Mountain Press).

Grotowski, J. (1967) 'He Wasn't Entirely Himself', *Flourish*, 14.

—(1969) *Towards a Poor Theatre* (London: Methuen).

—(1980) 'The Laboratory Theatre, 20 Years After: A Working Hypothesis', *Polish Perspectives*, 23.5, 31–40.

—(1980) 'Wandering towards a Theatre of Sources', *Polish Philosophical Quarterly*, 7.2, 11–23.

—(1995) 'From the Theatre Company to Art as Vehicle', in Richards, *op. cit.*, 115–35.

—(1996) 'Orient/Occident' in P. Pavis (ed.), *The Intercultural Performance Reader* (New York: Routledge).

Richards, T. (1995) *At Work With Grotowski on Physical Actions* (London: Routledge).

Schechner, R. and Wolford, L. (1997) *The Grotowski Sourcebook* (London: Routledge).

Secondary Sources

Auslander, P. (1997) *From Acting to Performance* (London: Routledge).

Ben Chaim, D. (1984) *Distance in the Theatre: The Aesthetics of Audience Response* (Ann Arbor: UMI Research Press).

Bennett, S. (1990) *Theatre Audiences* (London: Routledge).

Braun, K. (1996) *A History of Polish Theatre, 1939–1989: Spheres of Captivity and Freedom* (Westport, Conn.: Greenwood Press).

Grotowski, J. (1969) ' "I said Yes to the Past" ', *Village Voice*, 23 January, 41–42.

—(1996) 'A Kind of Volcano' in J. Needleman and G. Baker (eds), *Gurdjieff: Essays and Reflections on the Man and His Teachings* (New York: Continuum) 87–106.

—(1997) 'Tu es le fils de quelqu'un', *Drama Review*, 31.3, 30–41; revised version in Schechner and Wolford *op. cit.*, 292–303.

Kumiega, J. (1987) *The Theatre of Grotowski* (London: Methuen).

Osinski, Z. and Burzynski, T. (1979) *Grotowski's Laboratory* (Warsaw: Interpress).

Temkine, R. (1972) *Grotowski* (New York: Avon).

Wolford, L. (1996) *Grotowski's Objective Drama Research* (Jackson: University Press of Mississippi).

6

Boal's Theoretical History

Augusto Boal is probably the most influential of contemporary theoretical practitioners, and his books have become essential reading for a new theatre of commitment, whether in aspiration or in practice. Boal advocates what is in many respects a blameless theatre, in which all are participants rather than practitioners and receptors and are involved in an effort of social progress. The promise entailed is that of an absence of futility, which is a sense that may all too easily accompany many initiatives in performance or in other arts, and there is a comforting geniality to much of his writing which suggests that the theatre has the potential always to be kind, no matter what the circumstances. This in itself poses an interesting contrast to the definitions advanced by Artaud and Grotowski, discussed in the last two chapters, and Boal's popular theatre games convey a world of inclusion notably absent from the philosophies of these two practitioners. Similarly, *Games for Actors and Non-actors* is hardly a title which conjures up the systematic world of Stanislavski, with its assumptions of an institutional professionalism for actors in specialized schools, and neither *mise-en-scène* nor the arts of the director are apparently of the slightest concern to Boal. His initiative, then, may be thought to be timely, not just in the context of Latin American deprivation, but also in those contexts which have been found for the theatre of the oppressed in North America and in Europe, which demand a focus for activity and a purpose fundamentally separate from aesthetic aspirations.

The translation of Boal's theory and practice to these later contexts has been the subject of a number of studies, and connects firmly with traditions of dramatherapy and applied drama which have generally not achieved such prominence within theatre studies as his writings.[1] There is, unfortunately, still no detailed study of the origins of Boal's work in the 1960s in Brazil and (briefly) in Peru, and the narrative references to origins and development in Boal's own writings are often made in passing, or take the form of selective and illustrative story-telling, or anecdote.[2] Understandably, for someone who has been active in both the Americas and in Europe, Boal's writings have been published in several languages, and it is not always immediately clear from which language they have been translated into their English version. The theatre of the oppressed is Boal's presiding and relatively flexible concept; and while its permutations over the years in different contexts are tracked in *The Rainbow of Desire* and *Legislative Theatre*, its theoretical basis is presented in the early *Theatre of the Oppressed*, a book with which many find it easy to sympathize and which few find easy to read. Its style is distinctly unlike his later style, and has no pretensions to being reader-friendly or pragmatic in its immediate issue. This chapter will concentrate almost exclusively on reading that volume, because of its difficulty and because it is the definitive theoretical introduction to the theatre of the oppressed.

Theatre of the Oppressed is a complicated work for a number of reasons. It is not, as might have been presumed, a description by Boal of a theatre made by the oppressed, a kind of documentation of a phenomenon appropriate to a revolutionary period. Elements of documentation do appear, but they occur towards the close of the book, as a set of schematic or theoretical propositions about a possible practice, or as the account of the production history of a relatively conventional theatre company, the Arena Theatre of São Paolo. So within the book the theatre of the oppressed appears either as a possibility or as a necessity, and the critical arguments constitute a kind of charter for its existence, which Boal himself is either prepared to fulfil or to encourage others to do so. The chapters of which it is composed are disparate, and were written at different times. The earliest is apparently that on Machiavelli, which took shape in 1962 as 'an introduction to the performance of *Mandragola*, a comedy by Machiavelli, produced by the Arena Theatre of São Paolo in 1962–63' under Boal's direction (*Theatre of the Oppressed* = TO 52). The next in date is apparently the last, a series of articles on the work of the Arena Theatre over a decade written in 1966 to accompany another production, a play composed by Boal and Gianfrancesco Guarnieri (*TO* 158). The date of composition of the other chapters is not given, but that of chapter 4 'Poetics of the Oppressed' plainly comes after August 1973 when the work in Peru on which it is based took place. The 'Foreword' is signed in July 1974, and this suggests not only that the remaining theoretical chapters 1 and 3 were written in the same period specifically for (and to create) the book, but that the experience in Peru was formative. By this time Boal was in exile, after imprisonment in 1971 following the second Brazilian coup of 1968; so *Theatre of the Oppressed* has in some crucial respects a similar genesis to Paolo Freire's *Pedagogy of the Oppressed*, as an intense theoretical work of conviction by an exiled member of the intelligentsia.[3]

The theatre of the oppressed appears as both a product of Boal's growing conviction and a theoretical construct drawn from what Boal himself terms 'experiments' (*TO* 170) in Peru in 1973. It has, in those respects, all the hallmarks of a classic theoretical practice in the twentieth-century mode, and its written charter (or charters, if we include as we should the subsequent volumes) does not substantially help in tracing its evolution either as a practice or as an idea. Some indications in the later volumes would seem to confirm 1973 as the birth of the theoretical entity. At the opening of *The Rainbow of Desire* Boal describes 'how Forum Theatre was born' (*Rainbow of Desire = RD* 7), and states plainly that it came from the disruption of a presentation of 'a new form of theatre, which I named *simultaneous dramaturgy*', and which he introduced in Peru in 1973 (*RD* 3). Yet the same volume, in its autobiographical account of Boal's 'long journey', begins with attention to a period some ten years earlier, 'at the start of the 1960s', when Boal 'travelled extensively' with the Arena Theatre 'to some of the most poverty-stricken parts of Brazil: the interior of São Paolo, the North-East...' (*RD* 1).[4] Boal provides an extremely hazy impression of the work at that time – 'musical plays' and 'agit-prop' are the most significant hints (*RD* 2–3) – and his account of what he portrays as a formative incident, with a local man called Virgilio, is melded with the birth of Forum Theatre ten years later. More distinct indications arise in relation to the essay 'Categories of Popular Theatre' published in *Legislative Theatre* (= *LT* 211–46), but which Boal confusingly dates to both 1971 and 1973 (*LT* 211). The fourth and final category of popular theatre given there is 'Newspaper Theatre', and Boal dates its inception to the period following the second Brazilian coup in 1968 (*LT* 234). The essay as a whole shows no awareness of the theatre of the oppressed as a concept; but Newspaper Theatre occurs as one of several forms of 'The Theater as Discourse' in *Theatre of the Oppressed*, where it is introduced as a practice of the Arena Theatre in Brazil before Boal's exile. So the genesis is hazy, and Boal's terse account in *Legislative Theatre* leaves a great deal unexplained about that period in Peru in the few weeks of August 1973, and the theoretical practice that emerges from the grand historical scheme in *Theatre of the Oppressed*:

> The Theatre of the Oppressed started its development during the cruellest phase of the Brazilian dictatorship; its first manifestation was the Newspaper Theatre. It continued through various dictatorial Latin American regimes, during which time some of its other forms emerged – Forum Theatre, Invisible Theatre, Image Theatre (1971–76). (*LT* 4–5)

The theatre of the oppressed loses its particularity very early in the book that bears its name. The 'Foreword' makes it clear that this is not just some special kind of theatre practice in which we might take an interest, or which we might be inclined to support, but is effectively *the* form that theatre should take in the present. This is achieved in two complementary ways. In the first paragraphs of the 'Foreword' Boal asserts that 'all theater is necessarily political, because all the activities of man are political and theater is one of them', and politics and 'necessity' combine in an imperative of 'liberation' in which the theatre is an essential 'weapon' for which those opposed to the ruling classes must 'fight'.[5] So within three short paragraphs, and in under one hundred words, the theatre's duty has been bluntly defined:

> the theatre can also be a weapon for liberation. For that, it is necessary to create appropriate theatrical forms. Change is imperative.

What this appropriate theatrical form will be is established by the second means, which is an historical scheme which occupies the rest of the 'Foreword'. This scheme sees theatre passing from the possession of the people to the aristocracy and then to the bourgeoisie and back to the people in Brecht and in current developments in Latin America. Apart from the recourse to class, the most emotive concept is that of 'divisions', 'barriers', 'separation', all introduced by the aristocracy and their inheritors the bourgeoisie into a world of original unity, freedom and openness:

> 'Theater' was the people singing freely in the open air; the theatrical performance was created by and for the people, and could thus be called dithyrambic song. It was a celebration in which all could participate freely. Then came the aristocracy and established divisions...

This is, of course, a foundation myth for theatre of innocence corrupted, which goes well with a charter for current activity; the suggestion of deprivation of an original right permits the idea of a celebratory restoration, at the same time as it validates the contemporary activity by reference to the past. The work of the Arena Theater is in fact hidden in the 'Foreword' under a reference to (the later chapter in the book) 'Experiments with the People's Theater in Peru'; these experiments represent 'what is happening at present in Latin America'; what is happening in Latin America is 'what was lacking to complete the cycle' of return to an ideal, unitary origin. Particularity is subsumed in the greater theoretical picture, in which this activity is no less than 'the conquest of the means of theatrical production'. If the Arena is hidden in these formulations, then so is Boal, who merely puts his name at the close to a witnessing of theoretical truth.

The 'Foreword' is followed by an oracle in three pronouncements from the same source, which is Arnold Hauser's Marxist social history of art, a remarkable and influential work published after the end of the second great war. In the second of the quotations given by Boal, Hauser refers to the idea that tragedy '"owed its origin to the separation of the choir-leader from the choir, which turned collective performance of songs into dramatic dialogue..."'.[6] It would seem to be the case that Hauser's short statement is the authority for Boal's important theoretical concept of separation, division and barrier, although Hauser writes of the choir-leader and the choir and the creation of dialogue, while Boal alters or adjusts this into the aristocratic division between those who 'remain seated, receptive, passive' and those who 'go to the stage and only they will be able to act' (*TO* 'Foreword'). Similarly, in the third quotation Hauser writes of aristocracy retaining power in the 'imperialist democracy' of Athens. Boal's vision is significantly different, and suggests a scheme in which 'the people' were origin-

ally both free and creative and celebratory: 'Then came the aristocracy and established divisions' (*TO* 'Foreword').

Boal's vision undoubtedly relies on the notion of primitive communism, an idea which is particularly associated with Engels's *The
Origin of the Family, Private Property and the State* and provides a
foundation myth for modern communism, which can be seen to be
restoring an original and ideal condition (Engels 1972). Boal's historical scheme for the theatre is also – relatively crudely – Marxist,
allowing for significant moments of alienation and socioeconomic
development and organization in antiquity and in the advent of the
bourgeoisie. But it is a Marxism that would with great difficulty be
assigned to Marx, whose analyses of history in, for example, *The
German Ideology* like those of Engels allowed for a far greater complexity in social and economic evolution. It would also appear from
Boal's 'Foreword' that he is reliant on a relatively simple version of
the Marxist idea of base (or infrastructure) and superstructure, in
which base refers to dominant socioeconomic relations between
classes, themselves subject to change through class struggle, and
superstructure refers to ideology and so to art as a reflection of the
base. Boal uses the terms 'dominant ideology' and 'superstructures'
in the 'Foreword', with the latter paired or contrasted with 'social
forces' (or base). Boal's concluding reference to 'the conquest of the
means of theatrical production', of course, adds the term 'theatrical'
to a standard description of the objectives facing the proletariat in
Marxist thought. What is slightly odd here is the status of the
theatre in relation to theory; what Boal outlines in the 'Foreword'
is not just a theoretical scheme for the evolution of the theatre, but
also a historical scheme for the evolution of theatrical theory. So
there are two components of the superstructure, theatre and theory,
and the *'poetics of the oppressed'* (or the theory) is as much a necessary
result of historical evolution as is the practice of such a theatre. This
strongly suggests the Marxist notion of praxis, which is supposedly
a dialectical relationship between revolutionary theory and action,
and also suggests that a more accurate title for the book might well
be *Poetics of the Theatre of the Oppressed*.

Boal's summary in his 'Introduction' of ancient Greek contributions to a debate on the nature and value of poetry provides apparent quotations which are actually paraphrases. The style here is
affable and relatively casual, but the context is a little confusing.
Boal's major concern seems to be that of 'the relations between
theater and politics', and he insists on a continuity since Aristotle

of a division of 'themes and arguments', those that assert that art is 'pure contemplation', and those that find it to be political. But in the second paragraph, that in which the apparent quotations are made, his attention shifts to a different division (of themes and arguments):

> Should art educate, inform, organize, influence, incite to action, or should it simply be an object of pleasure?

Education, information, organization and influence might all be included in a doctrine of art as contemplation quite as much as pleasure, which confuses the supposed parallel between the two divisions as Boal summarizes them. The situation is not helped by a rather arbitrary selection and ordering of the figures for quotation: Aristophanes is a comic dramatist, Plato is a philosopher, Eratosthenes a scholar of comedy, and Strabo an historian and geographer who lived in the Roman period, some five hundred years after Aristophanes.

But a rather confusing prelude gives way to a firm statement of the terms of the enquiry:

> Is the relation of art to the spectator something that can be diversely interpreted, or, on the contrary, does it rigorously obey certain laws that make art either a purely contemplative phenomenon or a deeply political one?

Boal is suggesting here, as an alternative to open speculation, the idea that passivity in the spectator ('contemplative') is the creation of 'certain laws' which are presumed to govern all the artistic phenomena of a given society. The same laws will produce the contrary to this contemplative state in different circumstances, and the reference to the spectator makes it probable that 'political' here must involve action. Presumably, the theatre will take either a 'contemplative' or a 'political' form according to its place in the superstructure of a given society, and will appear as such in the ideological theory that accompanies it. The 'laws' that command rigorous obedience from the theatre are presumably those that relate superstructure to base, art or ideology to socioeconomic reality, and they will achieve different results in different circumstances. The confusing component in this proposition, as Boal drafts it, is that it contains two versions of the political. If the obedience to 'certain laws' is demonstrable, then the theatre will always (have) exist(ed) in relation to politics, whether the form it takes is contemplative or not. This would confirm Boal's statement of purpose in the opening of the 'Foreword': 'This book aims to show that all theater is necessarily political...'. But that is then confusing, because it leaves the other use of 'political' – for a form of theatre in some way opposed to 'contemplative' – dislodged from a clear or helpful definition. A strict interpretation of Boal's formula would have to insist that the theatre can only be 'political' in this second sense when the 'laws' allow it to be so, since it must 'rigorously obey' them. This is inevitably problematic, since it suggests determinism rather than active choice. It would also seem to demand a close analysis of what those laws are, and how they operate.

Boal on Aristotle

The role of theory in the tight grip of this relationship between base and superstructure is not at all clear; yet it is theory with which Boal is largely concerned, since he turns our attention directly to Aristotle. For his interpretation of Aristotle, Boal relies largely on works by Aristotle other than the *Poetics* and on the critical account by Butcher. The long chapter 'Aristotle's Coercive System of Tragedy' opens with a discussion of the key concept of 'mimesis', but the discussion is preceded by a small complex of associations around Aristotle's theory and his status. Boal concludes his 'Introduction' with a reference to 'the Aristotelian theater', and includes the phrase 'coercive system of tragedy' in the title of his first chapter. The impression given in these phrases is of a prescriptive role for Aristotle in relation to Greek (or Athenian) theatre practice, a vision which would perhaps begin to answer the question about Boal's view of the ideological role of theory. To approximate, the theory will then be the ideological means by which the class structure and the class struggle is guided into artistic practice. If that is the case, theory becomes a necessary instrument of the 'laws' that determine the relationship between base and superstructure, and result in the particular configuration of art (or theatre) at a given time, or in given socioeconomic conditions. As part of a 'dominant ideology', theory will be at the service of the 'ruling classes' (Boal's terms in his 'Foreword'). This instrumental function performed by theory would then be the hidden factor of reactionary 'change' in Boal's 'Foreword':

the ruling classes strive to take permanent hold of the theater and utilize it as a tool for domination. In so doing, they change the very concept of what 'theater' is. (*TO* 'Foreword')

Aristotle, according to Boal, fits firmly into this picture:

Aristotle constructs the first, extremely powerful poetic-political system for intimidation of the spectator, for elimination of the 'bad' or illegal tendencies of the audience. (*TO* 'Introduction')

Under this prescriptive influence of a theory serving the interests of the ruling classes, art is coerced (as presentation and as reception) into itself becoming 'a tool for domination'.

This powerful function for Aristotle in an apparatus of ideological coercion is unfortunately reliant on a significant omission by Boal, which is that Aristotle was writing virtually a century after the democratic tragedy which he was analysing. By the time the *Poetics* may have become known through teaching (it was not published as a text in antiquity), tragedy was in decline, and immediately after his death the Athenian state lost its independence. If the *Poetics* was prescriptive in intention, it had little opportunity to put this prescription into effect, and any observations Aristotle made about tragedy were attempted insights into the operation of an artform established well before his own birth. Despite his seemingly detailed account of Greek philosophy before Aristotle, Boal also fails to make clear from the beginning that Aristotle inherited the concept of *mimesis* from Plato, a point which is no more than implicit in Boal's paraphrase of Plato's view of imitation in his 'Introduction'. In the *Poetics*, Aristotle states that imitation is of things or of human actions, and that it is a natural activity (for human beings). He does not state that art imitates nature, and so there is no basis in the *Poetics* for asserting that this supposedly Aristotelian statement ' "Art imitates nature" actually means: "Art re-creates the creative principles of created things." ' (*TO* 1). Both Aristotle and any hope of meaning vanish, to little purpose, into this vortex of repetition.

The account of the early Greek philosophers that follows is puzzling because it seems to lack relevance, and the general chronology is extremely vague and confusing.[7] Nor is it obvious why Zeno's two stories of Achilles and the tortoise and the unending flight of the arrow 'are worth remembering' according to Boal (*TO* 4–5), unless it is as intriguing fallacies. It is, in fact, difficult to see why or how Boal's survey of Greek philosophy might clarify Aristotle's theory of dramaturgy or reception, even in the form that Boal represents it. The logic of the argument begins to reappear in the section 'What is the meaning of "Imitation"?', when Boal concentrates on Aristotle's belief in what he terms 'perfection'. If 'perfection' is understood as a tendency to come to completion or fulfilment, then the idea may be helpful in relation to the development of tragedy. But it does not mean that Aristotle anywhere stated that to imitate was to 'recreate that internal movement of things toward their perfection' (*TO* 8). Nor is it the case that Aristotle stated that 'the artist must imitate men "as they should be" and not as they are' (*TO* 8). What Aristotle proposes, early in the *Poetics*, is that all imitation of humans in action must be of those who are better or worse than we are, or of those who are of the same sort; and that tragedy imitates people who are better than contemporary people, as comedy imitates those who are worse (Aristotle 1996, 5). Later in the *Poetics* Aristotle reports the anecdote that Sophocles said that he portrayed men as they should be, Euripides men as they are, which may have become amalgamated with the earlier statements in Boal's mind (Aristotle 1996, 43).

The *Theatre of the Oppressed* is very hard to follow because of this process of amalgamation, synthesis, reformulation and ultimately misrepresentation of Aristotle's writings, from which summaries are repeatedly given without reference to any particular source. The influence of the commentator Butcher is extremely strong, and that of (statements or ideas in) the text of the *Poetics* is distinctly weak. In the section 'What, then, is the Purpose of Art and Science?' Boal returns to his idea of ' "re-creating the creative principle" ' which he attributed to Aristotle, and suggests that for Aristotle 'the purpose of art and science' is 'to correct the faults of nature, by using the suggestions of nature itself' (*TO* 9). What this means, Boal claims, is that the manufacture of clothing protects the skin, architecture builds bridges, medicine compensates for failing organs; and the arts are similarly corrective, like the sciences. But Aristotle's view in his work *Physics* makes a far simpler distinction: there are two kinds of human artistic skill, one of which produces what is not present in nature (for example a house or a bed), while the other imitates (what is already there): 'a skill either brings to fulfilment what nature has not accomplished, or it imitates' (*Physics* 199a). There is no place in this distinction for 're-creating the creative principles' in a work of art, or in theatre, or for a general principle of correcting the faults of nature in and through artistic works: these are imitative, as far as Aristotle is concerned.

The representation of Aristotelian poetics that comes in the next few sections is far from anything embraced by Aristotle's *Poetics*, and distorts the plainer statements of the *Nicomachean Ethics*, the work to which Boal refers as a source in his 'Introduction'. Happiness in the *Ethics* is an activity, and the ultimate happiness is contemplation, as one might expect from a philosopher, so Boal's conclusions in the section on 'What is Happiness?' relate to little in the *Ethics* and to nothing in the *Poetics*. The reference to Creon and Antigone (*TO* 15) in the first of two subsequent sections on virtue is drawn from Hegel, and is not the view of Aristotle, and as Boal's supposed definition of Aristotelian poetics continues to build it becomes more and more of a fantasia. The discussion of Oedipus and 'his flaws, his vices' (*TO* 19) is bound into this strange composition, ignoring the fact that the Aristotelian *hamartia* almost certainly refers to error, an action that is a mistake. Aristotle's attitude to politics suffers from the same neglect or distortion: it is not that 'the greatest good ... is the political good' (*TO* 21), because the greatest good is that happiness which is philosophical contemplation, but that the function of politics is to achieve the greatest good. There is a similar distortion in the representation of injustice, which in the *Ethics* is a vice, a motive for personal conduct like avarice, and is not discussed as a general principle in relation to equality. The climax of this misconstruction of a thing called Aristotle is then achieved: 'In the final analysis, happiness consists in obeying the laws. This is Aristotle's message, clearly spelled out.' Not particularly clearly, and certainly not by Aristotle, who in the *Poetics* – which appears in almost no direct quotations in Boal's fantasia – is hardly ever clear.

The reference to an Aristotelian system is hopeless, because Aristotle offers an analysis in the *Poetics* of dramaturgy (the components and composition of tragedy as an imitation) and of reception, not a system. But Boal's imaginative construction allows him to give a particular purpose to the *catharsis* of fear and pity and related emotions to which Aristotle draws attention in the *Poetics*. Boal's interpretation of *catharsis* is specifically attributed to his major source, Butcher, and includes the perception that *catharsis* implies both purification and purgation (*TO* 28–30). But Boal is obstinate in his refusal to read Aristotle without reformulation, and insists that what is purged or purified from the spectators of a tragedy must be different from pity or fear: 'Pity and fear have never been vices or weaknesses or errors and, therefore, never need to be eliminated or purged' (*TO* 31). This is like saying that what Aristotle says is not what Aristotle says, rather than offering an interpretation. Pity and fear are the primary emotions unleashed by the action of a tragedy in the spectators, and yet the artform of tragedy is salutary because in some way it purges the spectators of them: that is a rough summary of Aristotle. The purgation may produce pleasure, which Aristotle identifies as the purpose of tragedy, or it may justify tragedy. Pity and fear are two prominent emotions that can be manipulated by orators in persuading the people to take decisions: that much is apparent from Aristotle's *Rhetoric*, or study of the art of public speaking. In the *Poetics*, Aristotle is mounting a defence of tragedy and of imitation in general from its condemnation by Plato. For this reason he asserts that imitation is natural, and it may be that a purgation of powerful emotions such as pity and fear, which can unduly influence public decisions, allows tragedy to have a counteracting status to manipulative public speaking, which Plato despised. Aristotle never states his case fully or explicitly; but that is a possible interpretation of what he wrote.[8]

Boal achieves his own desired conclusions by way of his own definitions, which are given the dignity of quotation marks in their substitution for Aristotle. The fundamental conclusion depends on the invention of a missing emotion, which is not pity or fear, but which is mysteriously 'something *directed against the laws*'. This hidden motive Boal ascribes both to the characters and the spectators of Greek tragedy, and he implicitly associates it with the concept of *hamartia* as 'a social fault, a political deficiency' (*TO* 32). That association is made explicit in the following section, 'A Short Glossary of Simple Words', and the following sections aim to secure the proposition that the spectator identifies or 'empathizes' with the character and so follows the same course as the character in the action of the play. By this means the spectator '*is purified of the antisocial characteristic* which he sees in himself' (*TO* 40). Empathy, incidentally, is not an Aristotelian term, who discusses reception only implicitly and by oblique reference to the concept of *catharsis*.

Did Greek tragedy work like this? It is very difficult to say, since Aristotle is by any standards a remote and obscure interpretation of it, and Boal signally fails to discuss Aristotle's *Poetics* through many complex and tortuous pages. But Boal is confident that Aristotle (or tragedy?) is a 'coercive system', and that it – the theoretical system which is in some strange sense also plays, dramas, films – 'survived and has continued to be utilized down to our own time' (*TO* 40). That it 'cannot be utilized by revolutionary groups *during* revolutionary periods' (*TO* 46) is one obvious conclusion, which disregards the fact that tragedy was established and developed during a revolutionary period at Athens. The conclusive attribution of stability (of all things) to tragedy is extraordinary:

> In fact, only more or less stable societies, ethically defined, can offer a scale of values which would make it possible for the system to function. During a 'cultural revolution', in which all values are being formed or questioned, the system cannot be applied. (*TO* 46)

By all consensus, and by almost any standards, Athens was in exactly that state of 'cultural revolution' during the period in which tragedy developed and flourished.[9] But the function of 'Aristotle' and Greek tragedy in this discourse is clear: 'it is designed to bridle the individual, to adjust him to what pre-exists' (*TO* 47). The mention of the 'individual', when the preliminary discussion has been of classes, is interesting here, and will appear more transparently in later writings and formulations. The concluding theoretical moral is absolute, because it has to a large extent dictated the long presentation that has preceded it:

> if . . . we want to stimulate the spectator to transform his society, to engage in revolutionary action, we will have to seek another poetics! (*TO* 47)

Boal on Machiavelli and Shakespeare

Towards the end of his long chapter on Aristotle, Boal projects a scheme for the continuity of what he has advanced as the Aristotelian pattern for theatre in 'Different Types of Conflict: Hamartia and Social Ethos'. The projection includes two Greek tragedies, the morality play *Everyman* of about 1500 AD, a pairing of *La Dame aux camélias* by Dumas (1852) and *An Enemy of the People* by Ibsen (1882), and *Don Quixote* by Cervantes (1605–15). These works are given as examples of the 'modifications' of the Aristotelian system 'introduced by new societies', and 'capitalism' and 'the bourgeoisie' are introduced to the argument as descriptions of at least one major aspect of the 'new societies' (*TO* 44–5). The chapter on Machiavelli which follows seems designed, in the short introduction which Boal makes to it, to trace some of 'the transformations undergone by the theater under bourgeois direction' (*TO* 52), despite the general assertions of the continuity of the Aristotelian 'system'. Machiavelli, perhaps because his name is so notorious, is scarcely placed historically by Boal except in the broadest terms, and the first section of the essay written in 1962 concentrates for the most part on the middle ages and feudalism ('The Feudal Abstraction') as a precursor to bourgeois values and society. The opening paragraph (*TO* 53) sketches a Marxist theory of the artist rooted in the 'social sector... which sponsors him, pays him, or consumes his work', a situation that means that 'the dominant art will always be that of the dominant class'. This would seem to prepare the ground for the presentation of Machiavelli as an artist, although the title of the full chapter is 'Machiavelli and the Poetics of *Virtù*', which classes Machiavelli as a theorist. Some few details on Machiavelli may be helpful.

Machiavelli was for the first part of his adult life a diplomat and bureaucrat in the service of the state of Florence, for some years before and after 1500. In 1512 the Florentine republic collapsed, the Medici returned as effective 'princes' of Florence, and Machiavelli came into disfavour. He was then implicated in a conspiracy against the Medici, tortured, and excluded from the city of Florence. During this period he wrote most of his major works, including *The Prince* (1513), with which he may have hoped to regain the favour of the Medici; *The Discourses* (1515–17), a study of politics and the principles governing statecraft; and *Mandragola* (1518), a comedy and the most striking of his literary works.[10] Machiavelli drew on contemporary affairs and ancient precedents in his writing, looking in particular to his own experience of political actions and to the strength of ancient Rome, notably the Roman republic rather than the empire.[11]

Any Marxist historical scheme will be searching for capital and the bourgeoisie in the origins of the modern era. Boal makes use of the terms feudalism and the Renaissance (alongside the Middle Ages), but it is doubtful if these have much economic or social value. In discussing feudalism Boal comments on 'the insignificance

– the almost total absence – of commerce' (*TO* 55), which may be an acceptable shorthand in relation to the 'feudal manor'. But a little later, at the beginning of the second section of the chapter, Boal refers to 'the development of commerce, starting as early as the eleventh century' when

> life started moving from the country to the newly founded cities, where warehouses were built and banks were established, where commercial accounting was organized and trade was centralized. The slow pace of the Middle Ages was replaced by the fast pace of the Renaissance. (*TO* 59)

It is difficult to feel confident about this picture, and consequently about the characterization of feudal art that Boal, once again following Hauser, gives. His two primary examples of feudal plays, in fact, have to be qualified immediately by a bizarre contradiction:

> It is not so strange, after all, that the two examples cited – perhaps the most typical of feudal dramaturgy – were written when the bourgeoisie was already rather well developed and strong: the content becomes clear as social contradictions become sharper. (*TO* 57)

This contradiction is written into the theory of Shakespeare's plays that Boal presents. By his documentation of 'the coming of the individualized man' (*TO* 63) Shakespeare is 'the first bourgeois dramatist' (*TO* 64) according to Boal, even though Shakespeare 'did not portray heroes who were avowedly bourgeois' (*TO* 64). This has to be advanced as a theory of symbolism, in which aristocrats and monarchs represent the bourgeois characteristics of '*virtù* and praxis'; but even that frail hypothesis is subject to the observation that the fifth acts refuse to conform to the programme:

> Shakespeare expressed the new bourgeois values which were then arising, even if legality and feudalism are the apparent victors at the end of his plays. (*TO* 63)

Shakespeare supposedly was subject to a 'dichotomy', which was that he was sympathetic with characters such as Richard III, the 'symbolic representative of the rising class', but must also 'have been inclined, consciously or not, toward the nobility that patronized him and which, after all, still retained political power' (*TO* 63). This statement picks up the thoughts in the introductory paragraph to the chapter as a whole, which are of the artist rooted in the social sector 'which sponsors him, pays him, or consumes his work', the idea that I quoted earlier. Effectively, this means that through a crude theory of symbolism Boal is proposing that we see bourgeois values emerging in Machiavelli and Shakespeare, as artists of the Renaissance period, even though the presiding power is still that of the aristocracy (or monarchy). The complexity of the social and economic 'base' is rather left out of account, although in the idea of dichotomy, the contradiction about commerce, and the statement (drawn from Hauser) that 'Queen Elizabeth was one of the greatest debtors of the English banks' (*TO* 63) Boal attempts to allow for it. The situation in Machiavelli's Florence or in contemporary Europe is no less complex. But what matters for Boal is that the period embracing both dramatists yields bourgeois characteristics in the historical scheme, which can then be seen as modifications of the Aristotelian pattern that leads forward to modernity.

These characteristics are summarized by Boal in individualism and *virtù* and praxis. *Virtù* is not actually defined very closely by Boal, but is associated with a personal achievement by the (bourgeois) individual 'which owed nothing to his fate or his fortune', while praxis summarizes his reliance on practice for achievement rather than on traditions or concepts of right and wrong (*TO* 60); both are plainly qualities of individualism. It was in the context of a production of *Mandragola* by the Arena Theatre that Boal came to these conclusions, but the commentary on the characters in the play (section three, 'Machiavelli and *Mandragola*') and the surrounding sections do little to clarify why this version of *virtù* should be associated with Machiavelli. As Boal rightly says, 'Machiavelli himself criticized the bourgeoisie of his time' (*TO* 61), and the central, thoroughly bourgeois figure of Nicia in *Mandragola* is a ludicrous and pathetic figure who is satirized mercilessly. Consequently Boal has to make other figures, notably Ligurio the parasite and Fra Timoteo the friar, represent or symbolize this bourgeois value despite their lack of bourgeois status (*TO* 66–9): so, for example, Fra Timoteo is both ' "virtuous" ' and 'a symbol of the Church which makes its triumphant entry into the mercantilist era' (*TO* 69). Boal attempts to deal with this difficulty by suggesting a kind of false consciousness for Nicia – 'Like most bourgeois, he would prefer to have been born a prince or a count' (*TO* 70) – which leaves the supposedly defining and daring bourgeois characteristics in a strange state of limbo. An alternative is to put the qualities of *virtù* and praxis historically up for grabs, despite the fact that they 'were and are the two touchstones of the bourgeoisie':

> Obviously one cannot conclude from this that only he who was not a nobleman could possess *virtù* or trust in praxis, and much less that every bourgeois had necessarily to possess those qualities, under penalty of ceasing to be a bourgeois. (*TO* 61)

Nonetheless, despite all these qualifications and contradictions, the basic assertion remains untouched, because it is needed for the theoretical scheme:

> The bourgeois nature of the works of Shakespeare is not to be found in their externals at all, but only in the presentation and creation of characters endowed with *virtù* and confident in praxis. (*TO* 64)

Boal on Hegel and Brecht

Hegel was a nineteenth-century academic philosopher, many of whose influential ideas exist in reconstructions of lectures that he gave, collected as *The Philosophy of History, The Philosophy of Religion, The Philosophy of Fine Art* and *The History of Philosophy*, and a figure who had virtually no direct influence on theatre of any kind, unlike Marx. But Hegel is, in many respects, a greater presence in *Theatre of the Oppressed* than Marx, and some of his thinking appears intermittently in Boal's chapter on Aristotle, as I have noted. Towards the close of the first section of the chapter on Machiavelli we read of 'a fundamental principle of theater, which is conflict, contradiction, or some type of clash or conflict' (*TO* 57–8). This idea has only appeared briefly, and allusively, once before in Boal's argument, in a passing reference in the chapter on Aristotle to 'the creation of a conflict between the character's ethos and the ethos of the society in which he lives' (*TO* 40). As 'a fundamental principle of theater' this is distinctively Hegelian, manifested in the conflict between Creon and Antigone in Sophocles' *Antigone*, an exemplary instance for Hegel.[12] In the final section of Boal's chapter on Machiavelli,

Hegel is introduced as the saviour of the bourgeois principle in Boal's historical scheme (*TO* 73), although it is immensely difficult to see how Hegel's ideas relate to any redirection of theatre practice, even more difficult than it is to believe that Machiavelli can be associated with a 'poetics of *virtù*'. Boal gives a short summary of Hegel's doctrine of thesis–antithesis and resultant synthesis (*TO* 74), without explaining that this doctrine related to antiquity and Greek tragedy as far as Hegel was concerned as much as to any other period. The reason for this is that, apparently, Boal wished to associate Hegel with Romanticism in the theatre, a movement approximately contemporary with Hegel's life.

The problem, or the most important problem, with this scheme is that Romanticism is, according to Boal, both feudal and chivalric, and Hegel's adjustment to bourgeois values is 'a poorly disguised return to medieval abstractions, now in a theater formulated with greater theoretic precision and greater complexity' (*TO* 75).[13] Boal's Romantic theatre here is evidently and substantially a theatre of the mind, a theoretical theatre, and in a section in which he is heavily dependent once again on Hauser his examples of Romanticism include one play, Victor Hugo's *Hernani* (1830), and two novels, Octave Feuillet's *Roman d'un jeune homme pauvre* (1858) and Hugo's own *Les Misérables* (1862). What Boal wishes to assert is that the freedom of the bourgeois spirit unleashed in the Renaissance and represented in the 'poetics of *virtù*' is subject to a 'reduction', a term which now assumes considerable importance for him. Romanticism is 'the first serious reduction imposed on man in the theater', since through it 'he came to be weighed in relation to eternal, immutable values', with spiritual aspiration replacing material values in what Boal describes as 'the swan song of the feudal nobility' (*TO* 75). One might, I suppose, understand from this that Romanticism was a long-delayed form of cultural (superstructural, ideological) reaction, although how this fits into the continuity of the Aristotelian 'coercive system' is very hard to figure. So, incidentally, is the absence of any reference to the French revolution and the period of reaction which followed it, which might presumably provide the occasion (base or infrastructure), crudely enough, for these adjustments in the superstructure. But the argument fails totally in relation to realism, described as the 'second great reduction', for which no explanation is given.

In fact, Boal is moving very quickly at this point towards the modern, and objectivity, subjectivity (alternative modes, apparently) and psychology are all stages in what Boal casually terms 'the evolution' (of theatre) (*TO* 76). The sequence here ends in Hollywood, in a comparison of Dale Carnegie and Machiavelli, who both 'preach the slogan "where there's a will there's a way"', and in the 'most recent and severe reduction of man', which is the 'antitheater of Eugene Ionesco, who tries to take away from man even his powers of communication' (*TO* 78). A theory of 'reduction' has taken over from 'the poetics of *virtù*', but it is not clear how the two concepts can be reconciled with each other, or with the other components of the historical scheme that Boal has advanced. Modes of analysis or explanation are lacking, but the concluding assertion is that these stages and authors 'testify to the final phase of the bourgeois society and theater'. Reductions in the scope of bourgeois *virtù* are stages in the activity of 'dehumanizing man', even if the subject of Ionesco's drama, Bérenger, is 'the last bourgeois character' (*TO* 79). Quite why the bourgeoisie should wish to reduce or dehumanize itself in public is puzzling, but the scheme of decline has an evident theoretical function:

> In opposition to that theater, another must rise: one determined by a new class and which will dissent not only stylistically but in a much more radical manner. (*TO* 79)

This new theatre is 'dialectically materialist', and is to some extent the theatre of Brecht. In his third chapter, 'Hegel and Brecht: The Character as Subject or the Character as Object?', Boal apparently advances Brecht as a model of the 'gigantic transformations' and 'extraordinary changes produced in the theater by the contribution of Marxism' (*TO* 83). According to the general scheme outlined in the introduction, and the notion of 'laws', if the new theatre is 'determined by a new class' (the proletariat) then one might expect observations on that class and on the economic and political conditions affecting it and its ideologically operative theatre. Instead, Boal concentrates on an exposition of the theoretical position adopted by Hegel, and construes Brecht as a reversal of key values in that position: 'In reality, Brecht's whole poetics is basically an answer and a counterproposal to the idealist poetics of Hegel' (*TO* 84). At the same time, Boal makes a number of attempts to conflate Hegel and Aristotle. So in the first section of this chapter, 'The "Epic" Concept', Boal notes that Aristotle uses the term epic to refer to epic poetry and to its narrative mode, which tells of events that happened in the past. Boal then introduces Piscator, 'a contemporary of Brecht', 'who makes a type of theatre completely different from what Aristotle understands by epic poetry' (*TO* 84), a fact which is hardly surprising in itself. A little more detail would have explained more, and its omission is odd. The context of the *Volksbühne* ('People's Theatre') in Germany, Piscator's allegiance to the German Communist Party, his belief in a political theatre, the use of the term 'epic' to describe his production-work at the *Volksbühne*, his agit-prop outside the conventional theatre, and his relations with Brecht in the 1920s and later would explain the modern genesis of the term far better.[14]

In fact, Boal's emphasis on Hegel, and the contention that Brecht was mostly concerned (like Marx, one supposes) to overturn Hegel, is quite perverse, and is perhaps the most extreme example of Boal's curious attraction to a kind of pseudo-history of theatrical theory. The exposition of Hegel's leading ideas would be helped by a clear statement that Hegel discussed epic firmly in the context of genres of ancient Greek poetry and their relation to the 'spirit'. The simple reason for this is that Hegel wished to categorize drama in its original manifestation, in Greece, 'to consider the dramatic composition...in the contrast it presents to epic and lyrical poetry' (Paolucci 1962, 2). Boal's focus lies primarily on the admixture of 'objective' and 'subjective' that defines Greek drama in distinction to epic (objective) and lyrical (subjective) poetry in Hegel's thinking. But he might have added Hegel's contrast of the external world (largely of described actions in epic poetry) to the inner world of subjective experience (in lyric). The account is generally clear, and the theory is summarized as 'the Hegelian idealist poetics' to which Brecht, according to Boal, is *'squarely, totally, globally opposed'* (*TO* 92 and 93). But Boal remains worried by Brecht's choice of the term 'epic', because he feels it may be confused with the element in Hegel's analysis which refers to epic poetry, and so reprimands Brecht for not calling his theory 'by its name: Marxist poetics!' (*TO* 93). Boal then reproduces, in an altered form (*TO* 95), the outline of differences between 'dramatic' and 'epic' theatre drawn up by Brecht to accompany the published version of the opera *Mahagonny* (Willett 1964, 37). Boal has adjusted Brecht's comparative scheme to make the contrast one between 'idealist poetics' and Brechtian poetics, choosing to include 'differences mentioned by Brecht in other works' (*TO* 93), and suggesting obscurely that some of the 'differences shown by Brecht' (actually by Boal) relate to Hegelian differences between epic, tragic and lyrical forms (*TO* 94). The implication is that Hegel is directly in Brecht's sights, whereas in the essay Brecht is plainly justifying a new kind of opera in contrast to the standard form. Boal has drastically rewritten both sides of the scheme, including Brecht's own formulation of 'Epic Theatre'; the usefulness of this exercise is hard to grasp, except in the removal or destruction of the contextuality of Brecht's writings.[15]

The discussion of a number of Brecht's plays which follows is supposedly illustrative, but the morals drawn vary. The most important is stated immediately, which is that Brecht is opposed to 'all the idealist poetics (Hegel, Aristotle, and others)' (*TO* 96), which makes Brecht into the summation of the historic and Marxist scheme which Boal has outlined from the beginning. A secondary moral is that while Brecht shows that the proletariat in western countries is corruptible by capitalism, the situation in Latin America is different. This observation is based on an interpretation of *The Good Person of Szechwan* (*TO* 96–7), and in relation to *A Man Is a Man* Boal concludes that the play, like Sartre's story 'The Childhood of a Leader', is 'an almost scientific demonstration carried out through artistic means' (*TO* 99). *Arturo Ui* is cited to demonstrate Brecht's opposition of 'social or economic necessities' to the 'necessity of a *moral* nature' proposed by Hegel (*TO* 100). In a later section, 'Empathy or What? Emotion or Reason?' Boal opposes Brecht to Aristotle, and in 'Catharsis and Repose, or Knowledge and Action?' Boal links Hegel to Aristotle in their opposition to Brecht, since 'both see theater as a purging of the spectator's "antiestablishment" characteristics', and 'desire a quiet somnolence at the end of the spectacle' (*TO* 106).

Some of the allusions to Brecht are dubious. In the same section we read the following:

> Brecht contends that the popular artist must abandon the downtown stages and go to the neighbourhoods, because only there will he find people who are truly interested in changing society: in the neighbourhoods he should show his images of social life to the workers who are interested in changing that social life, since they are its victims. (*TO* 105)

The reference indicates that this statement will be found in Brecht's essay 'Can the Present-day World be Reproduced by Means of Theatre?' from 1955; but it is not, and the essay is not concerned with this issue. In earlier writings Brecht was interested in the particular audience that might become engaged with epic theatre, but Boal does not refer to the *Lehrstück* or to the essay 'The German Drama: pre- Hitler' of the mid-1930s, in which Brecht discusses his 'work outside the theatre' (Willett 1964, 77–81; my quotation is from 80). Nor does Boal confront the full implications of Brecht's supposed reversal of the Hegelian relationship of the objective to the subjective, in what Willett terms 'the individual's subordination to the collective', a conviction that Willett believes Brecht shared with Piscator (Willett 1986, 109). 'Transforming society', Boal's stated objective for Brechtian theatre, can see the individual ' "purged" of a flaw' (*TO* 106) in a thoroughly Marxist sense which Boal does not explore, as Brecht's *The Measures Taken* might reveal. Brecht is guarded about the possibilities for practising his epic theatre, and looks carefully to the prevailing conditions in the infrastructure, or the class struggle. He states clearly that 'the modern epic theatre ... cannot by any means be practised universally', and that 'favourable circumstances for an epic and didactic theatre have only been found in a few places and for a short period of time'. This is because that kind of theatre demands not only technology but also 'a powerful movement in society' which can defend 'against every contrary trend' its interest in 'vital questions' (Willett 1964, 76, from the undated 1930s essay 'Theatre for Pleasure or Theatre for Instruction'). Boal's introduction of 'the spectator–character relation proposed by Brecht' curiously concentrates on a massive but incomplete quotation from the poem 'On the Everyday Theatre' of 1930, which closely relates to the essay 'The Street Scene' of the late 1930s and to other, earlier essays on acting and the epic theatre. The result of this extended quotation is, ironically, to make prominent the emphasis Brecht lays on the accuracy of imitation, an accuracy largely achieved by the actor's 'disengagement' from the character or role, while also highlighting his rhetorical insistence that this actor is nonetheless 'an artist because a man' (*TO* 107–9).[16] Boal will later elaborate on this conception of the actor as the positive figure in theatre, in his continued attack on the passivity of the spectator.

Boal's fourth chapter, 'Poetics of the Oppressed', is one of the more important documents in the theatrical theory of the later twentieth century. Much of its methodology has become familiar through later publications by Boal, and through the secondary literature which has debated and discussed applications of its practice, notably in contexts from the northern hemisphere.[17] But its place in the grander theoretical scheme outlined by Boal in *Theatre of the Oppressed* is in various ways problematic. The problems start with the short preamble (*TO* 119), which resumes Boal's historical scheme of a return to origins originally formulated in the 'Foreword' to the book. The scheme places a large emphasis on what is plainly meant to be the Greek experience. The separation of the 'free people singing in the open air' by the ruling classes into actors and spectators, and then, among the actors, into 'protagonists' and the 'mass' was fundamental, and its reversal is only now happening. The 'oppressed people... are making the theatre their own', reversing the separation as 'the spectator starts acting again' and as 'the private property of the characters by the individual actors' is eliminated, which is the importance that Boal attributes to his original Joker system, outlined in the subsequent and final chapter.

What is curious about this summary is that it makes one wonder what the point of the theoretical bulk of *Theatre of the Oppressed* has been, since the primary situation of theatre, which stands to be reversed, can be stated so simply and so briefly. The changes to which Boal alludes are preliminary to Aristotle's theorizing, and so preliminary to Boal's extensive argument. Aristotle alludes in the *Poetics* to the speculative theory of his own day that tragedy evolved from the dithyramb, a song-and-dance in honour of the god Dionysos, but he clearly had no access to any kinds of evidence about the form that early song-and-dance took. The dithyramb, in a competition of choruses of 50 from the new democratic tribes of Athens, is known to have been vital to the new democracy, but so was tragedy, and both were established soon after the revolutionary institution of democracy just before 500 BC. But if the dithyramb, or other forms of choral song, existed before this point, then they will have been patronized by the tyrants of Athens who were expelled before the institution of democracy. Choral songs-and-dances were undoubtedly watched as well as performed at any time. The impersonation of particular individuals may have occurred in choral songs, as it may also have been a feature of epic recitation, and in so far as it became a feature of tragedy and the other dramatic forms (satyrplay and comedy) it developed under the radical democracy. The public productions of tragedies were financed by a form of taxation on wealthy citizens, and were placed in an ideologically assertive framework of surrounding events by the democracy.[18]

One of the major theoretical problems of the account that follows is the relationship to Brecht and to Marxism. Brecht was advanced by Boal, in the chapter on Hegel and Brecht, as the representative of a 'new theater, dialectically materialist' which was 'determined by a new class' in opposition to bourgeois theatre (*TO* 79, and the discussion above). The language in that chapter was itself Marxist, uncompromising and unqualified; but in 'Poetics of the Oppressed' Brecht slips from this paramount position in the theory. Brecht's poetics are indeed opposed to Aristotle early in this chapter, as 'an awakening of critical consciousness' is opposed to catharsis (*TO* 122). But Boal's vision of the original perversion of the performance of a 'free people' in pre-tragic Greece constitutes a very different kind of charter, in which the true reversal of an original corruption can only be accomplished by the methodology of the theatre of the oppressed. It is tempting to see here a reflection of Hegelian thinking: if Aristotle represents the thesis, and Brecht represents the antithesis, then Boal represents the synthesis. This may not be as far-fetched as it seems, because in later works Boal allows some kinds of relevance and value to the idea of catharsis as a partial truth (for example, *RD* 69–73). According to this scheme, the theatre of the oppressed is more Marxist than Brecht:

> I believe that all the truly revolutionary theatrical groups should transfer to the people the means of production in the theater so that the people themselves may utilize them. The theater is a weapon, and it is the people who should wield it. (*TO* 122)

The relationship of the theatre, specifically the theatre of the oppressed, to 'the revolution' is by no means as easy as this affirmative statement suggests. The incident with Virgilio, 'a huge peasant, a great big strapping colossus of a man' with which Boal opens his revision of the theatre of the oppressed in *Rainbow of Desire* is demonstrative in this respect. It dates from the early period of outreach by Arena under Boal's direction, when a performance of what Boal describes as 'agit-prop' with fake, theatrical guns was taken literally by Virgilio (*RD* 2–3). The performers were invited to take their guns and put them into action against the local, oppressive landowner, but 'lost their appetite' as their fear 'turned to panic'. Virgilio came to a critical consciousness that these artists were talking about spilling the blood of the peasants rather than their own, and left, leaving Boal unsure of the nature of the 'error', an artistic *hamartia* if ever there was one. Boal quotes Che Guevara – '*solidarity means running the same risks*' – and while retaining his belief in agit-prop resolves never again to write 'plays that give advice' or to send ' "messages" ' (*RD* 3). This incident, in the form that it is narrated, represents 'an encounter with a real peasant, in the flesh and blood, rather than an abstract "peasantry" ', an interpretation that fits well with the humanism and therapeutic emphasis of the later book. As Boal notes, with Virgilio he 'had learnt to see an individual being, rather than simply a social class; the peasant, rather than the peasantry' (*RD* 7); but the relation of this perception to the revolution remains unclear, particularly since the incident actually predates the *Theatre of the Oppressed* by a decade. Boal's concluding formula in 'Poetics of the Oppressed' is that 'the theater is not revolutionary in itself; but have no doubts, it is a rehearsal of revolution' (*TO* 155), which despite the lapse of years might have been a difficult concept to explain to Virgilio.

The framework of Boal's understanding of oppression is apparent in his account of the photographic aspect of the work in Peru; photography, like theatre, was one of the 'languages' apart from spoken languages in which 'literacy' was to be taught in the ALFIN programme (*TO* 120–1). The work here embraces, in the images, 'brothers equally exploited', the 'common condition: poverty on both sides', and 'the need to redirect their violent resentment' against the 'true enemies' in 'the wealthier neighborhoods' (*TO* 124). Beyond this national analysis lies the implicit condemnation of the fact that a photograph was 'in Kodachrome, "Made in the USA" ', and of the presiding role of imperialism:

What is exploitation? The traditional figure of Uncle Sam is, for many social groups throughout the world, the ultimate symbol of exploitation. It expresses to perfection the rapacity of 'Yankee' imperialism. (*TO* 125)

For the participants, the symbolic and analytic understanding of oppression may be different. The example of the child for whom oppression was a nail identifies the rental of a nail 'on the wall of some place of business' to hang the child's shoe-shining equipment overnight (*TO* 125). From its inception, the theatre of the oppressed confronts a local analysis which does not accommodate itself with ease to the ambitions of the revolutionary and Marxist frame in which it is offered to the participants. The leading example of simultaneous dramaturgy actually concerns an incident of marital infidelity in which the wife appears as the oppressed party, and it is 'all the women of the audience' who 'entered into a lively exchange of views' (*TO* 133). In the therapeutic context of *The Rainbow of Desire* this incident plays a significant role as the foundation myth of forum theatre from simultaneous dramaturgy, since in that version of the story 'a very large, powerful woman – built like one of those Japanese "sumo" fighters' intervenes in the performance, beating the actor-husband and ordering him to bring the dinner. In the earlier account in *Theatre of the Oppressed* those aspects are forgotten or ignored, as the actress-wife is instructed to beat the actor-husband and then sits down to dinner with him, discussing 'the latest measures taken by the government, which happened to be the nationalization of American companies' (*TO* 134).

The examples may be both local and revolutionary. A young woman literacy agent chooses, for Image Theatre, the public castration in her village of the leader of a rebellion which occurred, presumably, in her memory. In Image Theatre the actual image needs to go through transformation to arrive at the ideal image; the various transformations of this incident en route to the ideal seem almost inevitably confined to aspiration rather than feasibility (*TO* 136–7). Yet Boal's rumination on this exercise remains on the theme of revolution, and it acts as a distraction from the ruthless intractability of the actual image, offering instead a hesitant conceptual pluralism – 'each person will think of his or her "own" revolution, a personal conception of revolution' (*TO* 138). But feasibility is a functional rule of Image Theatre, and Boal emphasizes that 'the important thing is always to analyze the feasibility of the change' (*TO* 138–9). In the example of Forum Theatre, in which the participants are guided to telling 'a story containing a political or social problem of difficult solution', a young man tells of the exploitation of workers in a fish-meal factory. Feasibility here rules out machine-breaking, terrorist violence, and the strike, and the participants conclude on the formation of a small union (*TO* 140–1). By any Marxist standards, trade-unionism is not revolutionary, nor is it a 'rehearsal of revolution', which is the conclusion which Boal swiftly appends:

> Maybe the theater in itself is not revolutionary, but these theatrical forms are without doubt a *rehearsal of revolution*. The truth of the matter is that the spectator-actor practises a real act even though he does it in a fictional manner. (*TO* 141)

The guiding theoretical hand of the 'Poetics of the Oppressed' remains resolutely Marxist in its terminology. So we read, towards the end of the chapter, that 'The relations of production (infrastructure) determine the culture of a society (superstructure)', and that individual psychology is subject to class. If the work on social roles is organized effectively, the participants

> will realize that human actions are not the exclusive and primordial result of individual psychology: almost always, through the individual speaks his class! (*TO* 153)

It is not that Boal is introducing the concept of revolution or class-struggle only to mitigate those ideas in experience and practice, to acknowledge and recognize the local, 'the individual rather than simply the social class' in the retrospective vision of *The Rainbow of Desire*. The theoretical ascent in *Theatre of the Oppressed* is 'from the *phenomenon* toward the *law*; from the phenomena presented in the plot toward the social laws that govern those phenomena.'

> The spectator-participants must come out of this experience enriched with the knowledge of those laws, obtained through analysis of the phenomena. (*TO* 150)

So what is claimed for the theatre of the oppressed remains on the grand scale in the historical theory that has been constructed for it, and in the reversal of an original corruption that has divided the theatre. The Brechtian theatre may offer a poetics for 'the enlightened vanguard', but in it the spectator 'continues to delegate power' to the actors 'to act in his place'.

> The experience is revealing on the level of consciousness, but not globally on the level of action. Dramatic action throws light upon real action. The spectacle is a preparation for action.

> The *poetics of the oppressed* is essentially the poetics of liberation . . . (*TO* 155)

Boal and Freire

Plainly, Boal's theoretical practice is a pedagogy, and if he is compared to Freire and to movements in literacy like ALFIN, then the equation between language and the theatre must be examined. Is it the same to offer competence and confidence in the expression of a national language or a local language, and to offer the opportunity for action in a play? What is the relation between 'dramatic action' and 'real action'? Does participation in dramatic action transfer to real action, in the same way as participation in one's own language in a literacy programme transfers to use of it outside that programme, in the 'real' world? What is the role of the pedagogue? Almost the whole of Freire's theory is directed towards that central question, from the earlier essay 'Extension or Communication' of 1968 (Freire 1974) on the shortcomings of the standard approach of the agronomist-educator to the more familiar arguments of *Pedagogy of the Oppressed* (Freire 1970).[19] Freire also offers a subtle argument for pedagogy in relation to the need for revolution, which in summary is that if revolutionary thought is directed rather than based on dialogue then the revolution will fail. In this respect, Freire's sophistication could be well compared to that of Gramsci on intellectuals, and on the conceptual failure that would see intellectuals acting upon the revolutionary class.[20] Freire's terminology, his advocacy of *conscientização*, his early methodology (detailed in 'Education as the Practice of Freedom' (Freire 1974)), his attention to the 'student-teacher' are all points of intricate contact between his work and that of Boal. But they do not explain Boal's theoretical construct in *Theatre of the Oppressed*, nor do they allow for an untroubled transition between language and theatre. The configuration of theory in relation to practice is also very different in the two writers. For Freire, the experience of literacy programmes and methods gives rise to and entails a general theory of pedagogy, which may be applied to the agronomist-educator as much as to the revolutionary leader. For Boal, his theory of the evolution of theatre is a construct which justifies and provides a charter for the practice. Freire's theory of pedagogy may account for or help us to understand the genesis of Boal's pedagogical practice; but it cannot explain or justify Boal's theory of theatre.

One final observation should be made. Boal's theory is predicated on a condemnation of the role of the spectator, and on a correspondingly extremely high valuation of the actor. This relies heavily on a highly questionable but unqualified equation of the 'actor' with 'action', but is actually diametrically opposed to Boal's condemnation of the original division which brought the actor into being. The act of reception for Boal is either sub-human, or emasculated, according to our interpretation of 'man':

Yes, this is without doubt the conclusion: 'Spectator' is a bad word! The spectator is less than a man and it is necessary to humanize him, to restore to him his capacity of action in all its fullness. (*TO* 154–5)

This for Boal is 'the liberation of the spectator, on whom the theater has imposed finished visions of the world', and the concept of humanization recalls the final line of Boal's quotation from Brecht's poem about the actor in the 'Everyday Theatre': 'He is an artist because a man'. Boal is scathing about 'the bourgeois artist-high priest, elite artist, the unique individual', the 'star' (*TO* 109). But his theoretical hymn to the spectactor is perhaps the most lavish in its praises and its promises that has ever been sung. In this important respect, Boal's theory places him firmly in a twentieth-century and modern tradition of emphasis on the actor as the principal agent of theatre, and as the major subject of theatrical theory and of much theoretical practice.

Primary Sources

Aristotle (1953) *Ethics*, trans. J. Thomson (Harmondsworth: Penguin).
Aristotle (1996) *Poetics*, trans. M. Heath (Harmondsworth: Penguin).
Boal, A. (1992) *Games for Actors and Non-actors*, trans. A. Jackson (London: Routledge).
—(1998) *Legislative Theatre: Using Performance to Make Politics*, trans. A. Jackson (London: Routledge).
—(1995) *The Rainbow of Desire: The Boal Method of Theatre and Therapy*, trans. A. Jackson (London: Routledge).
—(1979) *Theatre of the Oppressed*, trans. C. and M.-O. Leal McBride (London: Pluto Press).
Brecht – see Willett, *op. cit.*
Gilbert, A. (1965) (ed. and trans.) *Machiavelli: The Chief Works and Others: Volumes 1–3* (Durham N.C.: Duke University Press).
Hegel – see Paolucci, *op. cit.*
Machiavelli, N. (1970) *The Discourses*, trans. L. Walker (Harmondsworth: Penguin).
—*Mandragola* – see Penman, *op. cit.*
—(1999) *The Prince*, trans. G. Bull (Harmondsworth: Penguin).
Paolucci, A. and H. (eds) (1962) *Hegel on Tragedy* (New York: Harper & Row).
Penman, B. (ed.) (1978) *Five Italian Renaissance Comedies* (Harmondsworth: Penguin).
Willett, J. (1964) (ed. and trans.) *Brecht on Theatre: The Development of an Aesthetic* (London: Methuen).

Secondary Sources

Anglo, S. (1971) *Machiavelli: A Dissection* (London: Paladin).

Babbage, F. (ed.) (1995) 'Working Without Boal: Digressions and Developments in the Theatre of the Oppressed', *Contemporary Theatre Review*, 3,1.

Engels, F. (1972) *The Origin of the Family, Private Property, and the State* (London: Lawrence & Wishart).

Freire, P. (1972) *Cultural Action for Freedom* (Harmondsworth: Penguin).

—(1974) *Education: The Practice of Freedom* (London: Writers and Readers Publishing Cooperative).

—(1996) *Pedagogy of the Oppressed*, trans. M. Bergman Ramos (Harmondsworth: Penguin).

Goldhill, S. (1986) *Reading Greek Tragedy* (Cambridge: Cambridge University Press).

Gramsci, A. see Hoare, *op. cit.*

Hale, J. (1972) *Machiavelli and Renaissance Italy* (Harmondsworth: Penguin).

Hauser, A. (1962) *The Social History of Art: Volumes 1–4*, trans. S. Godman (London: Routledge & Kegan Paul).

Delgado, M. and Heritage, P. (eds) (1996) *In Contact with the Gods? Directors Talk Theatre* (Manchester: Manchester University Press).

Hoare, Q. and Nowell Smith, G. (eds) (1971) *Selections from the Prison Notebooks of Antonio Gramsci* (London: Lawrence & Wishart).

Ley, G. (1999) *From Mimesis to Interculturalism: Readings of Theatrical Theory before and after 'Modernism'* (Exeter: University of Exeter Press).

Mackie, R. (ed.) (1980) *Literacy and Revolution: The Pedagogy of Paulo Freire* (London: Pluto Press).

McLaren, P. and Leonard, P. (eds) (1993) *Paulo Freire: A Critical Encounter* (London: Routledge).

Schutzman, M. and Cohen-Cruz, J. (eds) (1994) *Playing Boal: Theatre, Therapy, Activism* (London: Routledge).

Versenyi, A. (1993) *Theatre in Latin America* (Cambridge: Cambridge University Press).

Willett, J. (1986) *The Theatre of Erwin Piscator: Half a Century of Politics in the Theatre* (London: Methuen).

Winkler, J. and Zeitlin, F. (eds) (1990) *Nothing to Do with Dionysos? Athenian Drama in Its Social Context* (Princeton: Princeton University Press).

7

Conclusion: From Theoretical Practitioners to Theorized Performance

The best work of any practitioner might be considered theoretical, in the broadest sense, because it has a reflexive and thoughtful component to it. But it does not follow that all writing by practitioners is theoretical. Those theoretical practitioners that we have examined qualify for that description not just because they wrote down their ideas, but also because of the way in which they have expressed their thoughts. Their texts are sometimes prescriptive, often polemical, and frequently analytical. They have used written means to attempt to place their practice in a history or tradition of theatre (often one they re-make to suit themselves): to proselytize about their work, to quantify the purpose of their practice and to codify their working practices. The mode and rhetoric of this written material differ widely between practitioners, and may change through the working life of a given writer.

The selection of figures and of texts that we have included is not comprehensive, but it is characterized by the source of the initiative, which lies within or very close to the professional practice of theatre. This, however, has not been the only source of theoretical writing in the twentieth century. In the final decades of the century there was a noticeable if gradual shift in emphasis, as the significance of texts from theoretical practitioners became paired with what might conveniently be described as a substantial interest in theorized performance. There was a tendency in these decades for theoretical writing about theatre-making to be produced by people who were not primarily practitioners, while written theory from practitioners often demonstrated the support, or the encroachment, of academic concerns. This tendency might be seen as an economic response to the decline of patronage and postwar Euro-American

173

government sponsorship for theatrical activity. It has certainly manifested itself in the proliferation of theatrical research institutes and study centres. The rise of Drama or Theatre Studies, and now Performance Studies, as autonomous disciplines in universities undoubtedly encouraged this development.

The economics of the academy, which places a premium on publication, have certainly led to the domination of analytical points of view. In his introduction to a collection of *Modern Theories of Drama*, Brandt reflects that

> Twentieth-century analytical theories are not autonomous. They interact with related disciplines – with linguistics in the case of semiology, with anthropology in the case of structuralism, with sociology in the case of reception theory. (Brandt 1998, xviii)

This interaction might be considered a result of the establishment of a new discipline within the academy, which in the first instance drew on researchers from older disciplines. There are many areas where the application to the theatre of analytical approaches borrowed from literary studies or the social sciences has produced a body of writing about performance that lays claim to a coherent methodology for study. The developing discourse of theorized performance might include semiotics, theatre anthropology and interculturalism, and feminist or sexual politics or identity politics. For readers who may be less well-acquainted with these developments, we offer some brief guidance here in conclusion.

Elam (1980) provided an overview of the development of semiotics from Saussurian linguistics, through Prague School structuralism with its analysis of the theatrical sign to his own understanding of codes and discourses in the theatre. His commentary noted that theatre rather than literature began to be the subject of this kind of analysis only in the 1930s. His general introduction is continued in greater detail by Fischer-Lichte (1992) who attempted to distinguish a system of semiotic analysis geared to the specifically aesthetic realm of theatre. An emphasis on the context of reception and the complexity of post-structuralist thinking in the writing of Eco (1994) and Pavis (1982) has led semiotics into semiology and offered a richer analysis of the meaning-making activity of theatre. On the whole, detailed semiotic analyses have focused on performances which employ the conventions of western theatre, and theatre semiotics has been a major strand of theory since the 1970s.

The extension of the study of performance into areas like ritual, play and social behaviour can be largely attributed to Schechner, who was responsible for integrating experiments in theatre with the ideas of social scientists and social anthropologists. Schechner's *Essays on Performance Theory* (1977 and 1988) sought to synthesize these disparate fields of study under a methodological approach, performance studies, which would offer a unifying reading of the 'performative' in all behaviours. Schechner's exegesis of performance theory offered no specific origins for theatre, only a spectrum from animal behaviour, or as he termed it – 'animal ritualization' – at the one pole to human ritual at the other, with theatre somewhere in the middle. Victor and Edith Turner were two anthropologists with many years field experience, whose study of ritual and social behaviour had led them to use performance metaphors and models in their analysis; 'a cultural form [the stage drama] was the model for a social scientific concept' (Turner 1974, 32).[1] Victor Turner was, like Schechner, drawn to speculate on the theatre as one of many genres of performance in his later studies (Turner 1982 and 1986). In a move that reflected a tendency to explore beyond traditional western theatre aesthetics, and which shared a new-found interest of the Euro-American academy, Eugenio Barba created his International School of Theatre Anthropology in Holstebro, Denmark in 1980. In doing so he was led to define the school's remit and its theoretical approach:

> Originally, anthropology was understood as the study of human beings' behaviour, not only on the socio-cultural level, but also on the physiological level. Theatre anthropology is thus the study of human beings' socio-cultural and physiological behaviour in a performance context. (Barba and Savarese 1991, 8)

The practice and the language of Barba's work makes it clear that he is concerned primarily with explicitly aesthetic and performative traditions. He set out to discover laws or 'recurrent principles' of a performer's work, irrespective of their cultural context. These were, he surmised, situated in the 'pre-expressive' or pre-cultural body of the performer. Carlson's book (1996) traces other threads which have contributed to the location of performance, rather than theatre or drama, at the centre of recent written and theoretical inquiry.

Linked to this drive for a unifying methodology of approach across cultures and traditions as well as across genres of performance is the development of theories of intercultural theatre.[2] The attractions of intercultural connection range from 'rejuvenating' tired Western theatre aesthetics to saving our planet.[3] Despite these grand aspirations, there has been little extended discussion of theories of interculturalism, and few performances which can demonstrate exemplary intercultural credentials. The writings on this theoretical phenomenon are mainly edited articles grouped in collections from Fischer-Lichte (1990), Marranca and Dasgupta (1991) or Pavis (1996). Bharucha's (1993) wide-ranging critique is one of the few critical voices in the development of the fascination with interculturalism. In particular, his questioning of the possibility of 'exchange' draws attention to an idea which appears inherent in the language of the 'inter'- cultural, yet is rarely considered in the theory or practice of what passes as interculturalism.[4] There is one other collection, *Imperialism and Theatre* (Gainor 1994), which has offered a range of considered critical questions and helped to set the debate in a useful and illuminating context. Yet perhaps the most telling illustration of the ideological underpinning of interculturalism was demonstrated by Pavis's (1996) *Intercultural Performance Reader*. This grouped essays in sections, beginning with historical contexts and continuing with a laudatory section entitled 'From The Western Point Of View'. A few counter points are gathered in a much shorter section 'From Another Point Of View', by which the editor meant writers from the rest of the world. These critical assessments were given little breathing space before the conclusion, where those who originated much of this theory, including Barba and Grotowski, were introduced to clinch the debate. Studies of interculturalism have, at their best, offered insight into the influence of culture on culture, but have seldom provided a convincing rationale for the substitution of the idea of cultural exchange for that of cultural appropriation.

The impact of feminist thought and of the politics of gender, sexuality and identity within theoretical writing on theatre has come from a very different source. Feminism developed primarily as a political and cultural force outside the academy, and was only gradually taken up within it.[5] Wandor (1986) offered 'a critical history of the relationship between theatre, class and gender; it is about feminism, women and gays' (xv). She provided feminist critiques of plays, feminist and non-feminist, female and non-female authored, as well as non-playtext based feminist theatre. This multiplicity of approach has been echoed in much writing on theatre from feminists. Steadman (1991) provided an overview of writings on feminism and theatre, and separated feminist theoretical approaches to the theatre from studies of theatre groups with an explicitly feminist agenda or practice, and from studies of women playwrights or performance artists. Steadman also provided a publication history of feminist criticism. Much publication during the 1980s from feminists was influenced by the French academy, and showed a fascination with psychoanalysis. This produced a quite different texture to the writing from the politicized and polemical theory of the earlier period. The politicization of theory is still noticeable in the work of Dolan, Diamond and Phelan, from whose publications selections were given in Martin's (1991) *Sourcebook*. The impact of psychoanalysis, and the reclamation of that discipline by feminists, has led to some remarkable writing on identity politics. Butler's (1982) *Gender Trouble* seduced theatre theorists with its use of the performance metaphor for functions of identity, and much feminist theorizing since then has attempted to integrate Butler's approach into actual theories of performance.

The central problem of performance for Stanislavski was that of acting in a play in a theatre in front of an audience, and that problem formed the core of his theoretical system. Acting has remained central to the concerns of many of the theoretical practitioners discussed in this book, but alongside it the concepts of 'theatre' and 'performance' themselves have become sites of fluctuating debate and allegiance. This book has looked critically at some of the earlier events in the theoretical writing of the twentieth century, registering their diversity and examining their arguments in some detail. We hope that it has been not only a helpful companion to understanding difficult texts in a modern history of theories of performance, but also a stimulus to further interest and enquiry.

References

Auslander, P. (1997) *From Acting to Performance* (London: Routledge).

Barba, E. and Savarese, N. (1991) *A Dictionary of Theatre Anthropology*, trans. R. Fowler (London: Routledge).

Bharucha, R. (1993) *Theatre and the World: Performance and the Politics of Culture* (London: Routledge).

Butler, J. (1990) *Gender Trouble* (London: Routledge).

Carlson, M. (1996) *Performance: A Critical Introduction* (New York: Routledge).

Case, S. (1988) *Feminism and Theatre* (Basingstoke: Macmillan).

—(ed.) (1990) *Performing Feminisms: Feminist Critical Theory and Theatre* (Baltimore: Johns Hopkins University Press).

Eco, U. (1994) *The Limits of Interpretation* (Bloomington: Indiana University Press).

Elam, K. (1980) *The Semiotics of Theatre and Drama* (London: Methuen).

Fischer-Lichte, E. (1972) *The Semiotics of Theater*, trans. J. Gaines and D. Jones, (Bloomington: Indiana University Press).

—(1997) *The Show and the Gaze of Theatre: A European Perspective (Studies in Theatre History and Culture)* (Iowa: University of Iowa Press).

Fischer-Lichte, E. and Riley, J. (eds) (1990) *The Dramatic Touch of Difference: Theatre Own and Foreign* (Tübingen: Narr).

Gainor, J. (ed.) (1994) *Imperialism and Theatre: Essays On World Theatre, Drama, and Performance* (London: Routledge).

Keyssar, H. (ed.) (1996) *Feminist Theatre and Theory* (Basingstoke: Macmillan).

Laughlin, K. and Schuler, C. (eds) (1995) *Theatre and Feminist Aesthetics* (London: Associated University Presses).

Ley, G. (1999) *From Mimesis to Interculturalism: Readings of Theatrical Theory before and after 'Modernism'* (Exeter: University of Exeter Press).

MacAloon, J. (ed.) (1984) *Rite, Drama, Festival and Spectacle* (Philadelphia: ISHI).

Marranca, B. and Dasgupta, G. (eds) (1991) *Interculturalism and Performance: Writings from PAJ* (New York: Performing Arts Journal Publications).

Martin, C. (ed.) (1996) *A Sourcebook of Feminist Theatre and Performance: On and Beyond the Stage* (London: Routledge).

Pavis, P. (ed.) (1996) *The Intercultural Performance Reader* (New York: Routledge).

—(1982) *Languages of the Stage: Essays in the Semiology of Theatre* (New York: Performing Arts Journal Publications).

Schechner, R. and Appel, W. (eds) (1990) *By Means of Performance: Intercultural Studies of Theatre and Ritual* (Cambridge: Cambridge University Press).

Schechner, R. (1988) *Performance Theory: Revised and Expanded Edition* (London: Routledge).

Schmid, H. and Van Kesteren, A. (eds) (1984) *Semiotics of Drama and Theatre: New Perspectives in the Theory of Drama and Theatre* (Amsterdam: Benjanus).

Steadman, S. (1991) *Dramatic Re-Visions: An Annotated Bibliography of Feminism and Theatre, 1972–1988* (Chicago: American Library Association).

Turner, V. (1986) *The Anthropology of Performance* (New York: Performing Arts Journal Publications).

—(1974) *Drama, Fields and Metaphors* (Ithaca: Cornell University Press).

—(1982) *From Ritual to Theatre: The Human Seriousness of Play* (New York: Performing Arts Journal Publications).

Wandor, M. (1986) *Carry on Understudies: Theatre and Sexual Politics* (London: Routledge & Kegan Paul).

Notes

1 Stanislavski's Theoretical System

1. See Worrall's short but helpful conclusion on Stanislavski (1996, 204–8). On the doctrine of socialist realism that was imposed on Shostakovich, see Wilson (1994, 247–55).

2. In Part 1 of Stanislavski (1981) *Creating a Role* = *CR*. (Abbreviations to key texts under discussion will be made throughout the book and initially identified in this way.) These tensions may be reflected in the choice, for the first production by the Moscow Art Theatre, of a script which attempted to eliminate the verse rhythms of the play: see Worrall (1996, 171).

3. On *Julius Caesar*, see Worrall (1996, 152–4), Magarshack (1950, 248–9) and Benedetti (1991, 151–69); on the Meininger Company, see DeHart (1981) and the opening chapter in Braun (1982, 11–21); and on *The Lower Depths*, see Worrall (1996, 133–49).

4. Stanislavski (1924), with the biographies by Magarshack (1950) and Benedetti (1988).

5. See the summary by Benedetti (1989, 73) in his useful short introduction to Stanislavski. On Boleslavsky, there is the text by Boleslavsky himself (1949) and the study by Roberts (1981). Counsell (1996) has a good section on Method acting, particularly as it relates to film, and Krasner (2000) discusses Strasberg alongside Adler and Meisner, two further interpreters of the method; Strasberg (1988) provides a source.

6. One major study, tracking a generation of influence, was that by Edwards (1965).

7. Publications by Carnicke (1984 and 1993) have been prominent in this area.

8. Stanislavski (1981) and Stanislavski (1990), respectively.

9. On this influence, see Stanislavski's observations in his autobiography (Stanislavski 1924, 196–201), with the studies of the Meininger Company by DeHart (1981) and Braun (1982), noted above.

10. See the relevant letters in Benedetti (1991, 264–5 and 294–6).

11. Gorchakov (1954) and Toporkov (1979). The preparatory production notes (*mise-en-scène*) for Chekhov's *The Seagull* in the first season, on which Nemirovich-Danchenko and Stanislavski collaborated as directors, can be found in Balukhaty (1952), with discussion there and in Jones (1986).

12. On the first production, see Worrall (1996, 170–1).

13. In his autobiography Nemirovich-Danchenko repeats this claim, with reference to the early years (1937, 120–1).

14. For a provocative view of some of the modes of narrative of *My Life in Art*, see the discussion in Ley (1999).

15. There had been considerable interest in England towards the close of the nineteenth century on Diderot's dialogue *Paradox on the Actor*, which had been given an English translation, and the actor-manager Henry Irving had been involved in it: for details, see Archer (1957). Craig was a protege of Irving; for Craig's dialogues, see Chapter 2 of this book.

16. Elizabeth Hapgood, in the prefatory note to her translation of *An Actor Prepares*, made the connection between the character of Kostya and the young Stanislavski.

17. At *AP* 32, singing is included with gymnastics, dancing and fencing in a list of classes that are to be held daily.

18. For Ribot's work on affective psychology, and Stanislavski's interest in it, see Benedetti (1989, 31–2).

2   Proposals for Reform: Appia and Craig

1. For a fuller discussion and examples see Beacham (1987) and Volbach (1968).

2. Craig's work in London through small societies, even with unpaid amateur performers, lost money. Appia's experiment with Madame de Béarn's intimate theatre in Paris in 1903 was a one-off event, taking two years to prepare both space and light to his satisfaction.

3. This task has been usefully and accessibly carried out by the Directors in Perspective series, and such detailed studies as Senelick's examination of Craig's collaboration with Stanislavski on *Hamlet*.

4. For details of Dalcroze see Volbach (1968). Appia published the results of his collaboration and other theoretical works in a range of journals across Europe.

5. Interestingly when he represents this hierarchy diagrammatically, the drama is supported by the *mise-en-scène*.

6. This idea of unstructured space is linked in all Appia's arguments to festival, with all that that implies about communal participation. The Festival was a powerful idea at this time which had been bolstered by Wagner's Festival Theatre at Bayreuth, and was championed by others such as the designer and theorist Behrens, whose 1900 publication *Festival of Life and Art* echoed a call for communal celebration.

7. This is a sentiment which is echoed by Copeau writing his prospectus for his new theatre company at the Vieux Colombier in 1913, see Chapter 3 below.

8. Appia continues: 'Thus we have not one pattern of time, that is, a fictional pattern of time on the stage, for an audience living in another pattern of time in the auditorium, but in performance, music in the word-tone drama is *Time* itself' (*WLA* 16). Music is defined by its time durations, note/phrase lengths and so on, which are part of how it achieves its emotional effect. These directly relate to the audience, who understands the effect and the time durations at the same time; like other arts, music's form is equivalent to its expression.

9. The Foreword had originally been written as the catalogue introduction to Craig's Berlin exhibition the previous year. Having seen Craig's *Vikings of Helgeland* and *The Masque of Love* in 1903, Count Kessler invited Craig to the Weimar Court, an élite centre of German cultural life, and introduced his work to Otto Brahm and Reinhardt.

10. See Innes (1983) and Bablet (1981).

11. The publication record of the pamphlet, first in German in August, followed by an English version later in 1905 and by Dutch and Russian editions in 1906, indicates where Craig had found a level of patronage and interest in his work.

12. Craig's enthusiasm for Plato found its most demonstrable expression in a suggestion he made during his 1909 visit to Stanislavski in Moscow. His notes suggest that the Platonic dialogues should be read aloud in a specially designed open-air theatre, where people could wander in and listen to the *Symposium*, with its uncompromising hero, Socrates, for as long as they liked (Bablet 1981, 138). Stanislavski's reaction to this suggestion is not recorded. More recently, the dialogue form was used for theatrical debate in Diderot's *Paradoxe* (1830) or Goethe's *On Truth and Probability in Works of Art* (1798), two examples with which Craig may have been familiar. It was, of course, later employed in its fullest Platonic form, with narrative and multiple speakers, by Stanislavski.

13. Craig's article on *Theatrical Reform* (1910), which appeared in *The Mask* and his second collection of essays, *The Theatre Advancing*, indicates how much he knew about other movements for reform. With gentle wit he mocks the enthusiasts who set out to solve 'the riddle of the theatre' through open-air staging, or the reproduction of actual life, or communal theatre. He takes a swipe at Delsarte, the Futurists, Herr Littmanbachstein and 'the Socialist theatre reformer with his ponderous labour plays' (Craig 1979, 82). He dismisses this piecemeal reform, 'for the clever business man can take any one reform, and successfully tackle it, and turn it into a good paying concern, because when the show takes place the reform will not be noticed, but only a certain sense of novelty will be felt. That is just what he wants' (Craig 1979, 81).

14. Scathing comments about 'modern' theatre abound in Craig's writing, perhaps most demonized in his article 'Some Evil Tendencies of the Modern Theatre' which was included in *The Art of the Theatre*. For him,

modern theatre across Europe was filled with gentlemen 'continually on the rush' as if they were working 'for an oil business or a large grocery' (*OAT* 104).

15. Craig was finally to achieve a level of sponsorship from Lord de Walden in 1913, and for two years his school operated at the Arena Goldoni, Florence, although not along anything like the lines he proposed in his various prospectuses.

16. Craig's son acknowledges the vital support of Dorothy Nevile Lees, Craig senior's editorial assistant, and of Gino Ducci (Craig 1968). For a fascinating discussion of the economics of limited-edition printing and the exchange of ideas across Europe, see Lawrence Rainey's article, 'The Cultural Economy of Modernism' in Levenson (1999).

17. Craig's interest in the puppet had been signalled by his puppet plays, and presaged in the 'First Dialogue', when the playgoer wonders about how the actors will respond to being subordinated fully to the stage-director:

Are you not asking these intelligent actors almost to become puppets?...A puppet is at present only a doll, delightful enough for a puppet show. But for a theatre we need more than a doll. Yet that is the feeling which some actors have about their relationship with the stage-manager. They feel they are having their strings pulled, and resent it, and show they feel hurt – insulted. (*AT* 168)

18. Anatole France wrote in passionate admiration of the marionette mystery plays of Maurice Bouchor. Kleist's essay *On the Marionette Theater*, which Craig probably knew, argues along similar lines. The interrelationship between the mystery play and the puppet theatre was one which was to surface in Meyerhold's early, symbolist-inspired writing, see Chapter 3.

19. *The Mask*, V (1912), 100.

20. Although in 'The Actor and the Übermarionette' Craig, in the voice of the painter, was damning of Wagner for exactly this overwhelming personality:

'What an actor the man would have been, and what a personality he had!...Anyhow , it all turned out a great success – a success of personality.'
'Was it not a success of art?' asks the musician.
'Well, which art do you mean?'
'Oh, all the arts combined,' he replies, blunderingly but placidly. (*OAT* 72–3)

21. Craig's collection of essays, *On the Art of the Theatre* ends with a note on symbolism, dated 1910, which he reflects 'not only is Symbolism at the roots of all art, it is at the roots of all life' (*OAT* 294).

3 The Popular Front: Meyerhold and Copeau

1. Braun (1969).

2. Rudlin and Paul (1990). Copeau is reflecting with the benefit of hindsight in an article for the Buenos Aires journal, *La Nacion*, 1938. While he was engaged in his own practice during the 1920s and early 1930s, Copeau was much less aware of Meyerhold's work than this suggests.

3. Compare the genesis of the idea for establishing the Moscow Art Theatre, which in Nemirovich-Danchenko's original proposal was a reform of the Russian stage through a popular or 'open' theatre, drawing on government subsidy to provide free performances for working-class audiences. In the face of the censor neither crowds of workers in the auditorium, nor 'popular' in the title, were considered politic for the new company.

4. For a fascinating discussion of this interpretative development see Elin Diamond, *Unmaking Mimesis* (London: Routledge, 1997).

5. See J. Willett's *The Theatre of Erwin Piscator* (London: Methuen, 1986).

6. See Eaton (1985) and Hoover (1974).

7. Entry for January 1939 in Brecht's *Journals*, eds. J. Willett and R Manheim (London: Methuen, 1993), 20.

8. Alexander Bakshy's *The Path of the Modern Russian Stage and Other Essays* (London: Cecil Palmer & Hayward, 1916).

9. Several of these essays including Bryusov's, who was to greatly influence Meyerhold's own writing for the volume, are in Senelick (1981).

10. See Pyman (1994) for further details of the journal and a discussion of links between literary societies and the theatre.

11. In his edition, Braun has printed the essays in chronological order, so that this piece appears as the third section in his scheme.

12. S. Sergeev had powerfully employed the epithet 'mood' in his 1900 essay 'Glimmers of a New Trend in Art and the Moscow Theatre' to describe Chekhov's dramas, like *Uncle Vanya*, where 'the centre of gravity is transferred to the mood'. In an obituary of Chekhov the symbolist poet, Bely claimed him as a symbolist (Senelick 1981).

13. Meyerhold's practice of scoring movement and emotion in musical terms is recorded in the written notes on texts that still exist, for example the production notes for *The Lady of the Camillias* in 1934 (*MT* 274–8).

14. Nemirovich-Danchenko had noted many of Meyerhold's proclivities in a letter to Olga Knipper, which referred to his rudeness to a Nemirovich-Danchenko play, *In Dreams*, an attempt at the new drama:

    The Meyerhold movement has subsided, thank God! It was a muddle, a crazy mixture of Nietzsche, Maeterlinck and narrow liberalism verging on gloomy radicalism. (Braun 1986, 27)

15. The key element was the stage within a stage, the booth which displayed all its mechanics to the audience who 'sees the whole process' (*MT* 70). Many elements were maintained in the second staging of the play, in April 1914, by Meyerhold's students from the Tenishev Academy (Braun 1986, 127–9). *Balganchik* can be variously translated as the little showbooth, the puppet show, or the fairground booth.

16. It is difficult to imagine Meyerhold beginning a rehearsal period with a service of hymns and prayers, as work at the Moscow Art Theatre used to do (Benedetti 1991, 55).

17. Braun quotes an excerpt:

    What we are undertaking is not a simple private affair but a social task. Never forget that we are striving to brighten the dark existence of the poor classes, to afford them minutes of happiness and aesthetic uplift, to relieve the murk which envelops them. Our aim is to create the first intelligent, moral, popular theatre, and to this end we are dedicating our lives. (Braun 1986, 23)

18. *Cabotin*, the French for a strolling player, was almost always used pejoratively to imply a bad actor, the cheap and simplistic performance of a fairground entertainer or a mountebank.

19. Meyerhold was drawn as Pierrot by Nikolai Ulyanov in 1906, photographed in costume for the role in 1907. In February 1910 he danced Pierrot in first production of Mikhail Fokin's ballet *Carnival* at a ball organized by the Petersburg journal, *Satiricon* (Braun 1986, 71). Boris Grigoriev's 1916 double portrait of Meyerhold displays cubist tendencies and has Dr Dapertutto in the background. Aleksandr Golovin, his stage design collaborator at the Alexandrinsky, painted a curious image in 1917, with Meyerhold in pantomime smock and skull-cap sitting in front of a mirror so that the image is doubled.

20. See Leach (1994) and Kolocotroni (1998).

21. As in Chapter 1 above, for a discussion of the Russian tradition of training schools see Worrall (1989).

22. Asya Lacis, who was later to introduce Brecht to parts of Meyerhold's work, followed the development of Meyerhold's thought and of the Studio's experiments through the journal (Eaton 1985).

23. To be considered a foreign influence in the later years of Stalin's regime was dangerous; anti-Meyerhold vitriol in papers and journals even took to dubbing him 'that Jew'.

24. Excerpts from this essay in English are found in Cole and Chinoy (1970, 217–8) and in Rudlin (1986, 3–5, 7); the French version in full is found in Copeau's collected works, *Registres I: Appels* (1974, 19–32).

25. Compare the role of the journal and its editors in the development of Artaud's writing outlined in Chapter 4 below.

26. Looking back in 1941, he talks about the Little Theatres as the avant-garde movement of 1919, although at the time he resisted the epithet avant-garde (*CTT* 134). Notes from the lectures are gathered in *Registres*, with a few in Rudlin and Paul's selection, which are only half-written, degenerating into lists of key words and pithy one-liners.

27. Bradby and McCormick (1978).

28. The passage in which this phrase occurs talks of the theatre of the future as the temple rebuilt on perfect foundations. This is a New Testament metaphor echoing the language which implied the Jewish temple, a symbol of God's dwelling with man, would become post-crucifixion a church built in men's hearts. Copeau continues this metaphor in the passage and the theatre of the future, now cast as an immanent spirit within men rather than a building or show, would only be entered by consecrated men (*A* 260).

29. See Bradby and McCormick (1978) and Blanchart (1954).

30. The complete text is included in Copeau's *Appels* (1974, 277–313). Translated extracts in *CTT* are spread through the volume. The large extract pp. 186–95 is missing the first paragraph. A missing section on p. 189 has been translated on p. 134. Although the main extract finishes on p. 195, there are two further translated pieces of the essay to be found on p. 178, followed by p. 88.

4 Artaud and the Manifesto

1. As divergent examples of a continuing veneration, the critical philosopher Derrida added to his earlier essays on Artaud (Derrida 1978) a meditation on Artaud's graphics, originally published in German and then translated into English, despite the obstacle that the graphics could not be reproduced (Derrida and Thévenin 1998); while Finter (1997) has detected Artaud's influence in a variety of contemporary performances.

2. Barber's biography, for example, has little to offer on theory, and concentrates three out of its five chapters on the period from 1936 onwards. Barber repeatedly makes plain his thesis: 'The last period is an intensification of all Artaud's previous production' (Barber 1993, 12).

3. French disillusionment is probably best seen in Michel Foucault, with such works as *Madness and Civilization: A History of Insanity in the Age of Reason*, trans. R. Howard (London: Tavistock Publications, 1971).

4. The quotations are taken from a major study of a classical Roman poet: P. Hardie *Virgil's Aeneid: Cosmos and Imperium* (Oxford: Clarendon Press, 1986, 16).

5. From the 'Letter to Paul Demeny', Charleville, 15 May 1971; text with translation in Rimbaud (1966), 306–7. I have preferred the translation 'visionary' here.

6. *Ibid.*

7. *Ibid.*, 184–5.

8. *Ibid.*, 308–9.

9. *Ibid.*, 192–3 and 194–5 respectively.

10. For Jarry, see Braun (1982) and Deak (1993), with Jarry (1965); on Cocteau, see F. Steegmuller *Cocteau: A Biography* (London: Macmillan, 1970); and on Apollinaire's *The Breasts of Tiresias*, see Melzer (1977).

11. Braun (1982, 41); on the Théâtre d'Art, see Deak (1993, 134–83).

12. Since Deak (1993) claims Jarry's *Ubu Roi* for symbolism, Artaud's inheritance here is all the more consistent.

13. On dada in Paris, see Matthews (1974) and Gordon (1987) in addition to Melzer (1980).

14. The essential study is E. Said *Orientalism* (London: Routledge & Kegan Paul, 1978); compare Deak (1993, 132) on 'the proliferation of mysticism, the occult, theosophy, and Eastern religions' at the turn of the century in Paris.

15. On Vitrac, see Matthews (1974, 109–32); there is a good range of surrealist theatre-pieces in Benedikt and Wellwarth (1964), including Vitrac's *The Mysteries of Love*.

16. Of these three lectures given in Mexico, the first had the title 'Surrealism and Revolution'; the second is translated as 'Man Against Destiny' in Artaud *Selected Works* = SW 357–64; and the third as 'Theatre and the Gods' in Schumacher *Artaud on Theatre* = AT 130–6; the French text of all the lectures can be found in Artaud *Oeuvres complètes* = OC 8, 171–206. The abbreviations, with Artaud *Collected Works* = CW, are those I shall be using in the main text.

17. Bigsby (1972, 39–55) in his fifth chapter gives a helpful summary of the 'progress' of surrealism over this period; in general on surrealism, see Nadeau (1968).

18. The collections of Motherwell (1951) and Apollonio (1973), with Breton (1969) and Tzara (1977), and the manifestos translated by Victoria Nes Kirby in the 'Appendix' to Kirby (1971) provide a good range of documents.

19. I permit myself the liberty of composing a dada formula, whose relation to 'actual' dada would be a difficult theoretical issue.

20. Tzara 'Dada Manifesto, 1918' (Motherwell 1951, 76); compare Tzara (1977, 3–4).

21. Kirby (1971, 199), in the translation by Victoria Nes Kirby; see in addition the discussion by Kirby himself (146–7), in which he uses a different translation.

22. The versions of *The Theatre and Its Double* available in English vary rather oddly, and without editorial explanation. The separate edition published by Calder (Artaud 1970) includes fewer texts than the *Collected Works* Vol. 4 from the same publisher (Artaud 1974). Schumacher's collection offers a more arbitrary arrangement of a substantial but incomplete selection, which appends texts that were not included in the compilation. The French text can be found in *OC* 4.

23. 'Letter to Jean Paulhan', 25 January 1936 (*OC* 5, 272–3); compare *AT* 87–8. *The Theatre and Its Double* was published early in 1938, and contained material written from 1931 onwards.

24. All subsequent references to *The Theatre and Its Double* will be to this edition.

25. In a letter to Paulhan, 29 August 1932, Artaud commented of his manifesto of The Theatre of Cruelty that 'I believe this title is an attraction for the public'. The letter makes the populist intention quite clear; as he stated to his confidant, 'In reality it ought to be called "Alchemical" or "Metaphysical" Theatre' (*OC* 5, 139; compare *AT* 73).

26. The full text of the letter can be found in *OC* 5, 234–6.

27. *AT* 118, quoting from the journals of Anais Nin; see also Barber (1993, 62–3).

28. The first part of the essay is not given in Schumacher's selection, which rightly emphasizes that Artaud's subject is *mise-en-scène*.

29. In his much earlier essay, 'The Evolution of Set Design' of 1924, Artaud was abusive of *mise-en-scène* and 'retheatricalization' but in favour of the restoration of mysticism, which did not 'demand any really highfalutin', metaphysical operation' (*AT* 12–14; compare *SW* 53–5).

30. Kirby (1971, 19–27) provides a short chapter on this manifesto.

31. Breton had already tried his hand at some manifestos for dada; translation of these are given in Motherwell (1951, 199–206).

32. Stendhal's declaration came in the pamphlets that formed his *Racine and Shakespeare*:

Romanticism is the art of presenting to people those literary works that are capable of giving them the greatest possible pleasure in the actual state of their manners and beliefs. By contrast, classicism presents to them the literature that would have given the greatest possible pleasure to their grandfathers....

For Stendhal, compare M. Sidnell, *Sources of Dramatic Theory Vol. 2* (Cambridge: Cambridge University Press, 1994), 251.

5   Grotowski and Theoretical Training

1. Schechner and Wolford (1997, 490). Schechner bases his assertion on comments from Grotowski, notably in Richards (1995, x) and Grotowski (1996, 101).

2. In 1968 *Forefather's Eve* was banned again during an anti-Semitic purge because its author Mickiewicz was Jewish. It was only allowed back into the repertoire in 1973. The hardline behaviour of 1968 failed to save the administration of Gomulka, who was replaced in 1970 by Gierek, a Soviet choice. As Gierek's government became more established he felt able to relax some of the rulings on censored material.

3. In *Holiday*, written as he moved out of theatrical work, Grotowski dismisses political theatre:

   if instead of occupying oneself with politics, one makes politics in the theatre, then this is obvious escape. (*GS* 214)

4. Christopher Innes in *Avant-Garde Theatre 1892–1992* (London: Routledge, 1993) charts the connections before and after certain groups encountered Grotowski's work. Groups like Malina's Living Theatre, Chaikin's Open Theatre, Schechner's Performance Group were experimenting in this way. Brook and Barrault were also embarked in laboratory investigations which sought to utilize myth, ritual and ceremony in performance as a means to connect with a passive audience attuned to television.

5. In a piece of writing 'Methodical Exploration', which employs the metaphor of a scientific research institute to describe the Laboratory, Grotowski extends the idea of director as researcher: 'I do not put on a play in order to teach others what I already know. It is after the production is completed and not before that I am wiser' (*TPT* 98).

6. This also means that there is no contradiction when Grotowski later ponders the nature of method further in *Holiday*, and rejects the term:

   When they say that Grotowski's method exists as a system, the implication is that it is a false method. If it is a system, and if I myself have pushed it in this direction, I have contributed to a misunderstanding; it follows that I made a mistake and one must not go along that road, because it instructs 'how to do', that is to say, it shows how to arm oneself. (*GS* 221)

This resistance to acquisition of 'tricks' or a given creative method is entirely in keeping with the rhetoric of poor theatre.

7. Grotowski imagines that a very skilled actor will be able to achieve a unity of consciousness and body through the training of his reactions: 'allowing him to reveal one after the other the different layers of his personality, from the biological-instinctive source via the channel of consciousness and thought, to that summit which is so difficult to define and in which all becomes unity' (*TPT* 99). This is a concept drawn initially from the rhetoric of transcendental religious practice which, despite his difficulty in defining it, remains central to a great deal of his last phase of work at Pontedera in the 1990s.

8. Grotowski acknowledges this danger in the exercises:

    The elements of the exercises are the same for all but everyone must perform them in terms of his own personality. An onlooker can easily see the differences according to the individual personalities. (*TPT* 178)

    Again he suggests, 'it is I myself, as producer, who am confronted with the actor, and the self-revelation of the actor gives me a revelation of myself... My encounter with the text resembles my encounter with the actor and his with me. For both producer and actor, the author's text is a sort of scalpel enabling us to open ourselves , to transcend ourselves, to find what is hidden within us and to make the act of encountering the others...' (*TPT* 57). The act of encounter was to become increasingly important in Grotowski's work after the period of theatre productions had drawn to a close.

9. Bennett (1990) and Ben Chaim (1984) discuss Grotowski's work in the light of audience–actor proximity.

10. Although more difficult to find 'Wandering Towards A Theatre of Sources' and other contemporary interviews do exist as records of earlier work. Kumiega's book (1987) reproduces extracts from 'The Art of the Beginner' and the talk on Theatre of Sources given at York University, Toronto, parts of which find their way into the *Grotowski Sourcebook* version.

11. See Schechner, *Performance Theory* (London: Routledge, 1988).

12. In 'Wandering Towards A Theatre of Sources' Grotowski tries to distinguish between 'dramatic religion' and role-playing, which may share a form or exterior appearance, but only one is about 'encounter' (Grotowski 1980, 17).

13. Grotowski acknowledges the way in which actors are using his work at the Centre in his article 'From the Theatre Company to Art as Vehicle'. But here, where he is supposedly addressing himself to those who work on themselves rather than for an audience, he uses 'character' as a description of some of the work. This seems to deliberately provoke a theatrically allusive frame of reference.

14. In *Land of Ashes and Diamonds* Barba describes how, during his early work with Odin Theatre, he felt the presence of his Master in the corner of the room.

6 Boal's Theoretical History

1. Schutzman and Cohen Cruz (1994) and Babbage (1995) are good collections, the former having an interesting emphasis on the application of Boal's methods in Canada.

2. Versenyi (1993, 159–63) has a short section on Boal, but disappointingly does not examine the background of either Boal or the Arena Theatre.

3. Freire was a cultural theorist and educationalist who made a major contribution to literacy programmes; he died in 1998. His best-known book is *Pedagogy of the Oppressed*, which was first published in 1968 and translated into English in 1970. Freire was imprisoned after the first Brazilian coup in 1964, and went into exile later in that year: see, for example, the early biographical and publishing details on Freire in Mackie (1980, 3–8).

4. The interior of São Paolo refers presumably to the state, not the city. The north-east of Brazil includes the city of Recife, and is historically an area of great poverty and deprivation: see the political and economic summary given by Barnard in Mackie (1980, 12–38), which provides an essential background to both Boal and Freire. Freire's original initiatives were made in Recife and the north-east in the 1950s and early 1960s.

5. There are no page numbers for either 'Foreword' or 'Introduction' in *Theatre of the Oppressed*; but since each section consists of two pages only, references will not be hard to locate.

6. The quotations from Hauser occur between 'Foreword' and 'Introduction' in *Theatre of the Oppressed*, and like those two short sections lack pagination in the book. Boal's reference (*TO* 50, n. 1) is to Hauser (1957, Vol. 1, 83–7), which is the American edition from Hill & Wang; in the English edition, from Routledge & Kegan Paul (1962), the equivalent pages are 74–8.

7. A bare indication of some dates may be helpful. Athenian tragedy began just before 500 BC, and its major exponents Sophocles and Euripides died just before 400 BC; Socrates was executed by the Athenians in 399 BC, largely because he had been associated with reactionary aristocrats; Plato had been writing for many decades before his death in 347 BC, and Aristotle probably compiled the teaching notes that make up the *Poetics* in about 335–330 BC; Zeno belonged to the generation after Aristotle, and lived about one hundred and fifty years after Parmenides.

8. For a discussion of Aristotle's *Poetics*, and the relationship with Plato, see Ley (1999), ch. 1, and the references to reading included there.

9. Studies such as that by Goldhill (1986) make these characteristics abundantly clear.

10. For these works, see Machiavelli (1999) and (1970) and Penman (1978) respectively, or the comprehensive collection by Gilbert (1965).

11. Anglo (1971) and Hale (1972) are accessible and reliable accounts of Machiavelli's life, writings and activities.

12. Probably the most useful collection of Hegel's writings for theatre studies is Paolucci (1962); the index is essential for reference and cross-reference, granted the nature of the compilation from diverse sources.

13. The current Pluto Press edition of *Theatre of the Oppressed* has confusion in the printing at the bottom of p. 74, where the first line of the subsequent paragraph (on p. 75) has intruded upon and displaced part of the current paragraph. A comparison with the French edition reveals that the first two lines of the last paragraph on p. 74 should read 'Romanticism certainly represents a reaction against the/bourgeois world, even if only against its exterior ...'.

14. For these details, and on Piscator generally, see Willett (1986).

15. In this respect, it is important to note that Boal is referring to Willett's edition (1964) of a broad selection of Brecht's writings, which conspicuously provides that context in some detail; Boal is eliminating, rather than not providing, an available context.

16. For an analysis of the rhetorical strategies involved in Brecht's (illusory) advocacy of an everyday theatre, see Ley (1999), ch. 5,2.

17. The significant collections, as I have noted above, are Schutzman and Cohen-Cruz (1994) and Babbage (1995); but Boal and his approach to theatre are the subjects of continuing discussion in journals and elsewhere. See, for example, the interview with Boal in Delgado and Heritage (1996).

18. See the essay by Goldhill 'The City Dionysia and Civic Ideology' in Winkler and Zeitlin (1990).

19. The sequence of Freire's published works is initially a little hard to follow from the publication dates of the translations into English. Studies of Freire include Mackie (1980) and McLaren and Leonard (1993).

20. Freire's discussion of revolutionary leaders in section 4 of *Pedagogy of the Oppressed* might usefully be compared with Gramsci's writings (Hoare and Nowell Smith 1971), notably those on 'The Intellectuals' and 'The Modern Prince', in which Gramsci reads Machiavelli's famous work as offering perceptions for the role of a contemporary communist party.

7 Conclusion: From Theoretical Practitioners to Theorized Performance

1. MacAloon (1984) usefully charts one history of ideas related to cultural performance in his preface, where he placed Turner's work in a continuum with other anthropologists and cultural theorists.

2. Schechner describes performance theory as 'fundamentally interdisciplinary and intercultural' (Schechner 1988, xv).

3. Turner saw the interaction of cultures as 'a humble step away from the destruction that surely awaits our species if we continue to cultivate deliberate mutual misunderstanding in the interests of power and profit' (Turner 1982, 19).

4. On the history of the term intercultural, see Ley (1999).

5. Case (1988) has argued that only certain formations of feminist thought have been adopted by the academy over the last twenty years. The most notable absence has been employment for, and writing from, women of colour.

Index

193